Advance Praise for *Cool Wooden Box*

"There are books on acoustic guitars, acoustic guitar players, and acoustic guitar makers, but Rand Smith brings them all together for the first time as he explores and explains the evolutionary Big Bang that the acoustic guitar has undergone in the last five decades. An important work—and entertaining, too."

—**WALTER CARTER**, founder, Carter Vintage Guitars

"*Cool Wooden Box* is a freshly interpreted and exhaustively researched story of the establishment, development, disruption, and rejuvenation of the acoustic guitar industry and of the musical and cultural forces that shaped it, spun by a keen observer of equal-parts guitar aficionado, music lover, and historian."

—**DANA BOURGEOIS**, founder and CEO, Bourgeois Guitars

"We are so honored to be included in this obviously well-thought-out and well-researched effort. Rand's true love of the instrument and the people who make them on a small scale shines through."

—**MARK DALTON**, **KIMBERLY DALTON**, and **BRIAN DICKEL**, Huss & Dalton Guitar Company

"In *Cool Wooden Box*, Rand Smith has cleverly woven personal, social, and musical histories into a compelling narrative. In doing so, Smith has illustrated just how, well, *cool* the steel string acoustic guitar, its makers, and its players are."

—**JOHN THOMAS**, author of *Kalamazoo Gals: A Story of Extraordinary Women and Gibson's "Banner" Guitars of WWII*, field editor for *The Fretboard Journal*

"Rand Smith has contributed to the world of lutherie a unique perspective, of one involved with guitars in his early years to the present. Starting with visits to the local music store as well as doing extensive research and interviews with many of the current builders, from large and medium manufacturers to the small independent luthier. The book is a wonderful read and presents a unique perspective as to the evolution of the guitar."

—**MICHAEL GURIAN**, author of *An Instrument Maker's Guide to Insanity and Redemption*

"Rand Smith loves the acoustic guitar. In *Cool Wooden Box* he shares with us his own more than fifty-year journey of discovery and interest in the instrument. Along the way he has interviewed many prominent guitar makers (both small and large) and importers. The luthiers recount their experiences over the decades, as well as how and why guitar manufacturing has changed in that time. Rand's experiences will be familiar to guitar geeks of a certain age. At the same time, it is a valuable resource to help fill in the blanks for more recent generations."

—**STAN WERBIN**, co-owner, Elderly Instruments, www.elderly.com

Cool Wooden Box

W. Rand Smith

Cool
Wooden
Box

Transformation of the
American Acoustic Guitar

The University of Tennessee Press
Knoxville

The Charles K. Wolfe Music Series was launched in honor of the late Charles K. Wolfe (1943–2006), whose pioneering work in the study of American vernacular music brought a deepened understanding of a wide range of American music to a worldwide audience. In recognition of Dr. Wolfe's approach to music scholarship, the series will include books that investigate genres of folk and popular music as broadly as possible.

LIBRARY OF CONGRESS CATALOGING-IN-PUBLICATION DATA

Names: Smith, W. Rand, 1947– author.

Title: Cool wooden box : transformation of the American acoustic guitar / W. Rand Smith.

Description: First edition. | Knoxville : The University of Tennessee Press, 2023. |

Series: Charles K. Wolfe music series | Includes bibliographical references and index. |
    Summary: "This book is a history of guitar making in the US since the folk revival of
    the 1960s. Based largely on the author's interviews, it includes chapters on the rise
    of the modern independent luthier movement, recent developments at Martin, at
    Gibson, and at Taylor—especially regarding the use of technology and how it can
    tend either to erode or honor these companies' traditions—the changing, though
    still robust market, and the effect of foreign competition on American builders"
    —Provided by publisher.

Identifiers: LCCN 2023003043 (print) | LCCN 2023003044 (ebook) |
    ISBN 9781621907855 (paperback) | ISBN 9781621907862 (pdf) |
    ISBN 9781621907879 (kindle edition)

Subjects: LCSH: Guitar—Construction—United States—History. | Guitar makers—
    United States.

Classification: LCC ML1015.G9 S652 2023 (print) | LCC ML1015.G9 (ebook) |
    DDC 787.87/1973—dc23/eng/20230120

LC record available at https://lccn.loc.gov/2023003043

LC ebook record available at https://lccn.loc.gov/2023003044

To the memory of Allen Wier—

Writer, storyteller, music lover, friend

1946–2021

Contents

Illustrations

A Backward-Glancing Foreword

Charles K. Wolfe, *Cool Wooden Box*, and the
Transformation of American Music History

The year 2023 marks the fifteenth anniversary of the University of Tennessee
Press's Charles K. Wolfe Music Series, and this book—W. Rand Smith's *Cool
Wooden Box: Transformation of the American Acoustic Guitar*—marks the series'
fourteenth book. The books thus far published in the series have one thing in
common: each one explores some aspect of the vernacular music traditions
variously labeled folk, country, blues, bluegrass, old-time, roots, Americana
. . . the traditions that interested Charles Wolfe (1943–2006) throughout his
career and that interest me and many other people today.

In 2008, the University of Tennessee Press publicly announced the creation
of the Wolfe Music Series, a book series intended to honor the life and work
of a respected scholar who was also a prolific author of books and articles
exploring a broad range of topics in American music history. Dr. Wolfe was
simultaneously a professor at Middle Tennessee State University and a public
figure who was frequently consulted by the media to comment upon music-
related matters. I had worked with him on a book, so it was both logical and
meaningful that, after Dr. Wolfe's passing, I was asked by Press Director Scot
Danforth to oversee the Wolfe Music Series.

In 1999, I began teaching at East Tennessee State University, near the sites
of two historic music-related events that had inspired interpretive articles by

Dr. Wolfe: the Victor Talking Machine Company's Bristol sessions of 1927–1928 and Columbia Records' Johnson City sessions of 1928–1929. Since I lived literally down the road from where those influential recording sessions occurred, I read his pieces on those sessions and wanted to know more. During the 2001 meeting in Nashville of the annual International Country Music Conference, I asked Dr. Wolfe—a mainstay each year at the ICMC—if he might consider collaborating on a book to offer a comprehensive exploration of the events. He immediately said yes, and it certainly was a measure of his open-mindedness that he agreed to work with a junior scholar. Over the next couple of years, Dr. Wolfe and I produced a manuscript that became *The Bristol Sessions: Writings About the Big Bang of Country Music* (McFarland & Company) and was published shortly before Dr. Wolfe's 2006 death. The book was widely reviewed, and it received the Book of the Year Award from the Appalachian Writers Association. My intellectual indebtedness to Dr. Wolfe went well beyond that one book. Indeed, several of my subsequent research projects—specifically, three box sets (containing CDs of remastered historic recordings as well as curated books) exploring 1920s-era recording sessions held in Bristol, Johnson City, and Knoxville—owed their original inspiration to the work of Dr. Wolfe.

From the start, in order to properly honor the series' namesake, editors at the University of Tennessee Press and I committed ourselves to maintaining the highest possible standards for book-length manuscripts. Beginning in 2008 I spread word about the series through general announcements on the Internet and through direct invitations to individuals. While we received several book proposals, six years would pass before the arrival of a manuscript appropriate for launching the series—Ken Perlman's remarkably detailed study of Prince Edward Island fiddling. (From the beginning we sought manuscripts with an international scope, which is why the word "American" was purposefully avoided in the title for the book series.)

The Wolfe Series, like music itself, promotes an eclectic, wide-ranging approach to exploring its subject. Some of the books in the Wolfe Music Series have explored the life and work of individual musicians, such as Woody Guthrie, Waylon Jennings, Charley Patton, and Tex Morton, while other series titles have offered studies of various acoustic instruments and their makers. Some books in the series have stressed historical analysis, while others have conveyed personal experiences and observations.

Smith's *Cool Wooden Box* does not fit into any single niche; rather, it encompasses several categories, investigating diverse roots music styles while celebrating musicians who play these styles and the people who make a principal instrument. The acoustic guitar may be associated with several countries and cultures, but this book focuses on the *American* acoustic guitar—the steel-string, flattop guitar—and the major changes in both the playing and building of the instrument during the past six decades. Smith argues that those changes constitute a *transformation* of the American acoustic guitar.

In an interview I conducted with him for this foreword, Smith reported that he has long loved and played this instrument—in his own words, he has carried on an "instrumental affair" with the acoustic guitar over the past five decades. Smith also related that he has been an academic researcher as well as a keen observer of human behavior. Given Smith's skillset, this book is based on passion and analysis in equal measure. As he admitted, "I cannot separate my appreciation for the acoustic guitar—its colorful, striated woods; its curves and lines; and especially the sounds it produces—from my fascination with the worlds of those who play and make the instrument at a high level." Accordingly, *Cool Wooden Box* offers a blend of memoir, reportage, and assessment.

According to Smith, this book grew out of a life change—his transition to retirement after a career at Lake Forest College, where he had taught comparative European politics. He remarked, "I felt I had no more mountains to climb in my work on Europe, but I still enjoyed research and writing, and I wanted to keep on doing that."

That change involved a shift in research focus—from Europe (he had previously published a book integrating his long interest in the politics of France, Italy, and Spain) to the US, and from politics to music. And why the guitar? "The decision to focus on the acoustic guitar was easy for me," he said. "For decades I had played the instrument for fun. For me, the guitar was another form of learning and creativity, and I enjoyed the challenge of trying to develop some skill in playing it. I also came to enjoy writing songs and playing with other people."

Though his focus shifted, Smith's love of observational and interview-based research did not change. As he put it, "I've always loved the process of connecting with people from other cultures and of coming to understand how they viewed the world. In Europe, that meant going to specific countries and learning their languages in order to interview people." Research on the guitar may not have required learning new languages, but it did involve travel (visits to guitar-making shops, factories, and gear shows like the annual National Association of Music Merchants, or NAMM, Show) and conversations with luthiers about their work. Smith commented, "I hope this book conveys my appreciation for the openness and generosity of the people I encountered in the acoustic guitar world. I also hope it brings some new understanding about how that world has been transformed over the past few decades."

Cool Wooden Box will help readers more deeply appreciate an instrument that has enthralled so many people for so many decades; it will also increase general understanding of how the American acoustic guitar has always been a dynamic, ever-evolving, positive force across the US and around the world.

TED OLSON
East Tennessee State University

Acknowledgments

The reader will soon learn of my passion for the American acoustic guitar—for its beauty as a crafted instrument, its qualities as a music-making device, and, last but not least, its essential role in bringing creative joy to my life. But this book is no guitar-hero solo, far from it. It's the product of help and support from many people, and I'm happy to thank them here.

I still marvel at the willingness of virtually all the people I met in the acoustic guitar world to open their doors and answer questions from an inquisitive stranger. That willingness is a testament to the high level of trust and generosity one finds within this world. My only regret is that, for reasons of time and resources, I could not include even more people who devote their lives and livelihood to the acoustic guitar. I must therefore content myself—and, I hope, the reader—with a judicious sampling of that world's diversity.

I begin, then, with a collective thanks to the dozens of people who gave me their time, expertise, and reflections about the recent fate and possible future of the acoustic guitar. From Lewiston, Maine, to San Diego, California, and from Seattle, Washington, to Staunton, Virginia—as well as many places in between—I traveled and conversed with people engaged in supplying wood and making, selling, and promoting guitars. I apologize for not listing them all, but I wish to thank especially the following individuals for sharing their thoughts: Dick Boak, Dana Bourgeois, Walter Carter, Nick Colesanti, the late Bill Collings, Ashvin Coomar, Jim Craig, Mark Dalton, Ren Ferguson, Fred Greene, Michael Gurian, Richard Hoover, Jeff Huss, Richard Johnston, Richard Keldsen, Jean Larrivée, Chris Martin, Steve McCreary, Steve McMinn, Michael Millard, Andy Powers, John L. Rogers, Terry Straker, Bob Taylor, Bruce Van-Wart, Jason Verlinde, Bill Warmoth, Chris Wellons, and Stan Werbin. I also want to thank several people who facilitated my travels, contacts, and visits, especially Amani Duncan, Carolyn Grant, Carolyn Sills, and Chalise Zolezzi.

Closer to home, I'm so grateful for the support of family and friends who have expressed interest and even commented on various chapter drafts. I must start with my inner circle: my wife and true companion for the past forty-three years, Janet Kelsey, and our children, Caleb and Ellie. For sharp suggestions for revisions, I'm especially grateful to my brother, Rick Smith of Taos, New Mexico—a fellow guitar lover and fine musician in his own right. Others who offered both encouragement and invaluable critiques of earlier drafts include Anne Bishop, Adriana Bonewitz, Walter Carter, Jim Cubit, Pam George, Paul Lucas, Don Meyer, John L. Rogers, Terry Straker, Stephen Wade, and John Warnock.

In closing, I regretfully note the passing of a close friend of nearly sixty years who was instrumental in this book's publication. Allen Wier, superb fiction writer and emeritus professor at the University of Tennessee, recommended my manuscript to Scot Danforth, the director of the University of Tennessee Press. That connection led to a rigorous review process—including helpful insights from Scot and two anonymous reviewers—and a book contract. Alas, Allen passed away just before I received that contract, and so I was unable to celebrate the occasion with him. I find some solace in being able to dedicate this book to Allen's memory.

Cool Wooden Box

Introduction

COOL WOODEN BOX—
DISCOVERING A TRANSFORMATION

> After coming out of the disco and the Yamaha DX7 synthesizer
> era, when people rediscovered how cool that wooden box is,
> they just keep rediscovering it.
>
> —*CHRISTOPHER F. MARTIN IV, CEO, C. F. MARTIN & CO*

Imagine three store visits in search of acoustic guitars. I invite you to join me.

The first is in the year 1960, and we are in my hometown of Shreveport, Louisiana. I'm thirteen years old, and I'm taking you to the city's largest music store, Shreveport Music Company, located downtown on Texas Street. As we enter, we see that this store, true to its name, is indeed an all-purpose music store. Various types of instruments—pianos, drums, violins, and trumpets—grace the floor and walls, and we notice an array of cases, sheet music, and other music paraphernalia. You ask: wait, isn't there a *guitar* store in a city of 150,000? My reply: No, there's not. In the early 1960s, the public's demand for guitars—both acoustic and electric—does not financially support such single-product specialization in one store.

After passing the drums and trumpets, we come to a section along the back wall that displays a dozen or so new acoustic guitars, hanging on hooks and nestled in floor stands. A quick inspection reveals that almost all these instruments are marked Made in USA. The only exception is an inexpensive classical guitar, made in Mexico. Some of the American-made guitars bear one of two labels—Martin or Gibson. These companies have dominated the American acoustic guitar market for decades; both offer a variety of instruments, ranging from small-bodied parlor guitars, used for small-volume, fingerpicking musical styles, to larger dreadnought and jumbo instruments that are typically played with a plectrum (pick) in order to establish rhythm and perform occasional single-note solos in bands specializing in country, folk, and bluegrass styles. Within the guitar market of that day, Martin and Gibson occupied a high-quality/high-price niche.

We also see several lower-priced guitars bearing such names as Harmony and Kay. The salesperson informs us that these brands are mass-produced in Chicago, with only minor stylistic differences and the name on the headstock distinguishing one instrument from the next. She points out that these are the best starter guitars for beginners. Seeing no other acoustic guitars, we thank her and bid adieu.

We now time-travel to the present day and visit two other stores. The first is my local music store, Guitar Works, located near my home in Evanston, Illinois. The sign outside tells us this is a true *guitar* shop, not an all-purpose music store, à la the Shreveport Music Company of my youth. We are greeted by its owner, Terry Straker, a friendly, bearded fellow who has operated this store for more than forty years.[1]

We are first struck by the sheer size and scale of Terry's store, with the left-hand side of the store devoted to acoustic guitars and the right-hand side featuring electrics. On the acoustic side there are about a hundred instruments hanging on a large wall, and a comparable number of electric guitars on the other wall.

As we venture further into Guitar Works, we come upon a small test-driving room where one can sample the merchandise, hands on. We notice, hanging on these walls, several high-priced instruments, made in various places throughout the United States and bearing such names such as Bourgeois, Collings, Goodall, Huss & Dalton, Larrivée, Olson, Santa Cruz, and Taylor. Nearby we see some guitars with lower price tags, and owner Terry Straker informs us that these are "our starter guitars for beginners." Closer inspection reveals all of these to be imports. Those bearing names such as Takamine and Yamaha speak for themselves in terms of their Japanese origins. Other instruments appear to be all-American in name—Fender, Guild, Epiphone, Blueridge, Eastman, Kentucky, Johnson, Recording King, Washburn—but the interior label indicates their provenance as China, South Korea, Taiwan, or Indonesia.

Finally, we are reminded of the adage that the more things change, the more they stay the same: we notice that the old-line guitar makers, Martin and Gibson, have apparently held their own. Guitar Works carries an array of their new models. Also for sale are a few used Martins and Gibsons, made between 1920 and 1970. These, Straker tells us, are now considered vintage instruments, with prices that are typically several times higher than the new models.

As we head out the Guitar Works door, we turn left and walk three blocks toward the third and final store located . . . in my living room, which is where I usually keep my MacBook connected to wi-fi and internet. Though not a traditional commercial space in which buyers and sellers physically exchange money for goods, we are at a commercial crossroads nonetheless. In the "store" of online guitar shopping, I can quickly access countless sellers—actual stores as well as individuals—eager to sell me their instruments. Walk-in stores large and small—including Guitar Works and the still-kicking Shreveport Music Company of my youth—maintain their own websites. Stores such as these, as well as individuals, can also post their merchandise on aggregator sites such as eBay, Sweetwater, and Reverb. The latter's website, for example, states that it is "the largest online marketplace dedicated to buying and selling new, used, and vintage musical instruments. Since launching in 2013, Reverb has grown into a vibrant community of buyers and sellers all over the world." Connected to this online world, I have before me a virtually complete inventory of all the brands and types of acoustic guitars for sale throughout the country and even the world.

Considering these three store visits together, What have we just seen? What do these imaginary store visits tell us about the fate of the acoustic guitar during the past six decades?

• • •

In examining that fate, this book combines dispassionate analysis and personal passion. The analysis is my attempt to understand how the acoustic guitar has changed in recent decades, while the passion is my long-standing love for the instrument. Combining these two aspects entails conveying two related personal discoveries. The first is the realization that the acoustic guitar—both its use as an instrument and its making—has been essentially *transformed* during the past six decades. The other discovery is that of recognizing how my own engagement with the acoustic guitar has affected my life (in a very good way). Analysis and passion / passion and analysis—these are two sides of the same coin. I cannot separate my appreciation for the acoustic guitar—its colorful, striated woods; its curves and lines; and especially the sounds it produces—from my fascination with the worlds of those who play and make the instrument at a high level. So along with tracing the major changes that have occurred in the world of the acoustic guitar, this book also reflects my own experiences in that world.

DEFINING THE BOX

Everyone "knows" what an acoustic guitar is, right? But do you, really? I make no assumptions about the reader's knowledge of the guitar, although I presume everyone reading this book can distinguish between an acoustic instrument and a solid-body, electric guitar. But there are acoustics, and then there are acoustics, so let's specify.

This book is about one type of acoustic guitar, by far the most popular one: the steel-string flattop guitar.[2] Other variants can be grouped in the acoustic guitar family—including the classical, resonator, archtop, and lap-style (Weissenborn) guitar—but this book's focus is the steel-string flattop. With apologies to these other worthy family members, I use the term "acoustic guitar" to refer to this type of guitar (see photograph).[3]

Historically, the quest for enhanced projection, a.k.a. loudness, has driven much of the innovation in the acoustic guitar. As a general statement, this innovation grew out of guitar makers' responses to consumer demand. In the late nineteenth century, the guitar gained growing popularity in dance and ensemble orchestras, while instrument makers and retailers sought to meet

An acoustic guitar family (*left to right*): Johnson resonator (recent), Scheerhorn Weissenborn (2006, lap style), Martin D-18 (1947, flattop), Gibson J-45 (1943, flattop), Gibson ES-125 (1951, archtop). Photo by author.

that demand. For example, Lyon & Healy of Chicago, makers of Washburn guitars, adopted factory production techniques to lower costs, while mass retailers such as Sears & Roebuck and Montgomery Ward, also based in Chicago, promoted guitar sales through their catalog and mail-order services. These two pre-Amazon retailers also sold their own house brands: Recording King (Montgomery Ward) and Harmony and Silvertone (Sears & Roebuck).[4]

One such innovation that boosted the acoustic guitar's presence sonically was the use of steel strings, which were introduced in the late 1800s, first by the Larson brothers of Chicago and then later adopted by the Gibson Mandolin-Guitar Manufacturing Company of Kalamazoo, Michigan, and C. F. Martin & Company of Nazareth, Pennsylvania. By World War II, steel strings had become standard on most new guitars being produced in this country. In prior centuries guitar strings were mainly longer, fatter versions of violin strings made of catgut—strings made from the intestinal walls of animals (though not cats!). Steel strings, tuned at the same pitch as catgut, exert more tension on the guitar's top, producing greater vibration of the top and therefore more volume.

Another innovation to project more volume was simply to build a bigger "box." From the 1920s, larger body sizes—notably the dreadnought, so named for the gigantic British battleship HMS *Dreadnought*, built in 1906—became increasingly common, rivaling the smaller parlor and classical body shapes that had predominated until then.[5]

The greater tension of steel strings also drove other design changes in the instrument. Inside the box, luthiers—the general term for makers of stringed instruments, including guitars—devised heavier internal bracing that could withstand the increased pull of the strings; outside, they created a steel bar, called a truss rod, to fit inside the neck to resist warping.[6] These changes did not, of course, spell doom for catgut (and later, nylon) strings or the smaller, lighter guitars that used them. These instruments have retained their niches in classical, flamenco, and other styles. But steel-string guitars came to prevail in the acoustic field, becoming standard instruments in such popular solo and ensemble styles as blues, country, bluegrass, folk, and even rock and roll.

The term "flattop" refers not only to the guitar's surface, but also to the fact that the guitar's six (or in some cases, twelve) strings are anchored directly into the guitar's body via holes drilled through a bracing device (bridge) that is glued to the top. In guitar makers' never-ending search to produce a louder instrument, this design creates a direct transfer of energy from the vibrating strings to the guitar's top. The top's subsequent vibration reflects sound energy down into the box, or chamber of the guitar—its back and sides—which is then reflected from the top's sound hole out into the world.

As the central dynamic of the whole instrument, this energy conversion from vibration to sound waves depends critically on the types of tone woods that comprise the top, back, and sides of the box. Generally preferred by guitar makers is a combination of softer, vibrational wood varieties such as spruce for the top, and harder, reflective woods such as mahogany, maple, or rosewood for the back and sides. Complicating matters is that there are several species of each of these. Red (Adirondack) spruce, for example, is considered stiffer and therefore preferable to white (Engelmann) and Sitka spruce, both of which grow mainly in the western forests of North America. Similarly, rosewood from Brazil or Madagascar is widely believed to be tonally superior to the Indian variety. Beyond these woods, other tone woods such as koa, cedar, and walnut are often used, and so the possible combinations are many—if not endless.[7] A sure way to launch a lengthy, spirited discussion with any luthier, is to ask the question: Which tone woods do you prefer and why?

The flattop design just described contrasts with the other main type of steel-string acoustic guitar, the archtop guitar. As one writer colorfully puts it: "Flattops and archtops both look like guitars and walk like guitars, but they quack like two entirely different animals."[9] As the name indicates, an archtop features a curved, or arched, top. (The back is also typically arched as well.) Early versions of the archtop sported a round sound hole, but by the 1920s two f-shaped holes largely replaced the round version. As for the strings and bridge, the archtop's strings are anchored to the lower end of the instrument's frame, via a metal tailpiece, while a movable, or floating, bridge on the guitar's top holds the strings in place.

Because of differences in internal bracing, string tension, and tonal reflective qualities, the archtop tends to have a more cutting or punchy sound—that is, a stronger mid- to high range with less sustain—compared with the flattop's stronger low range and greater sustain.[10] During the early twentieth century, Gibson, the inventor of the archtop, was the primary producer of such instruments, whereas Martin focused on flattops. Both types of instruments remained popular throughout the pre-World War II period, with the archtop especially popular for jazz and swing styles and flattops for folk, blues, and country & western music. After 1945, as the guitar came to the fore as the most popular fretted instrument, the flattop's lower cost and versatility gradually gave it an edge over the archtop in public favor. Today the archtop retains its spot mainly as a jazz and swing-style instrument.

AN INSTRUMENTAL AFFAIR

My discovery of the acoustic guitar begins—where else?—with my own story. From the moment I undertook this book project, I knew I could not separate my study of the acoustic guitar from my own relationship with this instrument and the impact it has had on my life. To state it as directly as possible: this relationship has been enduring and liberating—one I continue to discover. To state it only slightly hyperbolically: my relationship with the acoustic guitar has been an extended love affair. I can trace the origins of this affair back to the early 1970s when I was a graduate student at the University of Michigan, studying for a PhD in political science. After I had been in Ann Arbor a few months, a friend invited me to a popular coffeehouse, The Ark, to hear some folk music. For the first time, I heard an acoustic guitar played through a good sound system to an attentive audience. My ears were captured, and, as corny as it sounds, my passion quickly followed.

I was no stranger to guitar-made music by then. I was eleven years old in 1958, when the so-called Folk Music Revival began with the Kingston Trio's version of an old murder ballad, "Tom Dooley." Like millions of other music lovers, I found the combination of a simple melody, the trio's tight harmonies, and a tragic narrative—backed by two acoustic guitars and a banjo—somehow compelling. It was a sound that seemed paradoxically new. There soon followed new acoustic-based groups such as Peter, Paul, and Mary, while long-time folksingers such as Pete Seeger found new fans. Then, of course, there was a skinny kid from Hibbing, Minnesota, who came on the scene sounding ancient but singing lyrics that spoke to the current human condition in such songs as "Blowin' in the Wind" and "The Times They Are a-Changin'."

Like millions of people, I watched musical variety TV shows such as *Hootenanny*. In my last two years of high school, I even sang in a folk quartet, performing such staples as "Chilly Winds" and "If I Had a Hammer." Even though our sole instrument was a baritone ukulele—played by a bandmate—I appreciated the sound of acoustic music featuring stringed instruments, with the foremost among them being the acoustic guitar. Truth be told, though, that appreciation never drove me to acquire an instrument and learn to play.

That all changed for me once I started going to The Ark and hearing a skillfully played acoustic guitar. I do not recall the first performer I heard there, but in the next few years, I heard such guitar-based artists as Norman Blake, David Bromberg, Guy Carawan, Michael Cooney, Elizabeth Cotten, Ramblin' Jack Elliot, Paul Geremia, Alice Gerrard, New Lost City Ramblers, Utah Phillips, Leon Redbone, Malvina Reynolds, Paul Siebel, Rosalie Sorrels, and Loudon Wainwright III. Whether it was the speed and clarity of Blake's flatpicking, the ragtime rhythm of finger stylist Cotten, or the melodic old-time blues of Cooney—all those sounds were, to my ears, both astonishing and incredibly enticing. For the first time in my life, I wanted to make music myself. I wanted to *do that*. I wanted to play what all these musicians played: an acoustic guitar.

This newfound motivation led to the decision to get my hands on a guitar. Fortunately for me, Ann Arbor not only attracted great guitarists, but it also attracted a young man destined for a successful career in selling musical instruments, Stan Werbin, who for decades now has owned Elderly Instruments in Lansing, Michigan. When, after visiting The Ark a few times, I mentioned to a friend that I would like to buy a guitar, he said, "Well, you should look up Stan. He's a grad student in biochemistry, but he's starting a business in his bedroom selling used guitars and other instruments." Lo and behold, I found Werbin's name in the telephone directory, called him up, and arranged to come see his wares in his lodgings in a fraternity house. I ended up buying a serviceable starter guitar in that frat house—a ten-year-old, Chicago-made Harmony Sovereign, price $75.[11] In the five decades since that encounter, I've applied myself to all things guitar, in the process learning new ways to play the instrument. In short, I have kept on discovering and appreciating the possibilities inherent in that simple wooden box. This endeavor has unquestionably enhanced the quality of my life.

The central dimension of my guitar education, as with most people who pick up the instrument, has been the social aspect: playing with other people. Playing informally with my brother and various friends has helped me develop timing, self-confidence, and perhaps the most important trait of a good musician: the ability to listen to and respond to the people you're playing with. My learning venues have included instructional classes of various types, most notably Steve Kaufman's summer Acoustic Kamps in Maryville, Tennessee, and classes at Chicago's legendary Old Town School of Folk Music.

My biggest advance came two decades ago when I cofounded an acoustic band with a group of Lake Forest College faculty, staff, and students. Since that time, our band, Fast & Cheap, has practiced weekly and performed many local concerts on campus and in the community. In the process, we have developed a repertoire of more than a hundred songs, several of which I've written. I have played a little mandolin, Dobro, and banjo in the band, but my main instrument remains the guitar.

Along the way, I also picked up a bug—a moderate case of GAS, or Guitar Acquisition Syndrome. For the serious guitar aficionado, having a single guitar is like eating a single potato chip—just one will not suffice. Over the years I have acquired (and sold) about fifteen acoustic guitars of varying quality, vintage, and type, including the ones pictured earlier. I have remained a fairly regular customer of my erstwhile fellow Michigan grad student, Stan Werbin of Elderly Instruments, as well as my local store, Guitar Works. A case of GAS such as mine requires knowledge of what you're buying, so I have tried to educate myself in the arcana of guitar history, materials, and construction. So not only have I paid attention to how guitars are played, but I have also tried to follow changes in how they are made. It is this dangerous bug of collecting guitars, as much as anything, that has driven my interest in the business of making guitars.

In the course of five decades, then, the acoustic guitar has been a constant companion whose creative potential I keep on discovering. During that time the guitar has helped me develop my admittedly modest abilities as a musician, not only as a player but also as a singer, songwriter, and one who "plays well with others" (or at least tries to). The acoustic guitar has been a literal instrument of personal discovery. Along the way, the instrument has also become a fascinating object of study, especially in terms of how the world of the acoustic guitar—both its playing and making—has changed over time.

AN INSTRUMENT AND AN INDUSTRY TRANSFORMED

What have I discovered about that world? In addition to personal discovery, I have also discovered—and come to understand—that during the past six decades the acoustic guitar world has undergone a *dual* transformation: a process of exceptional creativity that has produced greater craftsmanship and diversity in how the instrument is *made*, as well as greater virtuosity and variety in how the acoustic guitar is *played*.

A central claim of this book is that these two transformations are not merely coincidental but interrelated, driven by the interplay of the forces of demand and supply. Therefore, to return to our imaginary music store visits, one cannot understand the supply-side differences between the Shreveport Music Company of 1960 and Guitar Works of today without also taking into account the demand dimension—the public's attraction to the acoustic guitar. That attraction has depended critically on innovations in how the instrument is played.

Seminal changes in guitar playing began during the so-called Folk Music Revival extending from the late 1950s and through the 1960s.[12] To be sure, prior to the 1960s there were many innovative guitar virtuosos in a variety of genres. A short listing would include blues guitarists such as Robert Johnson and Blind Willie McTell; jazz guitarists such as Django Reinhardt, Lonnie Johnson, and Charlie Christian; and bluegrass/country musicians such as Maybelle Carter and Alton Delmore. All these players and many others were skilled at playing melodic lines and executing complex picking patterns. But a fair generalization is that in most ensemble settings, acoustic guitar players were assigned to provide strummed chordal and rhythmic accompaniment for other instruments such as violins and mandolins.[13] In the revival, however, the instrument itself, and those who played it, became a focus of attention.

As mentioned earlier, the revival as a mass phenomenon began with the Kingston Trio's surprise 1958 smash hit, "Tom Dooley," which was indeed a revived version of an old Civil War–era murder ballad, "Tom Dula." The young trio performed the song with all acoustic instruments—a banjo, a tenor (four-string) guitar, and a standard (six-string) flattop guitar—and thereby brought something new to the country's sonic landscape. Though some critics slammed the trio's smooth rendition as inauthentic, the consuming public voted with their dollars, apparently welcoming the shift away from the rock-and-roll and crooner sounds of 1950s popular music. Trailing not far behind was a cohort of young, acoustic guitar-wielding figures such as Bob Dylan, Richie Havens, Gordon Lightfoot, Taj Mahal, Joni Mitchell, and Joan Baez, along with television shows such as *Hootenanny*. There was also a renewed appreciation for such older folk styles as blues, bluegrass, old-time music (mainly Appalachian in origin), ragtime, and early jazz.[14] Nowadays these styles tend to be grouped under the broad category of roots or Americana music.

This stylistic shift coincided with a second factor, a demographic bulge: the coming of (teen) age of the so-called Baby Boomers, born in the postwar 1940s and early 1950s. This was a rising generation that in the 1960s was trying to define itself in a society that many of them found complacent, self-satisfied, and materialistic—in a word, inauthentic. One way to mark one's defection from the sheep-like masses and assert one's autonomy was through music, and so the acoustic guitar's new stylistic popularity fortuitously overlapped with growth in the very demographic cohort most attracted to that musical style. Its relatively small size and affordable price—along with the fact that it is fairly simple to learn basic chords—made the acoustic guitar not only a popular instrument, but also a signifier of one's cultural identity.

Since the 1960s, many other musical styles have gained popularity, and their fates have varied. Some styles have come and largely faded away, while others have endured. Despite these these ups and downs in popular styles, the acoustic guitar has held its attraction and prominence as a solo instrument. On this point, I concur with Chris Martin, who recently retired as CEO and sixth-generation scion of the family that, in 1833, created this country's most storied guitar company, C. F. Martin & Co. In our conversation, Chris remarked, "after coming out of the disco and the Yamaha DX7 synthesizer era, when people rediscovered how cool that wooden box is, they just keep rediscovering it."[15]

The term itself, with its prefix "re," suggests that the example of the disco-to-acoustic shift in musical tastes was not a unique event, but rather part of a larger cyclical process of back-and-forth swings in musical styles and orchestration. As just one example, in discussing current trends in country music, Chris Martin said, "what excites me about country music is getting back to basics. When country goes the way of orchestration, we suffer. When they come back to basics, we [Martin and other acoustic makers] are right there."

The acoustic guitar's so-called rediscovery therefore had much to do with innovations—in essence, a transformation—in *playing* the instrument in such genres as folk, bluegrass, country, blues, jazz, and even rock. I was indeed fortunate to have witnessed, in those concerts at The Ark, some of this transformation. In Chapter 1, I revisit my memories of those concerts as a springboard to reflect on that transformation.

In terms of *making* guitars, this book asserts that there has been a vital, enduring connection between playing and production. In simplest terms, I hold that the ultimate result of the acoustic guitar's growing role as a virtuosic solo instrument has been a rising demand for acoustic guitars in all ranges of quality and price. And those who build guitars have responded to the market's call. Chapters 2 through 6 recount my experiences in the world of these builders.

In my interview with him, Dana Bourgeois, a master luthier of high-end guitars bearing his name, captures a major part of this change: "You're writing a whole book because guys like me and a group of others have come along and kind of reinvented the wheel and spent an entire career doing it. So we're kind of back in a Golden Age of builders."[16] Bourgeois is referring primarily to the high quality of guitars being produced in the artisan-level portion of the market in which he operates. Indeed, other observers have remarked upon the current period as a New Golden Age of guitar making, comparable to the so-called Golden Age between 1930 and 1945. During those years, the two largest builders, Martin and Gibson, produced instruments of such quality that their best guitars of that period now fetch prices exceeding $100,000.[17] I agree with Bourgeois's use of the term "reinvention," but I would extend his basic idea beyond the artisan and small-scale producer segment of the industry. What has occurred is, in fact, nothing less than a transformation of the *American acoustic guitar industry as a whole*.

As a way of visualizing this transformation, let us return to our imaginary strolls through the three guitar stores separated by geography and time. Those walk-throughs reveal some major differences in the stores' offerings, the most obvious ones being those of specialization and scale. As for the two actual stores, as we saw earlier, Guitar Works sells mainly guitars, compared with the Shreveport Music Company's offerings of many types of instruments. Moreover, Guitar Works dwarfs SMC in terms of scale. Whereas the Shreveport store offered perhaps a dozen acoustics, Guitar Work displays about a hundred such instruments ranging across a price spectrum of several thousand dollars.

This difference in magnitude is not just a difference in the financial or entrepreneurial skill of different owners; it also reflects the industry's capacity to respond to growing demand for acoustic guitars. Since 1960 the acoustic guitar industry has expanded, albeit unevenly, in both units produced and overall sales. After averaging relatively strong growth in both categories during the 1960s, the industry, along with the economy in general, suffered from back-to-back recessions triggered by the 1973 and 1979 oil shocks—not to mention the public's proclivity for new musical styles such as disco. Growth resumed in the 1980s, but then declined again during the financial crisis of 2008–2009. Since 2010, acoustic guitar sales have followed an upward trend, driven by improving economic conditions and continued popularity of the instrument itself.[18] The onset of the Covid pandemic in March 2020, although it challenged guitar makers to adjust quickly to changes in both supply and demand, did not fundamentally reverse this basic trend.

One might have imagined that the rise in popularity of the electric guitar since the 1950s would have dampened demand for its older acoustic sibling. With its amplification, sound effects, and a certain cultural edginess, the electric guitar could have undercut the acoustic guitar's appeal and relegated the softer-voiced wooden box to campfire singalongs and living-room jam sessions.

Production and sales figures do not bear this out. Each type of guitar has found its musical niches and fans, with US unit sales of acoustic instruments slightly but consistently edging electrics every year during the past decade.[19] Why not enjoy both for what they distinctively bring to the musical table? For many guitarists themselves, there is no either/or. Bruce Springsteen, Jackson Browne, Bonnie Raitt, Richard Thompson, and Mark Knopfler—to name just a few—employ both types of guitars. What's good for the musician is also good for the maker, as several well-known guitar brands, including Fender, Gibson, Guild, and Taylor, produce both acoustic and electric guitars. Even a small company known mainly for its fine acoustics, Collings Guitars of Austin, Texas, also builds a well-regarded line of electric guitars.

Recall, too, another difference in the two stores that we noted in passing: Guitar Works today, unlike Shreveport Music Company in 1960, features many relatively high-end instruments from American makers who did not exist sixty years ago. These instruments represent what luthier Dana Bourgeois terms the "reinvention" of the acoustic guitar in recent decades: the entry of new luthiers and companies, such that there has been a reshaping of the competitive field of American guitar makers.

The result is a vastly expanded range of choices for the prospective guitar buyer. In 1960 the Shreveport store, as noted above, gave a prospective buyer a limited range: guitars by the two largest old-line producers, Martin and Gibson, along with a handful of low-end, made-in-Chicago brands such as Harmony and Kay. There were few high-end builders, either individual luthiers or small-batch companies, and virtually no imported guitars, except perhaps classical guitars from Mexico or Spain. Japan was just beginning to export cars, musical instruments, and other items, but the quality of their products was still largely deemed low by American consumers. As for China, the country was isolated economically and in the throes of Maoist-inspired, do-it-yourself technologies such as backyard furnaces for making steel.

The Shreveport store had a few used guitars for sale, but these were considered roughly equivalent to used cars. Who would want a scratched and battered instrument? In that pre-Internet era, there was no large, active market for used instruments. Yet to come were the huge offerings of eBay, consolidated sites such as Reverb.com and Gbase.com, and online store sales. Older instruments did not yet possess the character of vintage. Although the so-called Golden Era of guitar making during the 1930s had passed, few people in 1960 recognized it as such.

Today, the guitar market is virtually saturated with choices. Not only does one have immediate access to a range of used and vintage instruments online, but for the customer seeking a new guitar, there are still the long-established producers just mentioned, Martin and Gibson. These makers have been joined in recent decades by two new types of domestic builders, both of which are amply displayed at Guitar Works.

The first type is what I refer to, following Dana Bourgeois, as the "reinventors." These are the individual builders and small-scale companies—all makers who provide select materials, exceptional craftsmanship, custom orders, and, in many cases, direct personal engagement with the customer. A prime example is Michael Millard, who founded Froggy Bottom Guitars in Chelsea, Vermont, in the early 1970s. Today, finely crafted Froggy Bottom guitars—new and used—typically sell for between $8,000 and $15,000. Other celebrated individual luthiers include Linda Manzer of Toronto; James Olson of Circle Pines, Minnesota; and Wayne Henderson and his daughter Jayne of Rugby, Virginia, whose instruments on the used market start at $15,000.

There are also several small production companies making perhaps 300 to 1,500 high-quality guitars per year, ranging in price from $4,000 to over $10,000. On the wall in Guitar Works hang such instruments crafted by Dana Bourgeois himself and other makers noted earlier, such as Collings, Goodall, Huss & Dalton, Larrivée, and Santa Cruz.

In our walk-through of Guitar Works we also recognized several instruments bearing the name Taylor. These are made by a second type of new American guitar maker that is literally in a class by itself, namely Taylor Guitars, based in El Cajon, California, near San Diego. Starting from scratch in 1974, two young San Diegans, Bob Taylor and Kurt Listug, founded a small company bearing Bob's name; they struggled for a few years to become financially viable. But viable indeed the company had become by the early 1980s, and since then Taylor Guitars has risen to the point that it now outproduces Martin, averaging 80,000–100,000 guitars a year, all while offering a gamut of guitars from starters to high-quality acoustic and electric instruments. More than one observer has termed Taylor, due to its emphasis on growth and innovation, a "game changer" in the guitar industry.

A final difference in our two stores concerns imported guitars. Whereas Shreveport Music Company in the early 1960s carried almost no guitars made abroad, Guitar Works has a large selection of such instruments, bearing Japanese names such as Yamaha and American names such as Fender. Put in a larger context, our imaginary trip from Shreveport to Evanston highlights the acoustic guitar's globalization during the past six decades. Until the early 1970s, imported guitars were rare in the American market; however, at the beginning of that decade, imported instruments—almost all coming from Japan—began to gain market share in domestic US sales. By the 1990s, about half of all guitars sold were imports—now coming mainly from China. The acoustic guitar world has seen a strong push by foreign-owned and increasingly some American-owned companies such as Fender, to produce instruments abroad and export them to US and other world markets.

Our imagined walk-through of Guitar Works and our survey of Internet options impressed us with the rise and visible presence of new guitar makers. Compared with the relatively meager offerings of 1960, today's guitar buyer faces literal walls of new choices, not to mention the much vaster world of on-line sales. There is one component of the guitar industry, however, that has endured: the old-line companies of Martin and Gibson. C. F. Martin & Company dates from 1833, when Christian Frederick Martin Sr. emigrated from Germany to the United States and set up a small factory, first in New York City and later in Nazareth, Pennsylvania, where the company has continued to operate for nearly two hundred years. By contrast, the Gibson Guitar and Mandolin Company is still a relative whippersnapper, its founding dating from 1894 when Orville Gibson first established his instrument-making operations in Kalamazoo, Michigan.

The proliferation of new entrants to the ranks of guitar makers—what I am terming "reinventors," a "game changer," and "globalizers"—has apparently not swept these erstwhile household names into the competitive dustbin. The old guard is still represented on wall pegs in shops such as Guitar Works and easily obtainable from one's living room. The question remains, however: How have they fared amid this recent competitive onslaught? How has this old guard responded, and what has been their fate?

HOW THIS BOOK IS DISTINCTIVE

Based on a multitude of personal experiences connected to the acoustic guitar—from coffeehouse concerts in the 1970s to shoe-leather travel and research in recent years—this book recognizes and seeks to portray the dual transformation in the acoustic guitar world just described: a long, interconnected process of greater creativity and virtuosity in playing the instrument, along with a comparable leap forward in the craftsmanship and diversity in how the guitar is made. This book is my story of discovering the transformed world of the acoustic guitar.

In the interviews I carried out in my research, one of the first questions I asked guitar makers was "What makes your instruments distinctive?" I now turn the mic on myself and ask, "Among all the many books on guitars, how is this book distinctive?" My response: this book is distinctive in three ways—scope, research, and presentation.

Scope. No other book, I believe, attempts what this one does: to convey and interpret the major trends regarding an important American musical instrument during the past sixty years. I hope that this book will serve as an essential resource for any reader who wants to know what has happened to the acoustic guitar since the Folk Music Revival of the early 1960s, a movement that triggered renewed interest in acoustic instruments generally and the acoustic guitar specifically. This claim merits a brief comparison with other books on the American acoustic guitar, which tend to fall into one of three camps:

(1) Large format, photographic books on various types, brands, and models of guitars.[20] While pleasing to the eye, such books tend to be long on lavish pictures but lacking in historical perspective and analysis. While my book does have several photographs, these are mainly of performers and guitar makers, not of the instrument per se. Moreover, while not strictly speaking a history of the instrument, this book analyzes the ways the instrument's playing and making has been essentially transformed in recent decades.

(2) Single company profiles. These books present the history of a single major company such as Martin, Gibson, or Taylor.[21] While this book has chapters on each of these companies, its scope is broader, extending to the guitar-making industry as a whole.

(3) Artisan profiles. These books feature close encounters, via participant observation, with an individual artisan luthier or even several artisan luthiers.[22] There are many excellent books of this type, but their scope is generally narrower than mine, which seeks to identify and explain major changes throughout the entire industry.

Finally, I note that none of the types of books just cited focuses on the actual *playing* of the acoustic guitar; yet any account of the guitar's transformation is incomplete without such coverage. As mentioned, this book addresses the major changes in playing styles in the next chapter. While my admittedly personal account (drawing on formative memories of attending concerts at The Ark coffeehouse in Ann Arbor, Michigan, in the early 1970s) does not pretend to cover all genres and styles of playing, I trust that it provides a reasonably broad sample of innovative artists.

Research. I knew from the outset I wanted this to be an *experiential* book as much as possible. Through previous book projects I have found that I learn best—and, not coincidentally, have the most fun—when I go to where the action is and talk to people about what they do and how they view their world. So, for the guitar-*making* chapters of this book (Chapters 2–6), I visited shops and factories across the United States, from San Diego to Lewiston, Maine; from Nazareth, Pennsylvania, to Seattle; and from Staunton, Virginia, to Austin, Texas. I also attended the annual music industry trade show in Anaheim, California—a.k.a., the Winter NAMM Show—where I met dozens of makers and sellers. In all, I interviewed more than fifty luthiers, production managers, store owners, and other observers, and I extensively cite their direct testimonies when portraying and assessing how that world has changed.

Presentation. Despite my interest in direct observation and analysis, I make no pretense of being dispassionate about the acoustic guitar. On the contrary, this book seeks to convey my passion for the instrument—my "instrumental affair" with the acoustic guitar—by blending memoir, reportage, and assessment. So along with eyewitness accounts of shop and factory visits and extensive use of interviews, I also seek to convey my own engagement with the acoustic guitar. One might easily critique the subjectivity of my approach, to which I reply: guilty as charged. This is just one person's story—my story—but I hope that my vision of the acoustic guitar is sufficiently expansive to take in the big picture of the instrument's transformation in recent decades.

Chapter 1

DUG FROM THE ROOTS
New Sounds from an Old Instrument

You took from Woody, you borrowed from Pete,
You ripped Child Ballads right off the sheet.

For forty years you've dug from the roots
Seen a new past, invented old truths.

With tradition's clay you reworked the wheel
And left us more than we can ever steal.
Don't think twice, it's all right.

—*"STEALIN' (ODE TO BOB)," BY AUTHOR*

A good place to begin is with the sounds the acoustic guitar makes. What have I discovered, or, perhaps in the words of Chris Martin quoted earlier, "rediscovered"? My own rediscovery of the music emanating from that cool wooden box is certainly what drew me to the acoustic guitar decades ago. As recounted in the previous chapter, my acoustic guitar baptism took place in The Ark coffeehouse in Ann Arbor in the early 1970s. There I fell in love with the sounds generated by the instrument in the hands of skilled musicians coming through town on the folk music circuit. Since those halcyon days of my own personal rediscovery of the acoustic guitar, I have come to realize that these musicians were not just expressing their talents in the moment, they were also participating in and communicating a larger story of musical creation, emulation, and ultimately transformation in how the acoustic guitar is played.

The bigger picture here is that this transformation in *playing* remains a prime driver of a simultaneous and interactive process of transformation in the *making* of acoustic guitars that has occurred during the past six decades. That is, I maintain that the growing prominence of the acoustic guitar in various popular musical styles stimulated a growing commercial market in record sales, live performances, and general interest in the instrument beginning around 1960. In classic demand-and-supply fashion, this burgeoning demand for acoustic guitar-made music provided, in turn, an incentive for guitar makers to supply more and better guitars to the growing legions of people—largely but not exclusively young White males—desiring to play the instrument. I view the two transformations—of playing and making guitars—as intrinsically connected; therefore, attention must be paid to both. The transformation of the world of acoustic guitar making will be explored in subsequent chapters. This chapter focuses on the necessary dynamic that gave impetus to that world: the transformation in how the instrument is played.

My approach—a highly personal but, I believe, a revelatory one—is to begin with four musicians I experienced at The Ark. Chosen because of their distinct musical paths, these musicians serve as examples to tell at least part of that larger story of transformation. All four brought impressive musical skills—including guitar mastery—to the table, and all went on to careers spanning the next several decades. This chapter analyzes two aspects of these musicians' music. The first concerns the provenance of the musical traditions and influences that shaped these musicians' approach to the guitar, and the second is the musical pathways these musicians took, which likely influenced younger guitar players along the way. The four musicians—perhaps not household names but well-known to acoustic guitar aficionados—are David Bromberg, Norman Blake, Elizabeth Cotten, and Paul Geremia.

These musicians represent the overlapping yet distinct traditions of playing the instrument. These traditions—or what one might call "lines of lineage"—are the modern songster, the flatpicker, and the fingerstyle guitarist. All four made new guitar music out of the traditions they inherited and embraced. Other musicians, following in their wake, have done the same thing, keeping those traditions alive and evolving. The result has been an enormous enrichment—a process of deepening, widening, and ultimately transforming—of each tradition. For each of the four musicians considered, I address three questions. First, what were their major musical influences? Second, how did they incorporate and transmute those influences into new guitar music? Finally, who are some of the guitarists who have followed in the same musical lineage lines?

I draw on my own initial experiences, fully recognizing the inherent limitations of such an approach. At The Ark, I was hearing only a certain bandwidth of all the music then being made by the acoustic guitar. Knowledgeable readers will no doubt point out that I have neglected this or that musician or musical style. I stand guilty as charged; however, that is the risk of an approach rooted in one's own experiences and preferences. So while I do not pretend to be encyclopedic in this survey—that would take a whole other book!—I do trust that the reader will find this account convincing in its basic contention that the playing of the acoustic guitar has indeed been transformed during the past six decades, as creative guitarists have drawn new sounds from this old instrument.

THE MODERN SONGSTER TRADITION
DAVID BROMBERG—BEFORE AND SINCE

David Bromberg, born in 1945 and performing well into his 70s as of this writing, is a difficult musician to define, but there is no denying his talent as a versatile, all-around musician. He is a singer, songwriter, interpreter of a wide range of song genres, dynamic performer, and . . . a creative guitarist. Bromberg's repertoire and playing styles are so varied that I can think of no better term than to call him an heir to the "songster" tradition that originated in African American music in the nineteenth century. In his insightful book, *The History of the Blues,* Francis Davis states: "We draw a distinction between blues singers and songsters, recognizing the latter as transitional figures who performed many types of rural songs in addition to the blues."[1] I would term

Bromberg a "modern" songster in that he performs, in addition to the blues, a range of songs from many genres.

The modern songster tradition in contemporary acoustic guitar playing could be defined in several ways, but the essence is this: the guitar is just one element—albeit the key element—in an eclectic, evolving musical approach that embraces a wide range of playing/musical styles. In the process the songster incorporates singing, original material, cover songs, and even (gasp!) electric guitars. To be sure, the musician is a virtuoso guitar player, and there are musical passages, even whole tunes, when the musician showcases that instrumental prowess; however, the overall emphasis is on the song, with the guitar being figuratively at the service of the song itself, rather than the single star of the show. Think of the acoustic guitar as part of a musical ensemble that also includes other instruments, vocal arrangements, and a broad mix of styles and songwriting. The long career of David Bromberg exemplifies this modern songster tradition.

I recall, through the memory haze of five decades, the ambiance of The

The Ark coffeehouse in the early 1970s. Photo by Al Blixt.

Ark coffeehouse in Ann Arbor in the early 1970s as David Bromberg—in his mid-20s at the time—takes the stage. For David, that means picking a path—gingerly, with Martin guitar slung over his shoulder—through a crowd of about seventy-five young people sitting side by side on floor cushions. The "stage" is no more than a single microphone set up in a bit of open area in the living room of a rambling clapboard house on Hill Street, near the University of Michigan campus. At that time, the Hill House, as it was called, belonged to the First Presbyterian Church, which repurposed it as a coffeehouse, "to provide a warm, safe, peaceful place to come together free from drugs, alcohol, and the storms of academic life and personal stress. It was meant to provide a creative outlet for talent in music, poetry and artwork."[2] David Bromberg was just one of many "folk circuit" performers who came through town to play in a weekly concert series at the storm-free, biblically related Ark.

David cuts a singular figure by appearance alone: tall and gangly, with frizzy hair and beard. Barely acknowledging the scrunched-in audience gathered at his feet, he adjusts his guitar strap, does some final tuning, and launches into what was to become his signature mashup rendition of two blues standards—"Statesboro Blues" and "Church Bells Blues"—both first recorded in the 1920s by Blind Willie McTell and Luke Jordan, respectively.[3] Although McTell played "Statesboro Blues," as he did most of his repertoire, on a twelve-string guitar, Bromberg fingerpicks it on his Martin D-18 six-string, using Dropped D tuning. This tuning requires tuning the low E string—the lowest string in standard guitar tuning—down to D, thereby providing an alternating thumb bass line of a low D/high D (fourth string) that is used in many blues songs.

David begins the song softly, almost plaintively, slowly playing the melody and singing the classic lines:

Wake up, mama, turn your lamp down low
Wake up, mama, turn your lamp down low
Where in the world did you get the nerve
To turn poor Dave from your door?

Bromberg gradually builds the song, an extended rejected lover's lament, in volume and tempo with an increasing urgency. Lyrically, the song moves from a tone of sadness (in McTell's "Statesboro") to one of bitterness and anger (in Jordan's "Church Bells"), with the singer finally promising, "When I leave this time, I'm going away to stay."

After several verses Bromberg begins breaking with the repetitive verse structure as his guitar now mimics the propulsive clickety-clack of the train carrying the singer away from his lover toward the title town:

> Big 80 left Savannah, lord, it would not stop
> You shoulda seen that colored fireman when he got his boiler hot.
> Roll over Mama, hand me down my travellin' shoes
> You shoulda known by that I had these Statesboro blues.

Transitioning from McTell's lyrics of sorrow and regret, Bromberg slides to the hilarious vitriol of Jordan's lyrics. In one verse, the singer bitterly demands recompense for all that he has spent on the woman jilting him:

> Gimme back the hat I bought you, the big umbrella,
> Gimme back the shoes, I want the dress and all
> If you don't like your daddy, woman
> You got no right to stand and squall
> Gimme back the wig I bought you
> Let your goddam head go bald.

In this performance lasting a full five minutes, Bromberg takes just one twenty-second solo guitar break, all the while maintaining the head-bopping, bluesy tempo he has established. To add to the cumulative drama of this spleen-purging song, he spews forth denunciations with arms akimbo, eyes popping, and his expression grimacing, but with a wink that conveys: Hey folks, this is just a performance, and I'm having a blast. Following this bravura opening, Bromberg proceeds to work through a broad range of material, including the popular Jerry Jeff Walker tune "Mr. Bojangles," a medley of fiddle tunes, some original songs, and another old blues classic, "Delia."

Recalling that long-ago performance at The Ark and having followed his career since then, I conclude that Bromberg's music exemplifies two aspects of what I'm terming the modern-day songster tradition: "big ears" and respect. Big ears is my term for a musician's willingness and capacity to range widely and remain open to all manner of musical styles, and Bromberg has such qualities in abundance. A New Yorker, from the comfortable suburb

David Bromberg at The Ark, ca. 1977. Bentley Historical Library, University of Michigan.

of Tarrytown, David began frequenting Greenwich Village coffeehouses as a teenager in the early 1960s, in the process getting to know up-and-coming folk musicians such as Bob Dylan, Dave Van Ronk, Joan Baez, the brothers Artie and Happy Traum, and Ramblin' Jack Elliott.

Taking to the acoustic guitar as the default position for a folkie, Bromberg studied for a time with one of the rediscovered blues greats of that era, Reverend Gary Davis. David had also mastered the records of flatpicking virtuosi, most notably Doc Watson. One can easily identify several lines of musical lineage that constituted Bromberg's early guitar education: early twentieth-century blues, Appalachian styles (ranging from Carter Family old-time style to fiddle tunes), and the emerging modern folk movement featuring both revived traditional songs ("Tom Dula" / "Tom Dooley") and more recent ones such as the just-mentioned "Mr. Bojangles," performed with largely acoustic-based instrumentation.

Complementing this eclectic aspect of his musical interests is a strong sense of respect for inherited tradition. Bromberg conveys gratitude for this vast inheritance, but it is not the kind of respect that results in imitation. Bromberg's music embraces many styles, but he does not slavishly try to reproduce these inherited styles and songs. Rather, he puts his own creative stamp on them, as his mashup version of "Statesboro Blues" and "Church Bells Blues" demonstrates.

Perhaps the most definitive way in which David's songster sensibility has departed from folk-music orthodoxy with its characteristic acoustic sound is his incorporation of the *electric* guitar in his music. In his early years as a performer, including his concerts at The Ark, he played only acoustic guitar, but by the mid-1970s he was moving well beyond a sideman/solo act to incorporate a full band sound, and that required the amplification that an electric guitar provides. As his longtime friend Artie Traum remarks: "In a revolutionary way, David Bromberg was perhaps the first 'folkie' to bring a horn section, backup vocalists, unison fiddles, and electric guitars to his show—with electrifying effect."[4]

Bob Dylan, of course, had already "gone electric," not for the first time but notoriously at the 1965 Newport Folk Festival.[5] In that sense Bromberg was more evolutionary than revolutionary, but the point is that he does not see any particular Rubicon that he can or cannot cross. For him, acoustic and electric guitars make different sounds, to which he would say: *Vive la différence!* He would certainly concur with a recent study that concludes, "The electric guitar as we know it today is a substantively different instrument from its acoustic counterpart. It has its own unique sonic and physical identity. You'd rarely, if ever, mistake the twang, jangle, and crunch of an electric guitar, let alone its svelte shape, for the classic bulk and organic warmth of an acoustic."[6]

To Bromberg, it's all music and ripe for his own picking, whether that be his own original songs or those of others, playing acoustic guitar or electric guitar, or performing traditional versus modern music. As a rough quantitative gauge of this songster quality in Bromberg's music, consider the 1998 compilation CD of his thirty-year career. Of the fifteen songs chosen for this album, seven are original compositions, and the eight nonoriginals include a fiddle tune medley, songs by Dylan and Jerry Jeff Walker, and the McTell/Jordan blues songs mentioned above. He plays acoustic guitar on eleven of the tracks and electric guitar on four of them.

Becoming, in his words, "burned out" from touring, performing, and recording throughout the 1970s and into the mid-1980s, Bromberg retired from performing and established a successful violin shop in Wilmington, Delaware.[7] After more than twenty years away, he returned, in 2006, to recording and performing music, much in the vein of his earlier work, and in the years since, he has released five albums. To all appearances, Bromberg, born in 1945, is still going strong as of this writing. Reflecting on what I have termed his modern songster approach, he comments, "I pick songs that speak to me, that I can feel. There's no sense doing one I can't feel. You have to pick the right songs. If you write them, they probably have part of you in them already, so you're all right. If you don't write them, you have to see yourself in them."[8] His longtime guitar-playing friend and current producer, Larry Campbell, sums up David's musical approach: "Bromberg was Americana when Americana wasn't cool. It was blues, bluegrass, swing, rock and roll, Dixieland. . . . Anything that is real American music, he did with his particular authority."

The modern songster tradition in acoustic guitar playing, which David Bromberg introduced me to in the early 1970s, has been embraced by many musicians over the past five decades, and I apologize in advance for ignoring dozens of fine guitarists. Here I will underline the contributions of three musicians who are among this tradition's luminaries: Bonnie Raitt, Taj Mahal, and Ry Cooder. All of them embody not only instrumental virtuosity but also three qualities one sees in Bromberg. First, these performers showcase the song over sheer guitar brilliance. The guitar, to be sure, plays the key role in establishing the overall sound, but its job is to not to stand out as the exclusive instrumental focus but rather to integrate into a blend of vocals and other instruments. Second, these musicians embrace a wide, eclectic variety of roots styles ranging over the past century of American, and even non-American, music. Finally, all three project a respect for, yet a certain irreverence toward, those inherited styles. Put simply, all three can be said to operate with an unspoken motto: "Make it sound like you got it from somewhere, but make it sound like your own."

Bonnie Raitt's long career—stretching, like Bromberg's, over a fifty year period from the early 1970s to the present—exemplifies all of these traits. Born in 1949, Raitt, like Bromberg, came from a privileged background and began college at an elite school, only to drop out by age twenty to pursue music full time. In her early teens, she began playing guitar and listening to the folk and roots music around her. As a fourteen-year-old, she was especially impressed by an album, *Blues at Newport '63*, featuring performers such as John Lee Hooker. "From that point on," she said, "I was split into two parts. One side of me was all Joan Baez, my early idol, or Child-type ballads, while the other suddenly *had* to learn whatever the hell it was Mississippi John Hurt was doing on 'Candy Man.'"[9]

Over the decades, Raitt has remained "split"—not into just two parts, but into a wide range of musical styles including slow ballads, rock, reggae, gospel, folk, and of course, blues. Like Bromberg (not to mention Dylan before him), Raitt began as primarily an acoustic folkie solo act, playing a jumbo F-50 Guild guitar and performing the folk and blues standards popular at the time—songs by Dylan, Baez, Mississippi Fred McDowell, John Prine, and others. As she built a following and moved to larger venues, she incorporated—again à la Dylan and Bromberg—an electric guitar into her performances and recordings, even as she always reserved spots for her acoustic playing. On both instruments, a mainstay of her guitar work has been the "bottleneck" style: the use of a glass or metal slide on the middle finger of her left, fretting hand, to provide a legato, or note slurring, lead line. Although she increasingly became branded as primarily a blues musician, she retained her interest in a wide range of styles. As just one indication of her eclecticism is a 1995 compilation album of live performances that included not only her own original songs but also songs by, among others, John Hiatt, Chris Smither, Mississippi Fred McDowell, Michael McDonald, Richard Thompson, David Byrne, Bryan Adams, and Jackson Browne.

Seven years older than Bonnie Raitt, Taj Mahal (born 1942, né Henry Saint Clair Fredericks) grew up in Springfield, Massachusetts, surrounded by music. His mother was a gospel singer, and his father was a jazz musician hailing originally from Jamaica. Taj (as he is widely called) has been described in an encyclopedic survey of blues musicians as "a modern-day songster who incorporates into his repertoire country blues, ragtime, reggae, rhythm & blues, jazz, and folk music."[10] Like Raitt, he has had a long, up-and-down career, issuing his first recording in 1968 and still performing as he turned eighty years old. Also like Raitt, he began as primarily an acoustic guitar player, but during his career, he has also played keyboards, resonator slide guitar, and harmonica. In recent years, perhaps owing to his age, his recordings have featured mainly his emphatic vocals, leaving the instrumentation to a multiple-piece band.[11]

Like other guitarists in the songster lineage, Taj is fearless in putting his own stamp on his music. For him, there are no boundaries, no taboos. His own website states this vision: "Taj Mahal doesn't wait for permission. If a sound intrigues him, he sets out to make it. If origins mystify him, he moves to trace them. If rules get in his way, he unapologetically breaks them. To Taj, convention means nothing, but traditions are holy. He has pushed music and culture forward, all while looking lovingly back."[12] With well over fifty albums—studio and live recordings along with various compilations—spanning six decades, Taj Mahal has few peers in the musical tradition he has chosen.

A third musician in the modern songster tradition is Ry Cooder (born 1947), who, like Raitt, grew up in comfortable circumstances in postwar southern California. Cooder was also influenced by the folk and blues revivals taking place in the 1960s, and by age twenty had decided to pursue music full-time. Of the songsters considered here, Ry Cooder is certainly the most eclectic and virtuosic—often dizzyingly so. In the course of his career, he has delved deeply into the American roots songbook, covering songs by, among many others, Woody Guthrie, Blind Willie Johnson, Carter Stanley, Sleepy John Estes, Johnny Cash, Leadbelly (often spelled Lead Belly), Bix Beiderbecke, Skip James, and Josh White. Such a listing of musical influences only begins to describe Cooder's sponge-like sensibility. His vast output over the past five decades also includes several live recordings, albums of original songs, and scores and soundtracks for such movies as *The Long Riders*, *Paris, Texas*, *Crossroads*, and *Primary Colors*.

Another facet of Cooder's modern songster vision is that he seeks out and plays well with a variety of musicians, especially those from other cultures and traditions. In the course of his career, he has collaborated with many Latin and African American musicians—including Taj Mahal—and incorporated such styles as rhythm & blues, soul, gospel, and Norteño/Tex-Mex into his repertoire. He has also partnered with musicians from around the globe— including Cuba, India, and Mali.[13]

As with all three of the modern songsters I have portrayed—Bromberg, Raitt, and Taj Mahal—Cooder has no barriers in terms of the types of instruments he plays. He is, above all, a versatile multi-instrumentalist, proficient on mandolin, mandola, banjo, bass, keyboards, accordion, fiddle, and percussion. As a guitarist, Ry began his career, as did the other three musicians, playing principally acoustic guitar, especially the bottleneck style. As his career developed, Cooder expanded his guitar repertoire to include the electric guitar, although he still plays acoustic occasionally. His most popular recordings—for example, *Chicken Skin Music* and *Bop Till You Drop*—feature a distinctive, assertive electric slide guitar dominating the other instruments, thereby establishing a strong groove and clear melodic flow. But Cooder has always valued an acoustic presence in his music. On several songs he has played separate tracks on electric and acoustic guitar as well as mandolin or mandola.

As these brief profiles suggest, the modern songster tradition in acoustic playing has remained alive and well, even as it has been largely transformed. Listening to any of the recordings of Bromberg, Raitt, Taj Mahal, and Cooder, one is struck by what I have termed their big ears as well as their respect for their musical inheritance. Established American roots styles such as early country, Hawaiian, gospel, early jazz, protest songs, ragtime, and various subgenres of blues (Delta, Memphis-style, etc.)—not to mention such non-American styles as reggae, Cuban *son* music, and Indian *Hindustani* music—all are grist for the musical mill. Yet these styles are not worshipped or imitated; these musicians insist on asserting their own creativity in incorporating and adapting these styles into their repertoires. Above all, virtuosic acoustic guitar playing is evident, but that is not the dominating feature of their music. For these musicians, it's all about the song—the combination of groove, lyrics, vocals, and ensemble instrumentation—rather than featuring the guitar as the central showpiece.

THE FLATPICK TRADITION

Norman Blake—Before and Since

Another dive into my memory vault brings up another accomplished musician who appeared frequently at The Ark in the early 1970s: Norman Blake. Like David Bromberg, Blake began his evening performance by stepping carefully through a motley audience seated on the floor, final-tuning his road-worn 1930s Martin D-28 guitar, and then leaning into the one microphone in the house. The visual contrast between Blake and Bromberg was striking. Blake immediately came across as a quieter, calmer, and altogether more modest figure than Bromberg. Born in 1938, seven years before Bromberg, Norman Blake was a southern boy through and through, having been raised in Sulphur Springs, Alabama. Despite a traveling musician's life on the road, Norman still carried a strong southern accent. At about five feet, seven inches tall, he had none of Bromberg's looming, gangly, and sometimes blustery presence. What kind of sound could such a quiet, physically unimposing person produce?

The answer came immediately when Norman began to flat pick his first number: the classic, rapid-fire fiddle tune "Soldier's Joy." With little dramatic fanfare, Blake and his Martin guitar spoke with authority. Communicated instantly was Norman's paradoxical combination of relaxation and intense energy. One could easily imagine him sitting on a back porch "far away, down on a Georgia farm" (the name of a song he wrote), contentedly playing for himself and the flora and fauna around his southern retreat. With head down, eyes sometimes closed, and the hint of a smile on his face, Blake gradually built the well-known tune in drive and volume.

Norman and Nancy Blake at The Ark, 1975. Bentley Historical Library, University of Michigan.

Especially striking was the work of his right hand holding the flat pick to play the basic melody of "Soldier's Joy" the first time through the tune's AA/BB format, and then some slight improvisations in subsequent iterations. The terms "loose" and "relaxed" only begin to describe Blake's playing. His loose-wristed hand motion resembled that of someone flinging water off one's fingers or shooing away a fly, although those images imply a certain nonchalance and lack of precise control, which was not the case; his picking remained consistent and true throughout the tune. Every eighth note sounded clearly and cleanly, with none of the occasional fret buzz, inconsistent volume, and even "wrong" notes sometimes played by even experienced guitarists.

The rest of Blake's concert demonstrated those same qualities of laid-back but focused energy, as he ranged across a variety of songs that sounded somehow traditional, including several he wrote himself, most notably "Last Train from Poor Valley," and "Green Light on the Southern," and "Church Street Blues." As these titles indicate, Norman has a penchant for rural settings, hard times, railroads, and the blues. Consider a stanza and chorus of "Last Train," which he sang slowly and plaintively:

> The mines all shut down
> Everybody laid around
> There wasn't very much you could do
> But stand in that line
> Get your ration script on time
> Woman, I could see it killin' you.
>
> CHORUS
> Now the soft, new snows of December
> Lightly fall my cabin round
> Saw the last train from Poor Valley
> Takin' brown-haired Becky Richmond bound.

During his Ark concert, Blake also played mandolin, fiddle, and Dobro (resonator guitar), while singing in a tenor voice that sounded as if it was from a 1920s folk recording. That concert counts as one of those seminal moments in my musical life, in which a figurative seed was planted, prompting me to resolve to get a guitar and learn to produce sounds that might, however feebly, resemble the notes coming out of Norman's guitar.

Over a career that extends from the mid-1950s through the first two decades of this century, Blake has performed and recorded countless times in both solo and ensemble formats. For a time a touring sideman with Johnny Cash, he also recorded with, among others, Bob Dylan, Joan Baez, John Hartford, Kris Kristofferson, and Peter Ostroushko. His most durable (and presumably affectionate) collaboration has been with his wife, Nancy, a cellist and singer with whom he has made a dozen albums dating from the 1980s. It is impossible to put Blake's enormous musical corpus in a typological box—since it ranges freely among fiddle tunes, early country, modern folk, blues, and original songs—but on the whole, Norman has projected a musical vision and sound that embodies the term "traditional." To put it simply, he does not widely search out, or create, material that departs from an "old timey," rural feel.

With decades of hindsight, one can contextualize and assess Norman Blake's contribution to acoustic guitar playing. Although he is also a superb fingerstyle player, most of his recorded output is firmly in the lineage of the flatpick tradition. Within that tradition, I view Norman as one who has been both inheritor and progenitor. On the one hand, he inherited and further developed an emerging style of virtuosic single-note, acoustic flatpicking pioneered by Arthel Lane "Doc" Watson (1923–2012).[14] On the other hand, Blake has served as a progenitor—a collaborator, mentor, and inspiration—to a younger generation of flatpick acoustic guitarists, most notably Tony Rice (1951–2020), as well as a cohort of musicians born after 1970.

It would be impossible to exaggerate the influence of Doc Watson on virtually *anyone* in the past forty years who has seriously aspired to play American-style acoustic guitar with a flat pick. One begins, of course, with a small, triangular shaped pick, or plectrum, some basic chord shapes, and a simple up-and-down strumming motion. Once one achieves competence in these first steps, one is led to try to literally pick out a melody line of single notes. It is one thing to figure out how to play, however slowly and haltingly, the tune of "Mary Had a Little Lamb," and yet many aspirants have thrown down their picks in frustration at that point.

It is another musical feat entirely to flat pick the melody of a quick-step fiddle tune—a tune designed to keep a group of dancers moving happily and energetically. One must play the melody not only rapidly and flawlessly, but also tirelessly, since fiddle tunes always repeat several times. Fiddle tunes are aptly named because the fiddle is perfectly suited to this job, which requires furnishing a melody that is both loud and brisk. Compared to the fiddle, the acoustic guitar is not an obvious substitute, since it lacks both the volume of a fiddle and the relative ease of bowing back-and-forth across four catgut strings.

That is . . . until Doc Watson. Blinded as a young child by an eye infection, Watson was raised in the Appalachian crossroads of Deep Gap in western North Carolina. He was among the first musicians to find a way to elevate the acoustic guitar from largely a rhythmic, strumming, background instrument to a featured melodic role. That noted musical authority, William J. Clinton (forty-second US President), sums up the enormous impact of Doc Watson on the world of guitar playing: "There may not be a serious, committed Baby Boomer alive who didn't at some point in his or her youth try to spend a few minutes at least trying to learn to pick a guitar like Doc Watson."[15]

A self-trained musician, Watson was living in North Carolina and playing local concerts when he was first "discovered" by New York musician and folklorist Ralph Rinzler in 1960. Impressed with Doc's musical abilities as a traditional style guitarist and vocalist, Rinzler invited him to come to New York to record and play some concerts in the Northeast. That began a partnership between the two men — Doc as musician and Rinzler as his impresario—that lasted more than thirty years until Rinzler's death in 1994. Watson's talent was immediately obvious, and within a few years he had established a flourishing performing and recording career that lasted nearly five decades. Along the way Doc collaborated with many musicians across a range of styles, including old-time music (with banjoist Clarence Ashley), traditional bluegrass (with founder Bill Monroe), and the jazz-inflected "Dawg" music of David Grisman.[16] His longest running partnership was with his own son and fellow guitarist Merle Watson. For nearly twenty-five years, father and son performed and recorded twelve albums together, until Merle died in 1985 in a tractor accident.

Norman Blake acknowledged Doc Watson's impact on his guitar playing in an interview: "I was teaching guitar in the late 1960s in Chattanooga, Tennessee, and one of my students brought in an early Vanguard Doc Watson record. Until then, I played guitar with a thumb pick and one finger, much like Mother Maybelle, Lester Flatt, Riley Puckett, Carter Stanley, and others.

I used a flat pick for mandolin, but it never occurred to me to use a flat pick on the guitar until hearing Doc's LP that showed me this as an avenue one could go down."[17]

In the age of YouTube, one can readily appreciate Doc Watson's sheer virtuosity as a flatpicker as well as his impact on a younger generation of rising acoustic guitarists, most notably Blake himself. A perfect example comes from the 1979 Telluride Bluegrass Festival, when Watson is joined on stage by guitarists Blake and Dan Crary and fiddler Sam Bush—all three at least fifteen years his junior. With a quick count -off, Doc launches into the blazing cadence of the fiddle-tune chestnut, "Black Mountain Rag."[18] He plays the complex three-part tune with speed, clarity, and authority, then passes the tune to Blake, who picks it up seamlessly and with equal authority. About midway through Norman's solo, one hears Watson shout out, praise in his voice: "Aw, watch out there now!" Blake finishes and then passes the tune to Sam Bush, smiling in the process. After each of the other players completes his solo break, Watson plays the tune again to finish the five-minute performance. As he picks a brief bluesy tag, the other players smile at each other with palpable joy on their faces, while the crowd offers its applause and cheers.

This fiddle-tune jam from decades ago is also an apt metaphor for what one might term "intergenerational transmission of knowledge," as one generation gladly passes on its musical knowledge and encouragement to a younger one. Within the flatpick lineage, Norman Blake, as Doc Watson, has participated in this transmission process, both directly and indirectly. Most directly was Norman's collaboration on two albums (1987 and 1990) with Tony Rice (1951–2020), then still in his thirties. These two albums fit squarely within the Watson and Blake style of traditional music, and as such demonstrate that the younger Rice had mastered that style of flatpicking, especially on standard fiddle tunes such as "Salt Creek," "Blackberry Blossom," and "Whiskey Before Breakfast." One can fairly assume that Rice had "gone to school" on the albums of both Watson and Blake in his youth.

Unlike Blake, who continued to stay within the traditional sound of early, acoustic-based country music, Tony Rice worked on a wider musical canvas, incorporating jazz-inflected voicings into his singular guitar playing. Another key figure in Rice's musical development was Clarence White (1944–1973), whom Tony first met at age ten. By 1960, both the Rice and White families had relocated to southern California from elsewhere—Virginia and Maine, respectively—for promising job opportunities, and the two families got to know each other through musical connections, since the *pater familias* in each family was an accomplished acoustic musician who sought out other like-minded musicians.

As Rice recounts, in the dawning of the 1960s Doc Watson had not yet been discovered, and then-sixteen-year-old White had no established tradition of lead bluegrass guitar playing to follow. [19] Over the decade of the 1960s, however, that changed, and White gradually developed a synthetic style of guitar playing—first on acoustic and later electric guitar—that meshed elements of bluegrass, gypsy jazz (à la Django Reinhart), and even the folk-rock, Dylanesque stylings then coming into vogue. His originality was eventually noticed, and in 1968 he joined the Byrds, replacing Gram Parsons, who had quit. White remained in that popular group until the band dissolved in early 1973. Later that year, in June, White was killed by a drunk driver while loading equipment into a vehicle following a gig in Palmdale, California. At just 29, and with a still-promising career ahead, he had created a style of guitar playing that directly influenced Tony Rice and many others. As one authoritative report comments: "When the Byrds broke up, White was widely revered and in great demand. Not only was he a rock 'n' roll star whose guitar playing was admired by the likes of Jimi Hendrix and Jimmy Page, but the Kentucky Colonels [White's former band] were now idolized by a burgeoning acoustic music scene that was unafraid to acknowledge a love of both traditional and contemporary music."[20]

Certainly the younger Tony Rice was paying attention to, and learning from, Clarence White during the latter's short career. Rice eventually acquired Clarence's much-modified, and now iconic, 1935 Martin D-28 guitar and played it throughout his recording and performing career, which began the same year Clarence died.[21] Over the next three decades Tony Rice developed his own singular style of playing that combined and synthesized several styles, including the traditional solo flatpicking of Doc Watson and Norman Blake, the folk-rock voicings of White, and elements of jazz. In any pantheon of American acoustic guitar heroes during the past sixty years, Tony Rice would be in the very top echelon, along with Watson and Blake.

In addition to directly influencing Tony Rice, Blake was also an indirect progenitor—as a role model to emulate—for an even younger generation of flatpickers. Even a partial listing of fine flatpicking guitarists would neglect dozens of excellent musicians, and I do not intend to construct a "Top Ten" list or a ranking of any kind. Rather, I will draw from my own personal experience in recent years to indicate the range of outstanding flatpicking guitarists in the United States and elsewhere. That experience comes from attending several of the weeklong Acoustic Kamps—classroom instruction and nightly concerts by a corps of teacher-guitarists—all organized and hosted by Steve Kaufman. The Kaufman Kamp is held annually in early summer on a college campus in Maryville, Tennessee, about twenty miles south of Knoxville in East Tennessee.

Steve Kaufman is not only organizer and host, but also the star of the show, showcasing his talent in the nightly concerts. Steve can boast of a unique accomplishment: he is the only three-time winner of the prestigious National Flatpicking Championships, held annually in Winfield, Kansas. Given his "street cred" as a guitarist, Kaufman can draw from a deep reservoir of excellent musicians. An incomplete list of the flatpick instructors I had at the Kamp includes Stephen Bennett, Rolly Brown, Robin Bullock, John Carlini, Mark Cosgrove, Beppe Gambetta, Andy Hatfield, and Marcy Marxer. I can state with complete confidence that if you asked all these guitarists who have been their major musical influences, the name Norman Blake would be mentioned. In fact, in both classroom sessions and concerts, Blake was referenced several times.

It is worth noting that, in general, these guitarists do not hew to the traditionalist style of flatpicking that is Blake's mainstay. All of them, to be sure, can flat pick, at breakneck speed, the standard fiddle tunes that comprise one of the foundations of the genre; however, these are not just "johnny-many-notes" guitarists; they are all adept at diverse styles. For example, Rolly Brown and Marcy Marxer are primarily swing-style players, while Beppe Gambetta incorporates guitar-based tunes from his native Italy into his repertoire. Robin Bullock draws heavily from the Irish folk music tradition, while Mark Cosgrove has lately been recruited by David Bromberg to play backup and occasional lead guitar—on both acoustic and electric instruments—in Bromberg's band that features blues, folk, gospel, and other styles.[22]

An echelon of outstanding flatpick guitarists have followed in the wake of Norman Blake, Doc Watson, and Tony Rice. Any attempt to be completist would be futile, but a list of well-established guitarists would certainly include players such as Russ Barenberg, Chris Eldridge, Andy Falco, David Grier, Scott Nygaard, David Rawlings, Kenny Smith, Tim Stafford, Bryan Sutton, and Dan Tyminski.

What is perhaps most truly transformative about the growing list of excellent flatpickers is a rising generation of young women who are rapidly gaining recognition for their talents. This cohort includes the sisters Chelsea and Grace Constable, Courtney Hartman, Sierra Hull, Sarah Jarosz, Avril Smith, and Molly Tuttle. Their talents are especially impressive since most of these women play other instruments such as mandolin as well as they do guitar. And again, it would be inconceivable that any of these younger guitarists would not have been strongly influenced by the flatpicking prowess of Norman Blake, Tony Rice, and Doc Watson.

As I revisit my memories of The Ark in the early 1970s, I recall Norman Blake's performances as moments of Eureka-style discovery: I heard new, fresh sounds issuing from his old wooden box, as his hands and fingers moved and fretted the strings. Yes, I had listened to a few Doc Watson records, but I had never put eyes and ears directly on someone playing in the solo flatpick style that he and Blake were still pioneering at the time. Those moments, for me, were inspirational yet daunting. I wanted to do that, yes, but how could I ever approach Norman's combination of tone, speed, and melodic creativity? That's a question I still ask myself—now knowing well that the answer is "never"—but still I keep trying, hope against hope. The inspiration remains.

As it has for the generations of flatpickers who have come along since. What is striking, five decades later, is how much the flatpick tradition has indeed been transformed. As the examples of Clarence White, Tony Rice, and so many others demonstrate, that simple triangular piece of plastic (or tortoise shell) can produce many sounds and styles that depart from a classic fiddle-tune approach. Transformation continues to occur as well in terms of who is doing the picking; as noted, there is a young generation of female flatpickers coming to the fore. One can only be encouraged—and inspired—that the circle of accomplished guitar players is now widening from what historically has been largely a male-dominated preserve.

THE FINGERSTYLE TRADITION
ELIZABETH COTTEN AND PAUL GEREMIA—BEFORE AND SINCE

A consideration of the flatpick lineage does raise a relevant question: Why use a single plectrum, held between thumb and forefinger, when you can use all five of the fingers of your playing hand? Many creative guitarists over the decades and even centuries have pondered this question, in the process experimenting with types of picks and the use of those five digits. As in many aspects of the creative arts, there is no single way to do things. In the flat-picking tradition, for example, many guitarists use a hybrid style of playing in which one or more of the remaining fingers (usually the middle and ring fingers) simultaneously picks some notes while the flat pick provides both a driving bass rhythm as well as much of the melody line. Clarence White, Tony Rice, and many others have used this technique.

As for primarily fingerstyle players, one can, of course, use bare fingers, since picks fitted to the thumb and other fingers are not essential for play-ing the notes; however, thumb and finger picks do provide more projection (loudness) than playing without picks. (An alternative for many players is to have a nail salon install longer artificial nails on the same fingers.) Much of the fingerstyle repertoire uses some version of an alternating thumb stroke on two different lower-pitched strings to provide the basic beat, and one or more fingers to play melodic lines or repetitive finger rolls over fretted chords. As with flatpicking, there is also a hybrid style of fingerpicking that can approximate a flatpicking sound. This requires the forefinger grasping or stabilizing the underside of the thumb pick, thereby enabling an up-and-down motion with the playing hand while the thumb pick plays a rapid succession of single notes. A good example is Tommy Emmanuel, who often switches seamlessly between this hybrid and standard fingerstyle playing even within a single song (see below).

My introduction to fingerstyle guitar playing came through two musicians I saw at The Ark: Elizabeth Cotten (1893–1987) and Paul Geremia (born 1943). Both were skilled players, but it would be difficult to find two musicians whose styles contrasted more. Whereas Cotten, a Black woman from North Carolina who was nearly eighty years old at the time, generally played in a soft, fluid style, Geremia came on with gusto, often employing a thumping bass line and harmonica. Of the two, Geremia possessed more dexterity, range, and overall skill on his instrument, but Cotten's legacy has been more far-reaching.

Do you know the song "Freight Train"? Who hasn't at least heard it at some point? And what budding guitar player hasn't tried to master the easy-to-remember melody line that falls relatively easily under the fingers when playing in the key of C? That song was composed by Elizabeth Cotten, in 1905, when she was twelve years old. She recorded many songs in a musical career that came late in her life, but she is mainly remembered for that one tune, now a folk-song classic that's been recorded by, among others, Peter, Paul, and Mary, the Grateful Dead, and Pete Seeger.

When I saw her perform at The Ark, Cotten, with guitar in hand, walked slowly to the front of the room and sat down in a chair. Positioning her guitar, she looked up, smiled to the audience, and without a word began playing and singing another of her signature tunes, "Shake Sugaree":

> Have a little song
> Won't take long
> Sing it right
> Once or twice
> Oh, lordy me
> Didn't I shake sugaree?
> Everything I got is done and pawned
> Everything I got is done and pawned.

She then proceeded through a repertoire that included well-known gospel songs ("Jesus Is Tenderly Calling," "Jesus Lifted Me"), instrumentals ("Buck Dance," "Little Brown Jug"), and of course, "Freight Train."

Watching her play, I immediately noticed something I'd never seen before (and have seen only once or twice since): she not only played the guitar *left*-handed, she also did so with the strings tuned as for a right-handed player. Unless you play—or have tried to play—the guitar, it is hard to grasp how difficult it is to play this way. The difficulty comes from the fact that right-handed players typically—naturally—play the rhythmic pattern of the bass strings with their thumb and the higher-pitched, melody strings with the index and middle fingers. Without retuning an instrument set up for a right-handed player, a left-handed player must dance backward, that is, play the alternating bass strings with the index finger and the melody lines with the thumb. Nothing about this is intuitive or easy to master. Little wonder that lefties either retune the strings or, as in my case, learn to play right-handed from the outset. But Cotten somehow did it.

Another feat was the fact that she was in The Ark at all, playing before a crowd that knew her and her music. The circumstances of her life made such a musical fate highly unlikely. Born one of five children to a poor family in Chapel Hill, North Carolina, Cotten had little formal education and appeared, in all likelihood, destined for an uncelebrated life as a domestic for well-off White families. As a young girl she had exhibited musical talent, learning to play the guitar and even composing songs, but by the time she was in her late teens, she had largely put her musical interests aside, and for the next four decades, aside from church singing, her life was centered on domestic work and motherhood.

That life changed, however, in the mid-1950s when, strictly through a series of accidental contacts, she became the maid for a certain well-known musical family in the Washington, DC, area: the family of Charles and Ruth

Elizabeth Cotten at The Ark, ca. 1975. Bentley Historical Library, University of Michigan.

Crawford Seeger. In her free moments, Cotten apparently found time to practice the guitar a bit. By chance one day, one of the Seegers' sons, Mike, heard her playing in the house. Himself a budding musician and folklorist then in his twenties, Mike decided to record her. Seeger subsequently published her songs on Folkways Records and began performing with her, eventually introducing her to folk music audiences such as the Newport Folk Festival and the University of Chicago Folk Festival. From that time on—from the late 1950s into the 1980s—Cotten performed at festivals and coffeehouses around the country.[23]

Although she was a self-taught fingerstyle guitarist, she played within what is often called "Piedmont-style," with two of the lowest three strings providing an alternating bass beat while the three highest strings are picked for the melody, thus creating "the illusion of two guitars being played at once."[24] This style was deployed by many Black players who came originally from the Carolinas and Georgia, including Blind Blake (1896–1934), Blind Boy Fuller (1904–1941), Etta Baker (1913–2006), John Jackson (1924–2002), and John Cephas (1930–2009). Blues scholars have often contrasted this "more light-hearted, ragtime-influenced sound" with the more percussive Delta blues styles pioneered by Charley Patton (1891–1934), Willie Brown (1900–1952), Son House (1902–1988), and Robert Johnson.[25]

The other notable finger stylist I saw at The Ark, Paul Geremia, was skilled in both of these styles of playing. Though not yet thirty years old when I first saw him perform, he had already recorded two well-received albums. He subsequently he went on to a long career of performing and recording, and I had occasion to see him some thirty years later (see photo). Built along the slighter physical lines of Norman Blake, as opposed to the much taller David Bromberg, Geremia had a distinguishing facial feature: a walrus-like black mustache that nicely matched his mass of curly dark hair.

As all performers at The Ark had to do, Paul stepped through the floor-seated crowd to get to the performing space. He carried a guitar in each hand: one a six-string and the other a twelve-string. With no fanfare, he sat down, picked up his twelve-string and, with only a thumb pick on his playing hand, began the thumping bass line of "Silver City Bound," a tune Leadbelly wrote about his busking days in the 1920s in east Texas, with his guitar-playing buddy, Blind Lemon Jefferson. In a high tenor voice, Geremia began to sing:

Silver City bound, Silver City bound,
Well, I tell my baby, I'm Silver City bound,
And meet Blind Lemon, we're gonna ride on down
Silver City bound, Silver City bound.

I had heard a Smithsonian recording of Leadbelly singing and playing that song on *his* twelve-string, and to my ears, Geremia's version—both his almost note-for-note guitar playing and his tenor voice—sounded close to the original. That song set the pattern for the rest of the concert: a mix of acoustic blues songs by Black musicians, discovered and recorded in earlier decades, along with several original songs by Geremia himself, all in the blues vein as well. Here was a guitarist all about the early southern, acoustic-based blues of the 1920–40 era, as opposed to the postwar turn toward urban blues based on the electric guitar.

I left the concert impressed by Geremia's dedication to—and mastery of—a single genre of roots-based music, especially given his young age. One might think that a solo acoustic guitarist playing basically one style of music would get old quickly in a live performance. Such was not the case. Not only did Paul supply a wry, humorous, and even sometimes pedagogical about-the-blues patter between songs, but he also held his audience's interest by varying his musical approach. Most importantly, he played different types of blues in terms of tempo, lyrical theme, intensity of delivery, and accompaniment. On this last aspect, for example, he often played harmonica, held in place with a wire rack looped over his neck, to supplement his vocals and guitar.

As for his guitar playing, he also varied his sound. For a serious blues guitarist, it is essential to incorporate, as Geremia did, both a six-string and a twelve-string instrument. Some of the early blues giants—most notably, Leadbelly and Blind Willie McTell—preferred the heavier, more thumping sound of the twelve-string, whereas others—including Robert Johnson, Mississippi John Hurt, and Blind Lemon Jefferson—chose the lighter, clearer sonority of the six-string. Only by going back and forth between the two types of guitars can one fully convey the range and feel of the blues from this early era. Moreover, Geremia alternated between songs featuring standard fretted playing and other tunes using a bottleneck glass slide to produce a slurring, vibrato effect.

Years later, Paul spoke about how he developed an interest in the blues. There was a clear "Aha moment" for him: an experience that, at age twenty, put him on a path that changed his life's direction. As he recounted in a documentary film about himself and his music,

> The blues workshop at the 1964 Newport Folk Festival was the most incredible thing—I don't know if there will ever be the likes of it again. Almost every blues singer who had made records in the '20s and '30s, and who was still alive, was at that festival. You could just go there and sit on the grass and listen to these guys play and talk to them if you wanted to. It was an amazing experience. And two years later I decided that was what I wanted to make a living at, playing music. So that's what I've been doing ever since.[26]

By the time I heard him in concert less than a decade after Newport, Geremia was indeed making his living playing music, and he had already mastered the blues genre. In that Ann Arbor concert and on about a dozen albums, he has performed songs not only by Leadbelly and Jefferson, but also by other blues legends including Scrapper Blackwell, Blind Blake, Big Bill Broonzy, Reverend Gary Davis, Sleepy John Estes, Mississippi John Hurt, Skip James, Robert Johnson, Blind Willie McTell, Charley Patton, and Tampa Red. His own original songs also reflect, in their titles, classic blues themes of hard living and hard times, for example, "Gamblin' Woman Blues," "Cocaine Princess," "Out and Down," "Live Wire Blues," Where Did I Lose Your Love?" and "Stray Dog Shuffle."

Geremia makes no apologies about his career choice, one based on devotion to a musical genre—the style of early, rural blues—that he has sought to perpetuate and emulate. He views his own musicianship as combining tradition and originality. Tradition, of course, is a constant; he is working within a well-defined style. He comments: "What I do isn't far out. I write songs, I sing old-time songs. You don't have to be a graduate of Juilliard to understand what the hell I'm doing. But it helps to know where it comes from."[27] But there is also room for his own creativity, which Paul insists is a trait of the early blues players that he has also tried to achieve: "If you're going to be creative in this music, you have to write. All of those singers were songwriters, in essence. We are trying to emulate that tradition in that regard, in as creative a way as we can. It irritates me that blues singers are not looked upon as songwriters. You had to be creative. I mean, to be a real good blues artist you had to have something that was unique about you and the songs that you did."[28]

Paul Geremia at The Ark, 1974.
Bentley Historical Library,
University of Michigan.

As a coda on this brief portrayal of Paul Geremia—both as a young man playing at The Ark in the early 1970s and in the rearview mirror of countless concerts, a dozen albums, and endless travel during the past five decades—one is tempted to say "Mama, don't let your babies grow up to be . . . blues singers." This may be true for anyone who aspires to be an independent musician, but it certainly applies to those who are trying to carry on a rich tradition of creative music by African Americans who were largely from the rural South in the pre–World War II era. Those originators are, of course, long gone, and what remains of their original music are recordings of sometimes dubious quality—all of which complicates the commercial viability of the music that Paul Geremia provides.

Yet Geremia and others have recognized and willingly embraced this challenge. As he commented earlier in his career, "When the old-timers were around, it made it easier for guys like me. But now that the old-timers are gone, I've got to make my own way. I have to do it myself, which is what it's all about. They told us all that when they're gone, we've got to carry the ball, and it's not easy."[29] "It's not easy" could be the name of a good blues tune, but the phrase also applies to the small coterie of musicians who, like Paul Geremia, have chosen to carry on and deepen the acoustic fingerstyle tradition of African American blues. A sampling of some of the more prominent performers in this tradition—which includes both Black and White, male and female musicians—includes Rory Block, Roy Bookbinder, Guy Davis, Stefan Grossman, John Hammond, Corey Harris, Alvin Youngblood Hart, Steve James, Jorma Kaukonen, Keb' Mo' (Kevin Moore), Geoff Muldaur, Chris Smither, and Kelly Joe Phelps. What is striking about this cohort of finger stylists is the diversity of sounds and styles they deploy, even though they all started from the tradition of early acoustic blues.

The point is that these are not mere imitators of the now classic blues giants of yore. Rather, like Paul Geremia, they are *emulators*—rooted in the blues musical idiom but extending that idiom according to their individual creative vision, just as the early blues musicians did. Corey Harris, for example, has expanded his musical vocabulary to West Africa, having lived in Cameroon and collaborated, à la Ry Cooder, with the Malian guitarist Ali Farka Touré. Another example is Keb' Mo,' who has also written songs with more contemporary rhythms and lyrical themes. Like Harris and Hart, Keb' Mo' plays electric as well as acoustic guitar, and most of his recordings feature a band of bass, percussion, and other instruments besides his own guitar.

A third case, and perhaps the most stylistically distinctive in this sampling, is Kelly Joe Phelps (1959–2022), who combined three variations on the classic stereotype of the solo acoustic blues musician. First, he specialized in *lap-style* guitar, which, as the name indicates, first involves placing the guitar flat across one's lap and then "fretting" it—as one would a Dobro resonator guitar or a Weissenborn Hawaiian guitar—with a metal bar to make individual notes as well as chords. Phelps was certainly one of the very few who uses this style of playing for primarily blues-related music. Moreover, his renditions of blues classics bore his own creative stamp. A good example is his version of Leadbelly's "Goodnight, Irene," which resembles the original only in the lyrics; otherwise, one hears two different songs. In contrast to Leadbelly's chunky, emphatic fingerpicking of the song's three major chords on his Stella twelve-string, Phelps played it softly and sweetly melodically, using his bar to slide between notes and inserting minor-mode passages here and there. Finally, about half of Phelps's recorded output consists of his own compositions, which tend to have a blues sound but follow no standard format and often feature long, sometimes dreamlike improvisational passages.

All the artists just mentioned can be linked, in one way or another, to my Ark experience of hearing Paul Geremia perform his own version/vision of the blues. Over the subsequent decades I have learned that even a well-defined genre such as fingerstyle, acoustic blues is a very large tent indeed. This generalization applies even more to the fingerstyle lineage as a whole. At the risk of oversimplification, I perceive two other genres that broadly define the musical boundaries of the fingerstyle lineage. These are what I term the "Travis/Atkins" genre and the "boundary pushing" genre.

Merle Travis (1917–1983) and Chet Atkins (1924–2001) need no introduction for anyone who has even semiseriously taken up the guitar. I can clearly recall my early days of learning to play guitar, flatpick style, when I was at a point of being able to strum—with some sense of rhythm—the basic chords of G, C, and D, in first position, that is, on the first three frets nearest the peghead. And then I saw a young woman use her fingers—her thumb, forefinger, and middle finger—to play separate notes in a repeating pattern. Suddenly, a new sonic world opened up. Wow, what are you doing? How do you do that?" I asked. She said: "I call it pinch picking, but some call it Travis picking."

She proceeded to tell me about Merle Travis, the Kentucky-born guitarist who pioneered the style. Travis grew up poor in Muhlenberg County, coal country in western Kentucky. This region was made famous, and notorious, by John Prine's song, "Paradise," that describes a town that no longer exists because "Mr. Peabody's coal train has hauled it away." Along with writing two of the most famous songs about coal mining—"Dark as a Dungeon" and "Sixteen Tons"—Travis further refined and popularized a distinctive style of fingerstyle guitar playing—first developed by a local African American musician, Arnold Shultz (1886–1931)—that enabled the former to become a famous recording artist.[30]

The basics of the Travis picking style can be simply described for a 4/4 tempo: the thumb, adorned with a thumb pick, provides the quarter-note beats—the 1–2–3–4—while one or more of the other fingers—all without finger picks—provide the "ands" between those beats (1-and-2-and-3-and-4).

Those "ands" are typically used to provide a melodic line for a tune on the three highest strings, whereas the alternating thumb provides a steady bass beat using the three lowest strings. Travis, using only thumb and forefinger, incorporated all kinds of variations on this basic pattern, including jazz, swing, and country music stylings.[31]

Chet Atkins—another poor son of Appalachia, from East Tennessee—rose to become famous as a guitarist and record producer, and credited Travis as his major influence: "If it wasn't for Merle Travis, I'd be looking at the rear end of a mule."[32] Again, in the tradition of Paul Geremia, who looked to Black blues players as sources to *emulate,* not replicate, Atkins took the Travis style and made it his own, both technically and stylistically. In terms of basic technique, whereas Merle Travis used only his forefinger to play melodies, Atkins also used his third (middle) finger—and even occasionally his fourth (ring) finger—for that purpose, thereby giving his playing more fluidity and speed on the high strings. Stylistically, having studied classical guitar, Django Reinhardt's gypsy jazz, and other genres, Atkins had a broader musical palette than Travis and incorporated elements of these eclectic styles into his repertoire.[33]

Both these giants are long gone, but some have carried on the Travis / Atkins style, including Eddie Pennington, Jerry Reed, and Travis's own son, Thom Bresh. But one guitarist has carried this genre forward and innovated it more than anyone else: Tommy Emmanuel, an Australian born in 1955. Taking to the guitar at the tender age of eight or nine, Emmanuel soon became enamored with Atkins's playing style. By age eleven, he was adept at playing it, and even wrote a fan letter to Mr. Atkins. To little Tommy's elated surprise, Atkins wrote back a personal letter.[34] That sealed the deal on a combination of hero-worship cum friendship that lasted more than thirty years, until Atkins' death in 2001. Over the years the two of them collaborated musically, and Emmanuel never hesitates to credit Atkins with being the most formative musical and professional influence in his life.

As in the Travis / Atkins comparison, there is a similar distinction to be made between Atkins and Emmanuel, both technically and stylistically. On the technical dimension, as mentioned earlier, Emmanuel has perfected a method of shifting interchangeably and seamlessly between fingerstyle and flatpick styles of playing with his right hand. He does this by moving his index finger securely underneath his thumb, thereby forming a thumb-index finger hold on his thumb pick, such that the thumb pick can now be moved up and down, much like one plays a flat pick. This method gives Emmanuel remarkable speed in single-note runs that are required, for example, in fiddle tunes. Atkins could achieve respectable quickness with up-and-down alterations between thumb and forefinger, but not quite the velocity and even tonality on up-and-down strokes that Emmanuel attains with his quasi-flatpick style.

Stylistically, the two guitarists appear to be on different planets. Metaphorically speaking, as a performer Atkins is a glass of warm milk, whereas Emmanuel is a shot of espresso.[35] Where Atkins is laid-back, Emmanuel is caffeinated; where Atkins is smooth, languid, and melodic, Emmanuel is percussive, explosive, and rip-it-up fast. These are generalizations, and both were/are, above all, professional musicians able to play in virtually any style; however, I believe the distinction holds.

Part of this difference has to do with the type of guitar each man uses. Atkins was not, strictly speaking, an acoustic guitar player; rather, he mostly played a hollow-body electric: an electric guitar with a hollow acoustic chamber in the guitar's body. This type of guitar must always be amplified, since its acoustic-projection capability is limited, though it does provide a more acoustic-sounding tone than a standard, solid-body electric guitar. Atkins's main guitar was the Gretsch "Country Gentleman"—a hollow body he helped design that employs a metal nut and bridge and heavy top bracing. This guitar was so named, one assumes, for the kind of public image that Atkins conveyed, that of a mild-mannered, middle-of-the-road stylist. Hollow-body electrics generally provide a smooth sound that is favored by jazz musicians. By contrast, Emmanuel plays mainly acoustic guitars made by his countrymen at Maton Guitars of Melbourne, Australia. The key difference between the two types of instruments lies in the fact that an acoustic guitar can sonically tolerate rough treatment—hard strumming and percussive banging—much better than a hollow-body guitar. Tommy Emmanuel makes the most of that difference.

This difference translates directly into the two men's onstage personae. In performance, Atkins was unflappable, with head down, a slight smile perhaps on his lips, and all about making his hands move smoothly and certainly around the fingerboard. He might gesticulate with a head movement here, a body shift there, but overall he projected poise and equilibrium. Not so for Emmanuel, who is as expressive and hyperkinetic on stage as a rock star. Singing only rarely, Emmanuel struts, mugs, wields his guitar like a sword or machine gun or whatever other object he may conjure on the spot. At moments, he will indeed bang on the instrument's strings. He is all about conveying energy, joy, emotion, and wonderment at the music he is creating. But this expressive projection comes bundled with a virtuosity on the guitar that is often stunning in its dynamism, clarity, and creativity.

Without fail, to judge by the many videos easily available online, this is the kind of performance that his appreciative audiences expect and applaud. Perhaps the ultimate accolade that has been paid to Tommy Emmanuel is that uttered by none other than Les Paul (1915–2009), who said to Tommy directly: "You've carried this way beyond where we remember the Merle Travises and the Chet Atkinses and those people. You've got something going here that's fascinating."[36] In a show of humorous modesty that contrasts with his larger-than-life persona on stage, Emmanuel is quick to credit his predecessors, noting that Travis stole from Mose Rager and Ike Everly, and Emmanuel stole from Travis: "That's what we do—we're all petty thieves. That's how the language of music gets carried on."[37] Call it thievery, or the gentler term "emulation," Tommy Emmanuel is proud to credit his roots—the Travis/Atkins genre of fingerpicking.

Yet sometimes the language of guitar music seems to arrive as something strikingly original for its time, something truly transformative. The sounds may be recognizable as *music,* yes, but it's not music we have heard before. The sounds have not been "stolen" from a recognizable style or tradition; they may have been borrowed briefly from some style or tradition, but then the guitarists have pushed beyond the boundaries of that tradition to create something unique. These guitar sounds constitute a third genre of fingerstyle playing that I term "boundary pushing"—a catchall category that recognizes the outer limits of creative expression on the acoustic guitar. This genre includes an eclectic pantheon of guitarists, each distinctive in some way (or ways). Therefore, any generalization about this cohort is tentative and problematic, other than to say (a) these musicians pledge no allegiance to any specific genre, including the two—blues and Travis/Atkins—already discussed; and (b) their music bears above all the qualities of exploration and originality. Whereas guitarists working within the blues or Travis/Atkins genres generally remain identifiable as such, these Boundary Pushing guitarists elude such classification.

In the top tier of this group, I would place five seminal artists: John Fahey, Michael Hedges, Leo Kottke, Bruce Cockburn, and Richard Thompson. Each has his own distinctive sound, and all perform and record largely their own original compositions. There is little if any overlap in their playing, yet each musician has inspired a subsequent generation of guitarists to expand the creative boundaries of the fingerstyle tradition.

The oldest and most idiosyncratic of this group, John Fahey (1939–2001), reveled in pushing boundaries. According to a friend who knew him in high school in the Washington, DC suburb of Takoma Park, Fahey was "an outlaw, from start to finish. A gentlemanly outlaw, but an outlaw, outside the strictures of his background."[38] Unlike a Norman Blake or Paul Geremia, who chose to emulate an established musical tradition, Fahey was determined to chart his own path. Although he did initially borrow some stylistic aspects from early blues music, Fahey then added such elements as self-created tunings, dissonance, and endless cycles of repetitive rhythms. Self-taught as a guitarist, Fahey accepted the phrase "American primitive guitar" in reference to his unpolished style of playing, but he insisted on its originality: "Primitive means untaught—I didn't have any teachers. I taught myself." Some find his playing unmelodic and indeed repetitive, yet others view him as a true innovator. No less a guitar authority than Pete Townsend comments that Fahey's playing "seemed to me to be the kind of folk guitar playing equivalent of William Burroughs or Charles Bukowski. He had a really powerful thing we look for in American artists. He created a new language—modally speaking, harmonically speaking—and if that's not an iconoclast, I don't know what is, really. . . . He seems to be trying to create poetry, and if music is simply dividing time, he's dividing time in some new ways."

Fahey's musical influence extended beyond his own recordings, which numbered an astounding forty-nine albums; he also had a prolific side career as a record company owner and curator.[39] In 1959, at the age of twenty, he founded Takoma Records, and for the next twenty years, Takoma issued virtually all of Fahey's his own recordings, as well as albums by other musicians, including bluesmen Bukka White and Robert Pete Williams and innovative guitarists such as Leo Kottke, Peter Lang, and Robbie Basho. In the years since Fahey passed from the scene, a range of finger stylists, inspired by Fahey's "primitive" experimental style, have carried on that tradition; a brief listing includes Marisa Anderson, Jack Rose, Gwenifer Raymond, William Tyler, and Glenn Jones.[40]

A second Boundary Pushing pioneer, Michael Hedges (1953–1997), was just forty-three and in the midst of a rising career when he was killed in a car crash in northern California. Hedges created what is, to my ears, a singular body of work noted for intricate melodic patterns, innovative tunings, and percussive tapping to produce harmonic effects on the guitar's strings. Unlike Fahey, who did not sing, Hedges was also an expressive singer who included in his performances dramatically rendered covers of well-known rock and pop songs such as "Gimme Shelter," "All Along the Watchtower," and "Come Together."

A third pioneer, Leo Kottke (born 1945), remains active in what has been a remarkably long and influential career, beginning with his first recording in 1969. Playing both six- and twelve-string guitars throughout his career, Kottke builds his guitar solos off of an assertive right hand: alternating bass thumb strokes that propel and accentuate a seemingly endless variety of rhythms and melodies coming from his other four fingers. Like Hedges, Kottke is not strictly an instrumentalist; he varies his repertoire with songs featuring his capable, low-key, baritone voice. One observer notes Kottke's influence on those finger stylists who have come after him: "It is hard to exaggerate the impact Leo Kottke has had on the evolution of modern fingerpicking. Among post–Chet Atkins players, perhaps only Michael Hedges has found as many new and surprising sounds for the acoustic instrument or developed as distinctive and personal a compositional style."[41]

Two other pioneers also remain active well into their seventies. Canadian Bruce Cockburn—born, like Kottke, in 1945—is a songwriter, singer, and guitarist whose musical ideas seem to know no bounds. Cockburn admits to having borrowed a basic thumb-bass groove from early bluesmen such as Mississippi John Hurt and Big Bill Broonzy, but he also employs alternate tunings on various instruments such as six-string and twelve-string acoustic, metal resonator, and even electric guitars. Cockburn's music also reflects such influences as reggae, jazz, and even rock and roll. After fifty years of making brilliant music, Cockburn's advice is to keep pushing the bounds of one's creativity: "Don't stop exploring. . . . Always keep looking for a new angle of approach, or some new element to inject into your writing. That way, you're going to keep it interesting to *yourself*, if nothing else."[42]

Although Cockburn is an accomplished guitarist who has created, recorded, and performed solo instrumentals, his go-to method for songwriting begins with lyrics rather than the guitar: "Not necessarily a complete set of lyrics, but something that at least has a shape of its own. There's often an imaginary structure that the lyrics can kind of hang themselves around—a rhyme scheme, something like that. Then it's a question of finding the right music to give them rhythmic punch, if they need that, or an atmosphere—a kind of environment to exist in. That's where the guitar comes in."[43]

Given the importance of lyrics in his music, Cockburn has much to say, especially on subjects such as spirituality and social justice, which he connects through his understanding of Christianity and the Bible. He observes: "The mandate is: love your neighbor. Simple, dead simple . . . simple as a concept, but how do you execute? How do you love your neighbor and watch him starve to death? How do you love your neighbor and watch him be murdered? That can't be justified in Biblical terms."[44]

Finally, the London-born Richard Thompson (born 1949) is, like Cockburn, a durable, consistently creative songwriter, singer, and guitarist with dozens of albums to his credit during a career spanning over four decades. Although he generally plays with a small plectrum held between his right thumb and forefinger, he rarely strums the guitar but rather uses his free fingers to play melody lines on the higher strings, and so for that reason, I consider Thompson a finger stylist rather than a flatpicker. As for what he brings to the table musically, Thompson, like all the pioneers, is difficult to categorize. This is the reason they are pioneers after all: they have gone musically into new territory and forged new ways of playing finger style.

Perhaps the best term to describe Richard Thompson's guitar style is "fusionist," in the sense that his playing constitutes a distillation, compression, and fusion of several influences. In this respect, his guitar work bears little relationship to that of John Fahey, who prided himself on being a self-taught "primitive"—and therefore all original—guitarist, or to Michael Hedges, who was far more unconventional stylistically in his use of alternate tunings and tapping and other percussive effects.

By contrast, Thompson is closer to Bruce Cockburn in drawing deeply from various guitar styles or traditions yet refusing to identify with any particular style other than what he can create by, in effect, combining, mixing, and ultimately fusing various musical styles into a diverse body of work. In Thompson's case, those influences include British and American folk music, blues, gypsy jazz, slow ballads, and rock and roll. A fanciful yet concrete demonstration of this eclecticism can be heard in "Guitar Hero," on the 2015 Album "Still," in which Thompson lyrically extols some of his guitar inspirations—including Django Reinhardt, Les Paul, Chuck Berry, James Burton, and Hank Marvin of the Shadows—and then proceeds to play a break in each of their styles. Thompson has pushed the boundaries of fingerstyle guitar by, in effect, absorbing and fusing the various musical strains that already lie within those boundaries.[45]

NEW SOUNDS, OLD INSTRUMENT OF THEFT, ALCHEMY, EMULATION, DIVERSITY

As with any creative endeavor, fingerstyle and acoustic guitar playing in general continue to evolve beyond these "boundary pushing" pioneers. The most notable aspect of this change is in terms of *who* is playing the instrument. According to a recent article in the *New York Times*, "the genre has cast off its image as the province of white men."[46] To be sure, women and non-Whites, especially African Americans, have always had a visible presence and influence in the guitar-playing world, and I have already mentioned many of them, starting with my experience seeing Elizabeth Cotten at The Ark. Whole genres of music featuring the guitar—from blues to gospel to jazz in all of their variations—owe their very existence to African Americans. Nevertheless, the image of the guitar-wielding White male—from Dylan to Clapton to Mayer—persists. The times, however, indeed are a-changing. As the *New York Times* article states: "Long dominated by much mythologized white men like John Fahey, the form's demographic is slowly broadening to include those who have often been omitted, including women, nonbinary instrumentalists, and people of color. These musicians are paying little mind to the traditional godheads. They are instead expanding the fundamental influences within solo guitar, incorporating idioms sometimes deemed verboten in what was once a homogenized scene."[47]

Two successors of special note in this emerging generation of guitar players are Kaki King (born 1979) and Yasmin Williams (born 1996). Now in her forties, King has been performing and recording for over two decades, with nine studio albums to her credit by 2020. Defining her musical style is an exercise in futility, for she recognizes no boundaries and refuses to become wedded to any one technique or style. *Rolling Stone* magazine even asserted that she is "a genre unto herself."[48] The term "intricacy" only begins to describe the combination of melodies, tunings, and playing styles that King employs. Perhaps most distinctive among her playing innovations are slapping and hammering, as she searches for new ways to coax sounds from the box. Many of her compositions incorporate rhythmic percussive slaps with her right, playing hand, while her left, fretting hand hammers down on the strings from above. In her continual musical explorations, King has also embraced visual effects as a complement to her sound. For example, she has pioneered the projection of ever-shifting, abstract images onto the "face" (top and neck) of her guitar, as well as on a large screen behind her, while she plays.

The younger Yasmin Williams has clearly adapted some of her techniques from King, though she also credits the video game *Guitar Hero* as sparking her early interest in playing guitar. Like King, she is difficult to define as playing within a tradition—finger style or otherwise—but one immediately sees and hears the originality, complexity, and virtuosity in her playing. Although she can play the guitar adroitly in standard position, Williams especially excels in playing lap style where, in addition to taps on her shoes to provide a beat, she uses a combination of slapping, two-handed hammering, and even a thumb piano, or mbira, affixed to the guitar's top—all in a flowing melody.[49]

And so the beat goes on in the acoustic guitar world. Boundary pushing continues to take place not only within the fingerstyle tradition, but also within the modern songster and flatpicking traditions as well. Call it what you will: borrowing, thievery, alchemy, emulation, transformation. These are all synonyms for the creative process, which Richard Thompson defines this way: "You study your influences and at some point you emerge from behind them with your own synthesis of style—which becomes your style. That's what Aaron Copland did, it's what Charlie Parker did. Les Paul sounds like

Les Paul, but in a lot of ways he's playing Django. He's just doing it Les Paul style. You don't even think of it as Django. It's Les doing his thing."[50]

As I reflect on my early experiences, I have enough perspective to grasp what a privileged position I had, sitting on those floor cushions at The Ark, lo those many years ago. I was, in effect, witnessing demonstrations of this creative process in the guitar performances of David Bromberg, Norman Blake, Elizabeth Cotten, Paul Geremia, and many others. Call those experiences ones of enchantment, attraction, envy—all of the above. Call it discovery. These came to my eyes and ears as a "package" of music making that I did not, at that time, have the capacity to unwrap. To belabor this image, these moments also came wrapped with a big bow with a string that said: Pull on this and some of it can be yours, too. That was an offer too tantalizing to refuse. As I recounted in the previous chapter, I had to get myself a guitar and learn to play.

The term "emulation" was not yet in my musical vocabulary, but there were obvious first steps to follow, such as learning a few basic chords, keeping new sounds coming into my head, and paying attention to new styles of music and playing I encountered. All the while I kept learning about the history of musical traditions—especially American roots music—and the guitar playing that was a central element of that music. As mentioned, with much practice I learned to fingerpick the basic melody of "Freight Train" and to perform a decent rendition of Steve Goodman's "City of New Orleans." I also began playing with other people—an essential way to build one's friendships, musicianship, and musical inspiration. As a later effort to unwrap the package that my Ark experiences first gave me, I began writing guitar-based songs of my own. Though I never quit my day job of college teaching, my modest attempts to emulate some of the great guitarists who have transformed the instrument's playing during the past six decades have greatly enhanced the quality of my life.

To return to the basic argument that began this chapter, this book maintains that the transformation in acoustic guitar playing—a broad but by no means complete sampling of which I have just examined—has been the essential driving force behind a sustained mass demand for the acoustic guitar over the past six decades. That demand, in turn, has provided the equally essential economic incentive for increased guitar production at all ends of the price spectrum. The result has been a corresponding transformation in the making of the American acoustic guitar. The opening paragraphs of this book portrayed this transformation in imaginary visits to three retail stores separated by six decades. The next task is to examine the nature of this transformation. The next five chapters do so through an examination of the people, companies, and industry that make that "cool wooden box."

Chapter 2

REINVENTORS

The New Lutherie Movement

> I guess passion is the main ingredient—
> you gotta be a little nuts.
>
> —BILL COLLINGS (QUOTED IN
> ACOUSTIC GUITAR MAGAZINE, JULY 1995, 16)

> The most difficult part of designing a guitar is finding the delicate
> balance between keeping the instrument from ripping apart,
> while at the same time keeping the instrument as delicate as possible.
>
> —MASTER LUTHIER LINDA MANZER (QUOTED IN ZAK MORGAN,
> "THE LARRIVÉE TRADITION OF HANDMADE GUITARS,"
> CANADIAN JOURNAL FOR TRADITIONAL MUSIC, 1995)

What have I discovered about guitar *making* over the past five decades? Certainly a central one is of major improvements in the acoustic guitar's sonic qualities—that is, its capacity to produce beautiful projection and tone—as well as in its overall craftsmanship. To be sure, the Martin and Gibson guitars of the 1920s and 1930s continue to be prized as products of the Golden Age of guitar making. Many observers, however, credit the past few decades as marking a New Golden Age of guitar lutherie.[1] Master luthier Dana

Bourgeois, cited in the introductory chapter, goes so far as to claim that guitar makers such as himself have "reinvented the wheel" of guitar making. Rightly so. The overall quality of acoustic guitars being produced by individual builders and companies both small and large has vastly improved since the 1960s.

I would take Bourgeois's assertion one step further. In the process of improving the acoustic guitar's overall quality, *the guitar-making industry itself has become transformed.* This and the following four chapters convey what I have discovered about the "how" and "why" of this transformation on the part of the main components of the acoustic guitar industry, mentioned in the first chapter: the reinventors (the "new lutherie movement"), the game changer (Taylor Guitars), globalizers (import sector), and the old guard (Gibson and Martin).

REINVENTORS

An Introduction and a Note on Discovery

The initial driver of this transformation—the reinventors—was a generation of artisans who came of age in the late 1960s and 1970s. This group of guitar makers—individual luthiers and founders of small production shops—raised the quality standards of making guitars. In the process, these luthiers—sometimes lumped together as "the new lutherie movement"—threw down the gauntlet to the much larger and established companies, forcing them, in turn, to improve the quality of their own instruments.

I became aware of some of these new names appearing on guitar headstocks—Bourgeois, Collings, Huss & Dalton, and Santa Cruz—as I frequented guitar stores, took instructional classes at the Old Town School of Folk Music, and made new friends—with their new guitars!—at jam sessions. Other names such as Manzer, Olson, and Henderson were less familiar because they were built in small batches by individual makers, but everyone who played them praised their quality and sound. On one level, then, my discovery of this movement was gradual and piecemeal.

When I began research for this book, however, my interest in discovering more about this movement grew, and I began to formulate questions. Who are these reinventors? What drew them to building guitars in the first place, and how did they emerge as prominent guitar makers? What really drives them to do what they do? Specifically, what is their vision of what a great guitar—and a great guitar company—should be, and how do they try to bring that vision into being?

These questions were uppermost in my mind as I undertook my research, and I approached these issues as I would any topic requiring an understanding of motivation and strategy. I needed to sit down with some of these guitar makers and inquire about their lives and their work.[2] I regret that I could not visit and talk with all of the talented luthiers who make up this movement, but I hope that my account provides at least a representative sampling of this world. My travels took me to workshops and factories across the United States—to places such as Seattle; Oxnard and Santa Cruz, California; Austin, Texas; Staunton, Virginia; Chelsea, Vermont; and Lewiston, Maine.

Somethin's Happenin' Here: A Visit with a Pioneer, Michael Gurian

I drive my rental car near the Ballard Locks in northern Seattle and find a parking spot next to the water. As I scan the barge I am about to board, I notice that the lapping ripples of Salmon Bay, which itself flows into Puget Sound, cause the barge to rock ever so slightly. I also see that this is not your everyday barge made for hauling or pushing; rather, it is a boxy two-story building built on top of a barge. The building houses the production shop of Gurian Instruments, as well as the actual lodgings of its owner. Michael Gurian is a luthier and Renaissance man whose impact on the guitar industry in recent decades, as both an individual builder and a mentor of younger luthiers, has been large. Terming him "The Pioneer," one noted luthier, Rick Davis, says, "Simply put, Michael Gurian is one of the most important figures in 20th century American guitar making and he remains an essential part of the lutherie community."[3] Another observer notes, "Michael Gurian is a key figure in the development of the modern acoustic guitar, not only for the design and creation of his own legendary guitars, but in his core beliefs of sharing knowledge, passing it on through mentorship, and building a community of dedicated artisans committed to the music and the tools musicians need to make it."[4]

The unusual structure of Gurian's workshop cum apartment—built according to his own design and specifications—is just the first indication that the man I am about to meet prizes both aesthetics and functionality. I am here to learn not only what motivates him as a luthier but also how he views the development of the guitar industry. As I cross the gangway, Gurian comes out to greet me and we go up to a sunroom in his living quarters on the second floor. (In Seattle, you grab the sun when you can!) Quickly on a first-name basis, we settle in for a conversation about his life in guitar making.

Over the course of the next two hours, I learn that Michael has been a man not only *of* his times but a man *in* his times. Born in 1943, he was profoundly affected by the cultural ethos of his young adulthood, the 1960s, but he also helped reshape the culture around him—the world of artisan guitar making.[5] In the early 1960s Gurian was already, as he puts it, "part of the New York City scene." He was drawn, early on, to the nylon-string classical guitar, a musical instrument he could play as well as make. Becoming proficient as a guitarist, he performed for a time in basket houses—little clubs where patrons literally passed a basket to tip the penurious performers. There he became friendly with such fellow "basket cases" as Bob Dylan, Richie Havens, and John Sebastian. While a student at Long Island University, he also taught classical guitar. Along the way, Gurian got to know several classical guitar makers, including Manuel Velásquez and Victor Manuel Piniero, who encouraged him to try his own hand at the craft.

At one point, Michael tells me, he needed a new guitar but had little money. So he decided to build one himself, using a hand plane, sandpaper, "some kind of hand torch" to bend the sides, and bricks and ropes to hold things together. From that first guitar, he went on to build fourteen similar ones in the next few weeks, "waking up every morning covered in sawdust." He later destroyed all these guitars except the first one. Guitars #2 through #15 were, he says, "just practice and learning."

In making these guitars, Gurian was very much a part *of* his times. Throughout the 1960s New York increasingly became a hotbed of experimentation and rebellion against established forms—in art, music, theatre, education, and culture in general. Rebellion, of course, was in the air, at least in big cities and university towns and especially with the escalation of the Vietnam War in mid-decade. But large-scale rejection of the status quo went well beyond the war itself to a questioning of modern American society. For many young people, the struggle was not just against an imperialist war; it

Michael Gurian in his barge/shop/home at Ballard Locks, Seattle, Washington. Photo by author.

was also against a capitalist culture that celebrated the "organization man"—typically a male, other-directed, get-along corporate climber who had been socialized to accept the status quo without question.[6]

No wonder, then, that for many young people, an alternative mode of being based on personal independence, self-reliance, and self-expression was highly appealing. The buzzword became "authenticity": How to live an authentic life?[7] That such an alternative could even be pondered had much to do not only with a booming economy but also with certain skin, class, and gender privileges. As Tim Olsen, the longtime president of the Guild of American Luthiers, puts it in somewhat jaundiced fashion: "What happened was hippies came along. There came a situation where a lot of middle-class, white people had teenagers who had high opinions of their own native abilities and a relatively low urgency to get a regular job." At the same time, Olsen claims, many young people started building stringed instruments, "not so much as a career choice, but as an interesting pursuit. It just seemed like a fine thing to do."[8]

For someone with creative instincts, skilled hands, and, yes, perhaps a high opinion of one's native abilities, instrument making indeed held much promise. Such traits—creativity coupled with manual skills—describe a rising generation of guitar-builders born in the 1940s who went on to have successful careers. In addition to Gurian, this group includes, among many others, Richard Bruné, Bill Collings, William Cumpiano, Ren Ferguson, James Goodall, Wayne Henderson, Richard Hoover, Jean Larrivée, Michael Millard, James Olson, and Ervin Somogyi. A few years later came another group, born in the 1950s and early 1960s, that included Dana Bourgeois, Jeff Huss and Mark Dalton, Linda Manzer, and Bob Taylor. Such a list only begins to identify the dozens of luthiers of this generation who shared many of the same values and skills.

The reader will note that there is only one woman, Linda Manzer, and no African Americans or Latinos on this list. This rising generation of luthiers—however innovative and individualistic in their guitar making—was certainly homogenous in terms of gender and racial backgrounds. Manzer remarks about this context at the time of the new lutherie movement's emergence during the 1970s: "At the time, the guitar-making trade was 100 percent male. It may be hard to imagine now, but in 1974 people didn't want to buy guitars from girls. I'd go in a hardware store and no one would wait on me. They assumed I was someone's girlfriend."[9]

As for Michael Gurian, on the front end of this generation, he sought to live his own "do-it-yourself" life as an artisan guitar maker with his own approach and style. He makes this point with a personal example from his early New York years: "You can build a guitar out of an orange crate, and I did. I went to the local vegetable stand, and I said 'Gimme that box.' And I built a guitar out of it, and it sounded fine. It wasn't a great sounding guitar, but it sounded fine. So I can give you my bracing system and all the woods I use to make a guitar, and what you make will sound *completely* different from the ones that I make."

For Gurian, the true guitar-making method—by hand—is a two-part communication process. On the one hand, the guitar maker communicates personally with the eventual recipient, the buyer, to assess the latter's playing style and then craft an instrument with the most suitable ergonomic and sonic features. This means that components such as necks should be individually shaped, not mass-produced. Michael comments: "A good builder, you don't want all the pieces to be the same. You've watched the person play the guitar. That's what I used to do. I'd watch the person playing the guitar, and I'd say, 'Oh, the neck has to be this way, not that way.'" The buyer's needs defined, the luthier then carries on a kind of communication with the wood that will make up the guitar. Gurian describes this as a tactile process:

> In hand building, you start by checking the thickness of all the woods. You're feeling your wood as you're going. Inherently you're picking up the tonal sounds and vibrations of this wood as you're working it. From the base right on up, you're learning what this wood is all about in relation to the guitar you're building. In the end, it boils down to the builder, how he can build the instrument, how he sets it up, what he does with the woods—really, what the builder wants to achieve out of it. . . . I got to where if I wanted to design a fingerpicking guitar, I could do it. If I wanted to design a booming flatpick guitar, I could do that, because I knew where the guitar was at from step to step.

Guitar making, Michael says, has two basic methodologies—hand built or mass produced—and there is no question which one he prefers. "With hand building," he says," you watch the musician and design the neck based on the musician—whether he or she likes a thinner neck or a thicker neck, symmetrical neck or asymmetrical neck, depending on hand positions." By contrast, with mass-production instruments so prevalent in today's world, he claims "You've got to make something to suit the masses." The result is a uniform, technical exactness that comes at the expense of sound. "What you have now," Michael says dismissively, "is a lot of people making very fancy, beautiful guitars, and the guitars are that—they're very well put together, very precise. All CNCs, automatic tools, automatic this, automatic that. They look beautiful, but they sound like sh-t."

There is a certain irony in Gurian's critique of mass production in that once he became adept as a luthier, he built a factory operation in Hinsdale, New Hampshire. By the end of the 1970s, his company had seventy employees producing up to two thousand guitars a year. Despite Gurian's definitive departure from a solo, or even small-batch, approach, his guitars were respected for their quality. Today, Gurian guitars of that period sell for over $2,000 on the vintage / used market. Their maker proudly recounts that his factory was one of the most technically advanced guitar factories in the country: "Everything was automatic—carving, kerfing, etc. Load it and walk away."

Unfortunately, Gurian's flourishing guitar production literally went up in smoke in a factory boiler fire in 1979 that destroyed the building and everything in it—machines, tools, material stocks, and finished guitars. Michael claims that he did not want to reopen a production facility, given the country's recession at the time; however, he decided to do so in order to keep his workers employed in an otherwise poor local economy. Moreover, he received much support from the local population to rebuild, and within six months his new facility was producing guitars again.

This time, however, with the national economy in recession, the operation was unprofitable, and in 1982 he called it quits as a full-time guitar maker. He ceased production and closed the factory, never to build guitars at that scale again. Gurian did remain in the industry, though, becoming a supplier of instrument parts and tools—bridge pins, hand files, and the like—to other builders. He eventually moved his operations to Seattle in 1992 and has remained there ever since.

Of his times as an expert luthier, Gurian was also *in* his times as an engaged builder helping others learn the art and craft of guitar making. Even with his emphasis on technological efficiency, Michael recruited and taught a cohort of apprentices and young luthiers including Michael Millard, David Santo, David Rubio, and William Cumpiano—all of whom went on to successful careers as guitar makers. As mentioned earlier, Gurian believes in sharing his expertise and mentoring up-and-coming luthiers. Michael himself expresses this commitment to the guitar community: "Believe me, the group of people in my realm go back quite a few years. We're all good friends. We share information. If they need something, they get it from me. If I need something, they send it to me. We share."

This aspect of Gurian's legacy underlines a key trait of the luthier community that came of age in the 1960s and 1970s: the community's willingness, even eagerness, to help one another by sharing their hard-earned knowledge about the guitar-making craft. To become a luthier is to join a particular kind of community, one based on information sharing, cooperation, and reciprocity. Virtually everyone in this community received training and help along the way from more experienced and knowledgeable luthiers. A good example is Jean Larrivée's taking on Linda Manzer as an apprentice for several years in the 1970s. Manzer credits Larrivée and others in Toronto's lutherie community as all supporting each other. She says that the builders in that network were all struggling to get established; however, they "made a conscious choice to be friends and help each other. And it turned out to be a magical choice. It made us all better builders."[11]

Once established, most guitar makers feel obligated, in turn, to help train the next generation. By and large, luthiers, as Manzer remarks, do not see themselves as competing against fellow guitar makers for market share; rather, they feel engaged in a common pursuit: the building of a better guitar.[12] The ethos of this subculture is not so much *anti*-capitalist in an oppositional sense as it is *non*-capitalist in its rejection of what many of them consider "soulless" mass production. For a group whose members pride themselves on their self-reliance and individuality, the budding lutherie community in the late 1960s and early 1970s was also adept at organizing itself, beginning with the formation, in 1972, of the Guild of American Luthiers (GAL). The GAL's goal, according to its principal founder, Tim Olsen, was to "create a framework for information sharing." Olsen goes on to say that, in those early years, "it was really the idea of *getting* information because nobody had any." Starting with a list of forty names, the GAL has expanded over the decades to its present size of about 3,500 members.[13]

BRING UP A CHILD . . . NURTURE AND NATURE

What prompts a young person to build not just one guitar, but then another and another and another . . . until eventually he or she decides to make guitar making a profession? It's safe to say that few young people find such a prospect enticing. Aside from a capacity to endure penury and puzzled looks from concerned parents and relatives, what is the motivation that puts a young person on such a path?

As in the choice of any career, some mysterious mix of external factors and personality type shapes that choice. There is initially the factor of nurture in the form of family influences and socialization in the wider world. One's upbringing and early experiences interact with one's nature, that is, an individual's innate mental, physical, and emotional proclivities and abilities that relate to activities that bring a sense of engagement and fulfillment. Just as every individual is unique in some way, so too is the combination of nurture and nature that shapes that individual.

It is hardly surprising that many luthiers come from a family background that nurtured their creative engagement with the physical world. For virtually all the so-called reinventors I interviewed, parents and other family members and friends encouraged and facilitated their engagement in using tools and making things. For example, Richard Hoover, founder of the Santa Cruz Guitar Company, grew up in the San Joaquin Valley near Fresno, where his father was a window display designer and decorator who worked in wood, plastic, and metal. Hoover's dad had a shop at home, so the young boy was encouraged to make his own toys and, in Richard's words, "take stuff apart." His mother, he says, served as his "reference librarian" by going to the local library and finding material related to violin and guitar making. Another example is Michael Millard of Froggy Bottom Guitars, whose father was an architect as well as a professor at Yale. By his account, as a kid Millard was always around "building things," and he considers making guitars "an extension of my upbringing." Similarly, Dana Bourgeois says that he "grew up around tools" in his home near Portland, Maine. His father was an amateur woodworker, and his grandfather was a machinist; both had their own shops, which Dana knew well. Although he had no desire to use his granddad's tools, he says that "when the time came"—when he became interested in making a guitar—he was not intimidated by tools.

This kind of familial nurturing certainly paves the way for a person to develop the hand and eye skills required for lutherie, but that is only part of the story. The other part is a person's nature—the drive and desire in one's personality that influences, and perhaps dictates, the decision to become a luthier. That nature requires some combination of creativity, energy, independence, and will.

Few guitar makers have embodied these qualities more fully than Bill Collings, founder of Collings Guitars, who began making guitars in early 1970s. My encounter with Bill in a visit to the Collings factory in 2015 remains one of the most vivid memories of my research; alas, he passed away just two years after that visit.[14] The term "nature"—at least of the ecological variety—is a word that literally comes to mind as I drive into the Hill Country west of downtown Austin to visit the Collings plant on a hot morning in late

June. The operation consists of two low-slung beige buildings perched on a rise in the scrub mesquite hills on State Highway 290—the road to Dripping Springs. As I enter the main office, I'm met by the general manager, Steve McCreary, who tells me, "Bill's not here yet—he's at the gym, but he'll be in soon." Some moments later, McCreary hands me a cup of coffee and apologizes that the founder and owner, Bill Collings, is running late. Even though it's already ninety degrees outside, I soon conclude that I needed that shot of hot caffeine for what was to come.

After a few minutes, McCreary receives word that Bill has indeed arrived and is roaming around the factory floor. We head out to find him, eventually catching up with him in the finishing room. Bill has an empty coffee cup and some sweaty exercise clothes in his hands, and he's on the prowl for java. We shake hands, and he bids me to join him in his search. For the next fifteen minutes, Steve McCreary and I try to keep up with Collings as he hurries through the factory, asking everyone he comes across if they have some decent coffee. At one point we take a detour into a big room in the factory that Steve tells me is "Bill's hot-rod shop." Activity here is devoted to one of Collings's pet side projects: the restoration of old cars and pickup trucks. Bill takes a little breather by checking to see how one such restoration is going (see photo).

Even before we sit down to talk about his guitar life, I am impressed with the man's kinetic energy. In my real-time notes on that day, I wrote about Bill:

> The guy exudes dynamism. He's loud and brash and seems to love the attention he gets. He seems unable to sit still for very long. He seems to want to make things happen around him all the time. He's continually talking to people. Physically, though not a tall man—I'd guess he's about 5' 10"—he is thick through the shoulders and arms. He radiates a certain physical power. I especially notice his hands—they're not huge, but they look like a worker's hands, somewhat rough with powerful fingers. His forearms are muscular. All this to say he radiates fitness, energy, and strength. Yet he doesn't force this on you à la LBJ. But you are aware that this is a guy who is not afraid to take on physical challenges.

The term "force of nature" comes to mind to describe Bill Collings. One can easily imagine him as an eight-year-old telling his playmates how to line up for a touch football game. But there was certainly nurture in his early life that put him on a path to building things. Born in 1949 in Midland, Michigan,

Bill Collings (right) and Steve McCreary (left) checking out an old pickup truck in Bill's hot-rod shop. Photo by author.

Collings grew up near Cleveland, Ohio, in a family of engineers and managers who worked in the automobile and chemical industries. "I come from a line of inventors and builders," he says, with no hint of bragging. It was his nature, though, to break from the family mold and go off on his own. After college, he worked in a machine shop, gaining confidence in his ability to figure out how to get a job done.[15] Then he relocated to Texas in the mid-1970s and devoted himself to figuring out how to repair and build guitars.

For Collings, it was not about pursuing a specific career path; it was about the challenge of learning how to build the best guitar he could—a guitar that people would want: "When I started making guitars in my twenties, I started learning. I never really knew at that time that that was what I was going to

Bill Collings (right) with Bruce VanWart, director of lutherie. Photo by author.

do. I was just satisfying my own curiosity. And I kept repairing and building and existing—I did it for another fifteen years. I wanted to make guitars, but I wanted to make them so that people would want them. It was the challenge of seeing if I could make a good musician happy with it. My challenge really was to see if I could get that player excited, and if I did, I won. So it wasn't just making it, I had to get the answer."

Similar stories pour forth from other guitar makers. They enjoy the process of making the instrument for rewards both psychic and material. At some point, these luthiers realize three things: they like what they do, they're good at it, and it brings them recognition and a way to make a living. Jeff Huss and Mark Dalton make this point in recounting the beginning of their partnership in 1995. Jeff says, "First it was me by myself, building instruments, and I wanted a partner. We thought we could make fine guitars that people would buy, and so we started. After a while we had more people buying them than we could make ourselves, so we hired people." Mark adds, "The mission of our business was to make a living making guitars. And that's still all it really is. The mission is always for the business to thrive and be profitable, and to make guitars that are better this year than they were last year. If you don't do that—and the reason you're writing your book is that guitars are really good now—you're not going to be there."

TURNING POINTS

Mark Dalton is right: the main reason I'm writing this book is that acoustic guitars are indeed really good now, and many luthiers like Dalton and his partner, Jeff Huss, have worked to make it so. In seeking to discover why the guitars of Huss & Dalton, Collings, Froggy Bottom, Santa Cruz, and other small shops and companies are "really good" now, one must inquire about turning points—those key moments in their histories that enabled these makers to figuratively emerge from the pack of countless other guitar builders and become widely recognized for the excellence of their instruments.

There are few guitar makers who can match the diversity and range of experiences as well as the number of distinct turning points that Jean Larrivée has had in his long career. Born in 1944 in Québec to a French-speaking family, Jean also speaks English, German, and Russian, as well as some Chinese. (He says he has studied Chinese for nine years but is still a beginner.) This linguistic facility is a good clue to the man's capacity for geographic mobility, cultural adaptation, and personal independence. All of these qualities come into play when identifying the turning points in the history of his company, Larrivée Guitars.[16]

I visit Larrivée on a January morning at his factory in Oxnard, California, about 150 miles up the coast from Los Angeles. I had arranged this visit with him some days before when we met in the Anaheim Convention Center. The occasion was the Winter NAMM Show—a massive annual trade show of the National Association of Music Merchants (NAMM), which attracts more than 100,000 people involved in every aspect of the music industry, including agents, publishers, store owners, and manufacturers of audio equipment and every kind of instrument. Here, contacts are made, contracts are signed, and instrument makers—including virtually everyone in the guitar industry—show their wares in large display booths. At his booth, Larrivée had invited me to come up to Oxnard just after the show to visit his plant, and I eagerly accepted. A few days later, I arrive at the appointed hour in my rental car and park next to Larrivée Guitars' shop: a boxy, nondescript factory on the town's outskirts.

No one could accuse this compact, gray-bearded septuagenarian of easing off his workload as he moves through his proverbial golden years. As we settle in for an interview, Jean tells me his company runs production seven days a week with about fifty employees, and he comes in every day. A bit incredulous, I ask him, "So you work every day? You don't take a day off to go fishing or surfing?" He replies, "It's cheaper to go to Vonn's Supermarket and buy a fish and cook it." In one of the company's product catalogues, Jean is pictured—relaxed, arms crossed, and smiling—and the quote above his head reads: "I live and breathe guitars. . . . It's all I do."

In a career making guitars that stretches back to the early 1960s, Larrivée

Jean Larrivée at his factory in Oxnard, California. Photo by author.

identifies two types of turning points, the first being the challenge of relocating and gearing up production in different locales in both Canada and the United States. Jean has moved the operations of Larrivée Guitars four over times over the past six decades, with each successive move driven by trying to improve both the company's finances and the quality of its instruments. Since the 1960s, Larrivée guitars have been produced in Toronto (1967–77), then Victoria, British Columbia (1977–84), followed by Vancouver (1984–2001), and now, since 2001, Oxnard, California.

Taken together, these four moves were not just about relocation; they also entailed much dislocation and unforeseen problems. Larivée comments: "Every time we made a major move to another location—those were always turning points. A big one was when we moved from Toronto—which is where we had all the apprentices and where we had lots of one-on-one with many musicians—to Victoria, on Vancouver Island. There we became much more isolated. There were also too many problems with freight, and anything shipped overseas had a double whammy—you had to get it from Victoria to Vancouver, then from Vancouver overseas. It became much too complicated and too costly, so we moved to the mainland."

A second turning point involved a major change in Larrivée Guitars's relationship with the guitar-retailing world. By the late 1990s, the company had established a strong relationship with the major retailer, Guitar Center. According to Jean, during the period when it was producing guitars in Vancouver, the company was "growing like wildfire" and had become the largest supplier to Guitar Center. Around the year 2000, however, the giant retail chain wanted to boost their sales of Larrivée guitars and pressured the company to make some less expensive models, but the luthier insisted he was "a high-end builder." Guitar Center finally gave Larrivée an ultimatum—produce cheaper guitars or else. He says to me with a smile, looking at my voice recorder: "I can't tell you on the recording what I told them over the phone."

This refusal put the company on a different path. They lost Guitar Center as a customer but within a year had made up the loss with what Jean calls "Mom and Pops"—smaller guitar merchants. Up to that time, Larrivée was losing many of these smaller sellers because of his ties to Guitar Center. "If I told a Mom and Pop that I was with Guitar Center," he says, "they would back out. They didn't want to, or couldn't, compete with Guitar Center in terms of discounts and financing. When we parted company with Guitar Center, the Mom and Pops were suddenly interested in doing business with us."

Larrivée goes on to say that, for a company of his size at the time (about eighty employees), trying to supply both types of retailers had become a major burden, which he likened to an unsustainable human relationship: "You can't service two people—you just can't do that. It's like having a wife at home and a girlfriend next door. That doesn't work. Over the course of the next three or four months, we picked up all of the business we had lost through Guitar Center. That was a major turning point for us. For a company owner like me to decide to drop Guitar Center, well, not many people would do that. But they wanted more; what they wanted was to own me, and they even made that offer. But I refused."

At the end of my visit with Jean, I bid him *adieu* and set off in my car for the next part of my research travels. As I drive north, I reflect on the joy I find in listening to thoughtful, skilled, and successful luthiers recount the ways they embarked upon their careers and eventually reached their present situation. All of life, of course, is chancy and complex, but undertaking a career as an instrument maker is especially so, and there is no one way to climb that particular mountain. I am thinking of mountains in more ways than one as I drive my rental car toward the central California coast through the Santa Cruz Mountains.

The production facility of Santa Cruz Guitar Company, a low-slung building in the rear of a parking lot with a couple of industrial buildings nearby and a giant Costco across the street, is just as nondescript as the Larrivée factory. No sign out front indicates what goes on here. I walk through a glass door into a spacious room, and the receptionist, April, gives me a friendly welcome, as do two large, friendly dogs. I am here to meet the company's original owner, Richard Hoover.[17]

Like Jean Larrivée, Hoover is a bearded, compact man born in the mid-1940s, but their trajectories as guitar makers differ sharply. Whereas Larrivée has been a peripatetic producer, having relocated his shop four times in two countries, Hoover, a native Californian, has kept both his company's name and its production facilities directly tied to this specific geographical location. As well, Larrivée and Hoover took different approaches to the strategic question of whether to go it alone as a guitar maker or seek out partners to help share the financial and management burdens. As it turned out, Jean Larrivée did not have to face this question squarely, since he now has two grown sons who have joined him in running Larrivée Guitars. Jean says, "There's always somebody that wants to buy the company. But it's a family business—I can't sell it. I didn't necessarily want my sons to take over the business when I was young, but it automatically happens. It's like, 'Why would you work some-place else, when you can work here and make more money?' Plus I have a grandson. He comes here a lot and he plays around here, he likes it. We know he's going to be in the business, you can almost tell."

Hoover, on the other hand, has no heirs apparent, and so, early on in the mid-1970s, he decided to take on two partners in owning and running the fledgling guitar company he had created. The partnership had its difficulties and eventually dissolved; one of the partners left after two years, but the other one remained for nearly fifteen years, at which point tensions between Hoover

Richard Hoover in his shop, Santa Cruz Guitar Company, Santa Cruz, California.
Photo by author.

and his remaining partner over management and other issues reached a breaking point. Richard bought him out and has since remained the sole owner. Nevertheless, that partnership proved crucial for sustaining his company in its early growing years.

A second turning point for many guitar makers involves product development, specifically what types of guitars and models to build. Both Hoover and Larrivée have always produced a range of models, but Richard had the good fortune to craft a specific one—the Tony Rice model—that became a signature guitar for Santa Cruz during its early growth years in the late 1970s and 1980s. Tony Rice, the inventive virtuoso in various styles ranging from folk to bluegrass to jazz, was also known for the guitar he always played as he built his following and career: a 1935 Martin D-28 that had belonged to his close friend, Clarence White, who died in 1973 after being hit by a drunk driver. White, a trailblazing guitarist who had been one of the original members of the folk-rock band, the Byrds, had acquired that guitar for just $25 because it had been damaged, including two unusual idiosyncrasies. One was a whittled-out sound hole, done for unknown reasons by a none-too-skilled previous owner, such that the guitar's neck partially overlapped the sound hole itself; the other was that the original neck had been replaced by a blank neck (no position markers) off of a Gretsch electric guitar.[18] As Rice became increasingly known for his prowess on that guitar, which was eventually repaired but with the enlarged sound hole and Gretsch neck left intact, he had a dilemma: his fans expected to see him playing White's iconic guitar, but he cherished the guitar and wanted to protect it from the wear and tear of being an everyday road guitar.

Through mutual friends in the California music scene, Rice contacted Hoover in 1977 and asked him to make a close copy of his guitar. According to Hoover, "Tony wanted a few modifications to Clarence's guitar, but the guitar had to look right," meaning that it had to have an enlarged sound hole. Hoover took on the task, and Santa Cruz began producing its Tony Rice Signature Model, which quickly became known in guitar circles, giving Santa Cruz guitars a certain buzz and credibility, according to Hoover.

Every luthier I interviewed had a story, or several stories, about one or more turning points in line with the experiences of Larrivée and Hoover. Like Hoover other luthiers' instruments have become identified with a well-known musician; for example, Manzer and Olson guitars have long been favored by

Pat Metheny and James Taylor, respectively. Whatever the particulars of the situation, a turning point is an opportunity that presents itself and is seized. Imagine, for example, Tony Rice calling you up and kindly asking you to make him a copy of an iconic guitar that he can take on the road. In other cases, a turning point is forced upon you. Imagine, as another example, your main dealer, Guitar Center, calling you up and, not so kindly, requesting that you make a low-end model that you do not want to make. A takeaway here is that a turning point for a guitar maker cannot be predicted; rather, it can be discerned only in retrospect.

The vagaries of the market apply less to the question of how a guitar maker approaches his craft in the first place. The guitar maker must confront essential questions: What is your purpose in making guitars? What is your vision, not only for how to make a good guitar, but also—perhaps for more material reasons—what is your plan for making a living making guitars? Such questions are especially crucial in a world flush with high-quality luthier-crafted guitars from which to choose.

How to Be Distinctive

Answering the questions just posed requires a guitar maker to reflect on, and figure out, how to make one's guitars and one's brand distinctive in the market. Economists call this product differentiation; guitar makers would likely call it survival. But how can makers differentiate their guitars when tradition-bound buyers consider a 1930s Martin D-18 or D-28 to be the Platonic ideal of what an acoustic guitar should look and sound like? This question was uppermost in my mind as I traveled to shops and factories and interviewed some of the luthiers of this Reinventor generation.

Michael Millard is one of this generation's most eloquent members on this topic.[19] Born in 1947 and brought up in New Haven, Connecticut, Millard was a budding luthier in 1970 when he met the "other Michael," Michael Gurian, who persuaded him to move to New York City and come work for him. Millard even remained with Gurian when the latter moved his shop to southern New Hampshire a few years later. Ultimately, however, Millard went off on his own, setting up his own small shop in the woods near Sharon, Vermont, making guitars under the name Froggy Bottom Guitars.[20]

Froggy Bottom found success as a high-end, hand-building luthier; however, the company reached its own turning point in the year 2000. By that year, Froggy Bottom, now with seven employees, was making three hundred guitars a year and selling its instruments through fifty-two dealers worldwide. The expansion produced its own organizational problems, and Millard now admits "We got way too big." Following a series of gradual cutbacks over the next two decades, the shop now has three employees and makes about seventy-five guitars a year, almost all custom orders.

Froggy Bottom's time-tested strategy for guitar making could be summarized as higher quality, lower production, and higher price per instrument. Michael reports happily that "It's working out really, really well." The price of a new, custom-made Froggy Bottom guitar is, of course, to be negotiated with Millard himself, but a quick internet search reveals that a used instrument typically sells in the $8,000-$16,000 range.

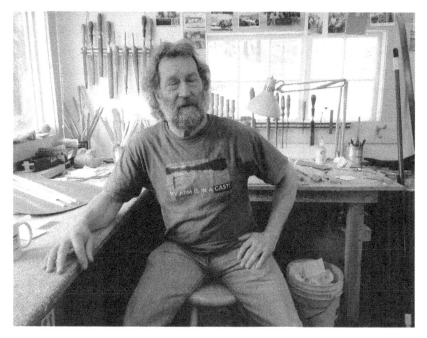

Michael Millard in his Froggy Bottom Guitars workshop near Chelsea, Vermont.
Photo by author.

"Innovation"—or least, the capacity to be flexible and build a guitar suited to the individual buyer—is built into Millard's mode of operation. As we discuss his work over cups of coffee in his shop, he explains how Froggy Bottom guitars are distinctive: "My business plan is to be me. Everything is organic. We respond to what the world around us is asking for. Everything in our methodology is based on flexibility, unlike anybody else I know who makes guitars. We can change anything in a guitar that we want to change. Anything. For us everything is about function. Only after we get through the basics about function do we begin to talk about other aspects that have to do with appointments and appearance." Though he himself does not use the term "innovation" Millard certainly considers his guitars original in that each is virtually one of a kind—made for a specific buyer. He says, "The real alchemy in making a guitar at the highest level lies in the ability of the builder to communicate with the client as a unique individual, one on one. The better I understand what motivates you, the more that understanding will be incorporated into the instrument I build for you, and the more satisfied both you and I will be." Michael then describes the extensive interview process he conducts with an interested buyer. "Why is the most important question. What do you want to do, and why?" He then asks about the scope and kind of music the customer plays. Millard wants to find out, in his words, "where are you heading musically?" Referring to my current and former hometowns, he asks metaphorically, "Are you going to Chicago or Shreveport?" His interrogatory eventually delves into other details such as playing style (finger style or flat pick), string gauge (light or medium), and preferred tunings (standard or open tuning). He concludes, "You need to know that I am totally here for you and that I really know what I am doing."

As we finish up our conversation, I ask Michael how he assesses his contribution to guitar making. He immediately responds: "It's the scope of my work. I'm trying to make very traditional guitars; I haven't tried to reinvent the wheel. I've tried to take the scope of what I think is possible with the steel-string acoustic guitar and address that comprehensively." He likens his craft to that of a blues singer: "It's a fairly narrow genre, but when you get into it, it's like, wow, the subtlety and refinement are endless. You've got body size, scale length, strings and string gauge, wood selection, music being played, and proportion. I want to know that when a person gets my guitar some months later, they consider it the best guitar they've seen in their life."

On the same trip I took out east to visit Froggy Bottom and interview Michael Millard, I paid a call on a fellow New Englander, Dana Bourgeois, who runs a small shop in a refurbished warehouse in Lewiston, Maine.[21] A lifetime Mainer, Dana was born in Portland in 1953 and graduated from nearby Bowdoin College in 1975. At that time, he knew two things: he wanted to stay in Maine, and he enjoyed working with his hands. Since, as mentioned earlier, he was familiar with his father's wood shop and his grandfather's machine shop and therefore, in his own words, "not intimidated by tools," he began repairing and later building acoustic guitars.

Bourgeois quickly fell in with the growing community of acoustic guitar makers. In recounting his early days, he specifically mentions a national convention of the Guild of American Luthiers (GAL) held in Boston in 1979, where he met and became friendly with other regional guitar makers including Nick Apollonio, Michael Cone, Michael Gurian, and Michael Millard. In the late 1970s, he says, it was relatively easy to become a guitar maker. In addition to a flourishing DIY culture and a sharing ethos within the guitar-building community, there was also strong demand for acoustic instruments from folk, bluegrass, and blues musicians.

DIY culture and a sharing community were shaping factors in Dana's development as a luthier, but perhaps the key element was what I will label "instructional input" that he gleaned from professional musicians. He describes his approach as one of intentional listening: "My whole career has been driven by trying to find and get to know the best players I can have access to. I show them my guitars and listen to them play. Then I listen to what they have to say, and then go back and scratch my head and figure out what should I do next." This feedback process has been critical to his success: "The stuff I'm now learning from great guitar players is fairly subtle, but a good player can bring out so much in a guitar. You may think your guitar is a great instrument, but you as a builder need that affirmation that it really is. All of this information gets soaked up and sloshed around. Every little voicing decision you make is going to be informed by something, and it's the cumulative experience of all that feedback that makes a huge difference."

Naturally enough, the emphasis on "player feedback" leads to a discussion of how Bourgeois seeks to make his guitars stand out in a competitive field. He does not shrink from comparing his approach to that of two companies—Collings and Santa Cruz—that are often mentioned in the same breath as Bourgeois Guitars. Going slightly geeky, Dana waxes eloquent on the nuances of construction, string action, voicing, and projection, concluding that "All three of us—Collings, Santa Cruz, and Bourgeois—we're all working with traditional styles of guitars. We're not trying to do anything radical or experimental in design. We're all going after that elusive vintage sound, but we have different pathways of getting there."

Collings, for example, has always focused on power, achieved in part through heavier construction. Collings, Dana claims, builds guitars with sturdy tops that "like to be played hard" and stiffer backs that "reflect sound with greater efficiency." Santa Cruz, by contrast, builds with thinner, lighter tops than either Collings or Bourgeois. This is perhaps due, Dana says, to the influ-

Dana Bourgeois, founder/owner of Bourgeois Guitars, Lewiston, Maine.
Courtesy Bourgeois Guitars.

ence of their longtime endorser, Tony Rice, who played with a relatively light, articulate touch but still produced a massive sound. Rice's iconic, heavily altered 1935 Martin D-28 had a thinned-out top that sounded best when played close to the bridge, whereas the typical "sweet spot" on most guitars is located closer to the sound hole. Bourgeois claims that Santa Cruz also employs a light top construction, further noting that "guitars built in this style cannot be played as hard as guitars made with stiffer, heavier tops, but the difference is made up in the instrument's unique combination of fullness, clarity, and presence."

Bourgeois Guitars has developed a "voicing system," based on its owner's skill at tap tuning the top, that enables them to create, in Dana's words, "good note-to-note and string-to-string balance no matter the size of the guitar we build." His approach, too, has its price to pay, as this sonic balance, he admits, "comes slightly at the expense of overall volume." Bourgeois goes on to say that he has borrowed building ideas from the great vintage Martin and Gibson guitars of the prewar years. "I build with a Gibson-style back and a Martin-style top" he says. Traditionally, he explains, the backs of Gibson guitars were relatively light and therefore more resonant, and so the back functioned as a kind of secondary soundboard to the primary soundboard, which is the top. This construction increased the guitar's overall "frequency range." A relatively thick or "tighter" (i.e., more heavily braced) back, by contrast, acts more as a reflector of sonic vibrations produced by the primary soundboard, the top.

Bourgeois claims that a Gibson-style back improves harmonic fullness, thereby reducing the playing time needed to "break in" a new guitar. As for his Martin-style top, Dana says he has adopted the Martin top-bracing system of the classic 1930s instruments, which features a "forward-shifted X brace" This means the X-shaped brace that is glued to the top's underside is positioned farther forward—that is, more toward the sound hole and away from the bridge—compared with conventional guitars of the postwar era. Such is the arcana that luthiers live with every day, but I come away impressed by the nuances of how a skilled guitar maker deals intimately with questions of wood thickness and brace positioning.

The question of how a luthier's instruments "stand out" in the crowd of other high-quality guitars is not just a matter of professional identity; it is also one of practical survival. As Bill Collings tells me, "When I started making guitars, I started learning. I just wanted to make good guitars. I just did it for me. Money was secondary, but making good guitars became a way to make a living."

Not surprisingly, all the luthiers I interviewed had thoughtful, detailed answers in response to my question of how their instruments and instrument making are distinctive. Collings makes the point that his company is notable for the sheer range of instruments and models that his factory of about one hundred employees produces. He then proceeds to detail the number of different models produced, not only of acoustic guitars (14), but also of electric guitars (17), archtop guitars (7), mandolins (14), and even ukuleles (4). Bill explains this diversification: "That was done for one thing: I wanted to give my dealers something to sell. I never wanted to make a lot of things cheap, so I spread out this way. I never wanted to make a low-price instrument—you can buy those anywhere, from China, from Taylor. So we wanted to be this higher end thing, but we couldn't be a one-trick pony, because people own many guitars. So that was done on purpose."

As a final example, Richard Hoover quickly identifies Santa Cruz Guitar Company's distinctiveness: "We are a custom shop." Echoing Michael Millard's attention to customer needs, Richard also underlines Santa Cruz's capacity to make guitars to order; however, there is a major difference: because it has the capacity to do so, Santa Cruz sells only to retailers rather than directly to individual buyers à la Froggy Bottom. This difference is due to the companies' dimensions. Though still a small company by most standards, Santa Cruz is much larger than Froggy Bottom. Making five hundred guitars a year with fifteen guitar builders and a small office staff, Santa Cruz dwarfs the size of Froggy Bottom's lean operation of Millard and two other employees making a few dozen guitars a year.

This size difference requires a different approach to the logistics of ordering and supplying. Yes, an individual customer may custom order a Santa Cruz guitar, but not directly from the company; the order must be run through one of its dealers, which submits the order and ultimately sells the guitar. As Hoover says, "We became a custom shop, and we now have four decades of practice. Large companies can't manage that, and small companies might not know how. So that's where we decided to take our niche. So over 75 percent of our work is custom."

In my conversations, I eventually asked these luthiers to assess the chief challenges they foresee going forward. The term "challenges" is not uppermost in my mind, however, as I drive through the beautiful Blue Ridge Mountains of southwestern Virginia. The only possible challenges to living here that I could imagine would be the crick in my neck from gazing at the picturesque peaks and the dizziness in my head from the twisting roadways. My destination is the small city of Staunton, where the youngest company of the reinventor lutherie generation, the Huss & Dalton Guitar Company, runs its operations. Upon entering their shop, I am greeted by a friendly woman, Kimberly Dalton, who oversees the office. She quickly summons her husband, Mark Dalton, who in turn calls out to his partner, Jeff Huss, to join us. I shake hands with both men, who look to be in their early- to mid-50s, and then we settle in to talk about their life in making high-level guitars, along with the occasional banjo.

Jeff Huss grew up in North Dakota, graduating from college and law school and even passing the bar there. Soon after, however, he realized that he had no desire to be a lawyer. In the meantime, he had fallen in love with bluegrass music featuring that characteristic "banjer sound." So in the mid-1980s he migrated to the warmer climes of Afton, Virginia, near Staunton. Huss's goal: to learn how to build banjos with the well-known maker, Geoff Stelling, who had recently moved his operations from San Diego to Virginia and was recruiting new employees. Once hired on, Jeff found that he enjoyed and was good at making banjos; eventually, in his spare time, he extended his instrument making to acoustic guitars.

While working at Stelling, Huss met Mark Dalton, a native Virginian who is described in one magazine article as "a blustery southern-Virginia hay farmer who raises mules and draft horses."[22] Notwithstanding their background differences, the two men became friendly and found a common bond: a love of playing and making guitars. Becoming business partners in 1995, they began producing their own instruments under the Huss & Dalton name in a small shop in downtown Staunton. More than two decades later, they are still at it. They and their ten employees produce about three hundred guitars a year.

After talking about their beginnings together and their current operations, we turn to the road ahead, the likely future. I finally put the "C" word—challenges—on the table and ask them what they see as their biggest challenge going forward. Without hesitating Huss says, "our main customer base." He then proceeds to talk about demographics, or more specifically, the demographic decline of the Baby Boomer generation: "That's a real concern for everybody in this industry. When we started in the mid-1990s our main customers were 40- and 50-year-old male professionals with disposable income. That's who has fueled this boom, because those are the guys buying all these high-end guitars. And now they're 60 and 70 years old and selling their guitars or giving them to their kids or grandkids."

Mark Dalton then recounts a recent phone call with one of their dealers who noted that fewer 30- and 40-year-olds are buying the kind of handcrafted guitars—with price tags of $4,000 and up—that Huss & Dalton produces. Trying to stay optimistic, Mark expresses hope that this younger generation

Huss & Dalton Guitar Shop. *Left to right*: Mark Dalton, John Calkin (luthier), and Jeff Huss, Staunton, Virginia. Photo by author.

will eventually have the disposable income to sustain demand for high-quality guitars. For the present, however, neither luthier sees a quick replenishment of their principal customer cohort.

I then ask where they would like to be in the next five or ten years in terms of production and market position. Logically but cautiously, Huss says that depends on the market: "We have followed the market. It would be useless for us to say, 'We want to be building 600 guitars a year.' If we can't sell 600, what's the point of doing it? And that's how our line has developed, responding to people or dealers asking us to build a guitar of this or that type."

That approach—responding to dealers and others requesting a particular type of model—has its risks. Case in point: Huss & Dalton attempted in 2010 to introduce a new line of models into an uncertain market. At that time, in the wake of the so-called Great Recession of 2008—the economy was slowly recovering. They tried to adjust to lower demand by making a lower-cost line called the "Road Series." Jeff remarks: "We DID—past tense—have a Road Series. It was a response to the recession, and people weren't buying guitars. But dealers told us that if you can make a guitar with a street price of about $2,000, we can sell those. So we went into it with a leap of faith. We thought we'd try to see if we could make some money out of a less expensive model, but in the end we found we couldn't."

At first, Dalton adds, they got a rush of orders for the simply appointed, lower priced Road Series model, but they soon realized that their operating costs, especially for labor, were too high to turn a profit with that model. "The question was whether it could break even," Mark says. He continues: "The idea was to keep our employees' jobs. Our jobs—Jeff's, Kimberly's, and mine—weren't in jeopardy, but everyone else's was. You try to keep these people who are so hard to train—it takes forever to train them. Plus, it's a small shop, we're working here together, we like each other, and you don't want to lay anybody off. Besides all that, it doesn't make business sense to let people go who took that long to train. And who knows, they might take a job someplace else, and you can't get them back." To anyone who ever thought guitar makers were idealistic, dreamy hippies unconcerned with earning filthy lucre, Mark Dalton's conclusion stands as a corrective: "I'd like to do the Road Series if we could make money at it, but I don't want to build any guitar I can't make money at."

IS THERE A CONCLUSION TO THE REINVENTOR GENERATION?

As Huss & Dalton's ill-fated Road Series initiative indicates, all individual and small-scale luthiers—not to mention virtually anyone in a private business of any kind—must deal with a complex mix of factors including the costs they incur versus the prices they can charge. There is nothing inherently mysterious or ineffable about the interplay of supply and demand in the market-competitive environment of acoustic guitars. As just two examples, supplies of premium woods—notably spruce for tops, and mahogany, rosewood, and maple for backs and sides—will likely become scarcer and more expensive over time because of deforestation, especially in developing countries, while the public's demand for "that acoustic sound"—and therefore acoustic guitars—will always be subject to shifting, unpredictable musical fads and tastes.

Demand is also related to demographics, as already noted. Dana Bourgeois adds his voice to Jeff Huss and Mark Dalton in worrying about the *possibility* for growth, given the gradual but inevitable dwindling of the Baby Boomer cohort. He notes: "There was a period when the industry was growing by leaps and bounds. Most of our customers are people our age, and the trends we see happening are that large guitar collections are being consolidated. People are saying, 'Well, I've got 20 guitars, but I really want to get it down to four or five nice ones that I really like.' So part of what we're doing is not only competing with other high-end builders and the big companies, but we're also competing with our own used guitars now on the market. It's difficult to look at that and ask, 'How do I grow?'"

However worrisome, these basic economic and demographic factors are, to employ the infamous but suggestive terms of a former US Secretary of Defense, largely "unknown knowns." One knows that supply and demand factors must be faced and managed, though their exact dimensions cannot be predicted. What *can* be predicted for this reinventor generation of luthiers is indisputably a "known known": they will not work forever. The question, then, is whether—and if so how—to carry on their legacy of guitar making once they retire or pass on. The German sociologist Max Weber developed a concept that describes the dilemma that many luthiers of the reinventor generation face: the "routinization of charisma." How can these companies sustain a founding luthier's reputation for producing superior instruments *after* the founder has passed from the scene?

The luthiers I interviewed are all of an age when such a question naturally arises, and they have all considered it. Dana Bourgeois is especially thoughtful and candid about this prospect: "I'm past 60, and I'm not going to build guitars forever. As long as I'm healthy, I want to have a hand in this, but the challenge for me and companies like Santa Cruz, Collings, and others is how to outlive their founder." As we shall see in Chapter 4, Dana has found a path forward to ensure the survival of Bourgeois Guitars well into the future.

Bourgeois goes on to mention the "Taylor model" as a possible template for other guitar makers contemplating retirement. He notes that in 2012, Bob Taylor, the cofounder of Taylor Guitars of El Cajon, California, designated a much younger master luthier, Andy Powers, then just thirty years old, as his successor and the public face of the company. Powers, says Dana, is now doing much of the R&D work that Taylor himself used to do, and the company is heralding Powers as the creator of a new bracing system, among other innovations. Bourgeois adds that Bob Taylor currently devotes most of his work to acquiring new wood sources and setting up supply chains to ensure the company's long-range access to natural resources. We explore these and other changes in Taylor Guitars in the following chapter.

As noted earlier, Bill Collings was incredibly charismatic, but the company's general manager, Steve McCreary, today claims that Collings Guitars is carrying their founder's legacy forward. Collings passed away at age 68 in July 2017, and though his widow and daughter still own the company, it is now run by a trio of top managers headed by McCreary. He emphasizes that many of Collings's top luthiers have been with the company for many years, during which time they worked directly with its founder, absorbing his knowledge and commitment. "Bill was all about designing and executing the coolest stuff there is," McCreary notes. "Everybody in this company has been affected by what Bill stood for, and that was: no quarter given, attention to detail, do it right, make it nice, make it beautiful, give the buyer more than what he or she paid for. That spirit is pervasive in all that we do."[23]

Jeff Huss and Mark Dalton, in contrast to the brash, outspoken Bill Collings, have tried to project a different image. Huss says, "The only theory we had from the beginning was that we didn't want to make ourselves rock-star luthiers," a characterization he says is thrust on them often. "We wanted to make a company that would maybe outlast us. We looked at everybody and asked ourselves: 'What's going to happen to Collings when Bill Collings is gone, or Santa Cruz when Richard Hoover is gone?'"

Dalton describes this tendency metaphorically: "People really want their guitar to have been built by an elf in a tree," he says. "You gotta walk the line between being that elf—that is, some kind of magic figure—and then NOT being that elf, so that the company can survive our retiring at some point." A family succession is not in the cards: Dalton has no children, and Huss's children are not interested in taking over the business. Dalton concludes: "We both want to be able to retire at some point, so we're hoping somebody else will buy this business, and that the people working here can keep their jobs."

NOT JUST A MAN'S WORLD ANYMORE

As for the long-term endurance of the artisan luthier segment of the guitar-making world, perhaps the most hope lies in an emerging generation of female guitar makers. Just as women are increasingly making their mark in guitar playing, the same trend is evident in guitar building. This is not to say that women luthiers have been invisible in the profession. As indicated previously, Linda Manzer was "in there among the boys" as a female pioneer in the 1970s, and she has remained so in the decades since, constructing highly esteemed guitars alone and almost completely by hand. It would be difficult to imagine a nicer accolade being paid from one luthier to another than this one: "In the modern age of lutherie in North America, Linda Manzer belongs at the forefront. She is a pioneer in a craft long dominated by men. Linda creates instruments at the top of the craft, and she expanded the definition of the acoustic guitar at a time when there were almost no women in the field."[24] Other women luthiers have been active over the years, including Canadian Judy Threet, whose guitars, known especially for their exquisite inlays, have been played by well-known musicians such as Tracy Chapman. But there's no question that despite the presence of Manzer, Threet, and a few others, male luthiers have continued to dominate the field, at least numerically.

This dominance appears to be changing, albeit gradually, as a generation of younger female guitar builders is gaining respect and customers for the quality of their instruments.[25] Three such examples are Jayne Henderson, Rachel Rosenkrantz, and Maegen Wells.

Henderson (born 1983) is likely the most immediately recognizable name, given that her father is Wayne Henderson, who was born, raised, and still lives in Rugby, Virginia, of Grayson County, population eighty. Over the past forty years, Henderson *père* has become a revered maker of fine hand-built guitars and mandolins; he has made custom instruments for, among others, Doc Watson, Eric Clapton, Vince Gill, and Tommy Emmanuel.[26]

If both "nature" and "nurture" play a role in one's becoming a skilled luthier, how could his daughter Jayne not have had some of her dad's talent rub off on her? The short answer is that such "rubbing" is no automatic process, and in Jayne's case the spark to make guitars came a bit later and more unexpectedly than is the case for many luthiers. For one thing, her parents divorced when Henderson was small, and she was raised largely by her mother, not her dad, in Roanoke. Although she visited him occasionally, she showed no early interest in guitar making. Asked where she got her "vision and skill set" to make guitars, she replies that it came mostly from her mom, an artist who always encouraged Jayne to be creative and use her hands to make things.[27]

Committed to finding more sustainable ways to live, Jayne studied environmental law at Vermont Law School and then took a job with a nonprofit environmental organization in Asheville, North Carolina. But she had one problem: a load of student debt. So she asked her dad if he would make her a guitar that she could sell to pay off her debt. (A new Henderson guitar on the open market will easily fetch at least $20,000.) Her dad proposed an alternative: making one together. Semi-coerced to agree to Wayne's proposal, Jayne soon had a revelation: Not only was she good at the handcraft, but she also found joy and fulfillment in the building process itself. Within two years of working with her father, she decided to quit her day job and make instruments full time.

Henderson now specializes in small-body guitars and ukuleles and operates much as her father does: she builds to order, emphasizing the handcraft techniques Wayne taught her and viewing the relationship between the builder and the instrument as a highly personal one that develops through the communication process between the human creator and the wood. Jayne uses words like "soul" and "personality" to talk about an instrument she is making: "To me, it's not a thing, it's a being. Each instrument has its own personality, and I cannot wait to meet it. My favorite thing—I love to string that E string [as] the first string, and I always pluck it just to hear it—its first little cry."[28] In so doing, she sees herself not only as a kind of artist using the skills both parents taught her, but also as someone "working to alter gender stereotypes in a male dominated field."[29]

Female guitar-makers can alter gender stereotypes by demonstrating not only virtuosity in building skills but also diversity, and it would be difficult to imagine another luthier—of whatever gender—who could be more different from Jayne Henderson in upbringing, background, and approach than Rachel Rosenkrantz (born 1981). For starters, Rosenkrantz is French and was raised in Paris. Demonstrating an early interest in art and design, she eventually came to the United States and studied for a year at the Rhode Island School of Design, in Providence. She eventually got work in the States designing commercial lighting fixtures and furniture; however, along the way she rediscovered an early love of music and decided to apprentice with Daniel Collins, a classical guitar maker. By 2016, she had established her own shop in Providence, Atelier Rosenkrantz, and was already immersed in several different projects at once: building a gypsy jazz guitar, four classical guitars, and for good measure . . . a violin and a ukulele.[30]

She has continued to pursue such varied projects ever since. Not wedded to any one type of instrument, style of building, or wood combination, Rosenkrantz constantly experiments and seeks out new challenges. Although she is committed to handcrafting her instruments as much as possible, she is no self-conscious traditionalist, hewing to past practices. A good example is her collaboration with guitarist Kaki King. As mentioned in the previous chapter, King herself constantly experiments with different playing techniques and tunings. On her 2021 album *Modern Yesterdays*, King uses a second bridge on her guitar, designed and crafted by Rosenkrantz. This portable wooden device, called a *passerelle* (French for footbridge), is inserted under the strings on the fingerboard itself and thereby divides the strings into two playable sections, making the instrument comparable to a Japanese koto or a Chinese *guzheng*.[31]

Rosenkrantz credits her own musical background as foundational for her guitar building; in her words: "I play upright bass, bouzouki, and guitar in various styles; I have played in bands, ensembles, and solo, too. Once you have that experience, you can absolutely put yourself in your client's shoes and understand their needs. Making a guitar is more than designing and building an object. It is addressing a bigger picture about having a creative lifestyle."[32] Not surprisingly, when asked whether she considers herself a traditionalist or an innovator, she responds without hesitation: "I am more drawn to innovation and experimentation. It is part of my fabric, as it is in what and how I teach. Innovation and risk were also encouraged during my studies and what I focused on as an industrial designer before my career shift to lutherie. The more I build, the less I am interested in confirming what we already know. Past instruments that get my attention were innovative in their time, like Maurice Martenot's Palme Diffuseur or Jean-Baptiste Vuillaume's octobass. I don't like to follow blueprints."[33]

A third example of a rising female builder is Maegen Wells (born 1987), who had neither a famous luthier parent nor an upbringing in Paris. She does, however, credit her parents with fostering an interest in doing and making things that ultimately led to a career as a luthier. How many luthiers link their interest in making instruments to an early love of mowing the lawn because they got to operate the lawn mower? Maegen Wells does so as she recounts her origin story. What she learned by watching her parents do such things as mow the lawn, chainsaw trees, and replace kitchen tiles put her on a DIY path of creativity that led to a love of playing guitar and eventually woodworking.

That interest led, in turn, to several years of lutherie training—in the Master's Program at the Galloup School of Guitar Building and Repair and an apprenticeship with well-known luthier Tom Ribbecke—before going on her own around 2015. Working out of a house in the redwood trees near the small town of Forestville in northern California, Wells crafts primarily guitars and mandolins.[34] A savvy social-media presence, she is still actively building her brand as of this writing, even as she keeps a part-time job at the all-purpose lutherie supplier, Luthier Mercantile International (LMI), and also makes wooden pedal boards for West Coast Pedal Board—both located in the nearby town of Windsor.

If Wells is representative of the upcoming generation of female luthiers, the future looks promising. When asked if she sees a benefit to being a woman in a traditionally male-dominated field, she is forthright: "Honestly, I rarely think about the fact that I am in a male dominated industry—I just don't see it that way. These are some of the coolest, most amazingly talented, and supportive people I've ever met in my life. . . . Ever since I started building guitars thirteen years ago, I've been met with an overwhelming amount of encouragement, and I would be completely lost without the support of this very special community, that just so happens to be mostly men."[35]

Let us leave Maegen Wells with the last word on the topic of artisan and small-scale production of guitars. Her advice to any aspiring luthier transcends both gender and craft: "Think long term. Learning this craft is a lifelong mission. I've been completely devoted to building guitars since 2006 and I'm just now getting to a point where I feel like I might have some sort of understanding of what I'm doing. Stay focused on your work and true to your vision, while also allowing room from that vision to change and grow. There's going to be a lot of failure; learn to love it for what it has to teach you."[36]

Chapter 3

GAME CHANGER

Taylor Guitars

> I believe in the power of manufacturing. I believe a lot of things
> exist because somebody wants to make it . . . before somebody
> wants to buy it.
>
> —BOB TAYLOR (AUTHOR INTERVIEW, JANUARY 23, 2015)

> Bob Taylor's a game changer. He's definitely a driver in the industry.
>
> —REN FERGUSON, MASTER LUTHIER (AUTHOR INTERVIEW,
> JANUARY 22, 2015)

One of the surprising and wonderful things about working on this book has
been the serendipitous meeting of guitar lovers both famous and obscure. I
begin this chapter on Taylor Guitars with one such unforgettable encounter.

During October 2016 I was engaged in one of my periodic book-writing
stints—monastic weeks during which I am the sole inhabitant of my cous-
in's 150-year-old farmhouse forty miles east of my hometown of Shreveport,
Louisiana. Yes, it does get lonely out there among the cows, pastures, and
pine trees, but the ambiance is perfect for pushing prose along. One day,
after writing and transcribing interviews all morning, I decided to break the

routine and go out for lunch and a few hours in a library. That meant driving eight miles to Arcadia, a small town with a fine public library and Sharon's Café, a popular lunchtime restaurant. Arcadia is most notoriously known for its proximity to the roadside site where, on May 23, 1934, Bonnie Parker and Clyde Barrow met their bloody fate at the hands of Texas Ranger Frank Hamer and his band of lawmen.

Having polished off Sharon's lunch-plate special of beef tips, rice, and mustard greens, I was halfway through my dessert of banana pudding when who walks in but James Burton, lead guitarist for Ricky Nelson, Elvis Presley, Roy Orbison, and many others. He has been termed a "Master of the Telecaster," and his name appears on one list of great Tele players alongside the likes of Keith Richards and Jimmy Page.[1] Then seventy-seven, he was still a guitar god to just about everyone who plays the instrument. I had never seen Burton in person, much less met him, but I recognized him from photos. I also knew that he had grown up in Shreveport and had established a foundation there that promotes music education in schools and hospitals.[2] He had clearly kept his north Louisiana roots although he had traveled the globe and played before countless millions. James walked into Sharon's with a single friend, no entourage, but the waitresses seemed to know him and greeted him with smiles.

Who would not want to talk guitars with James Burton? I sat there for a while, too shy to approach him on my own. But the journalist/interviewer voice within me whispered "This is too good to pass up—you'd never forgive yourself if you just finish your pudding, pay your check, and walk out." Then I had an inspiration. I called over my friendly waitress, whom I'd seen chatting with Burton a few minutes earlier, and quickly explained my guitar book project to her. I then asked for a favor: "Would you mind introducing me to James?" My waitress didn't hesitate. "Why sure, honey," she said, and went over to Burton. Within thirty seconds I was sitting down with him and his friend, and we proceeded to chat about guitars for a good half hour.

I happened to have with me a small folder of articles about Taylor Guitars, and I mentioned that Taylor was one of the companies I'm studying. At that, James smiled and said, "I know Bob Taylor well and highly respect what they do at Taylor. They make great guitars, and when I play acoustic, I play Taylors. Everybody says their acoustic guitar necks are slim line, pretty much like electrics, and it's true. I never have any issue going from my Telecaster to a Taylor. Not only that, almost all their acoustics have pickups, so I can plug in any time I want. And every Taylor I've ever played sounds great and plays so smoothly. Tell Bob hi for me when you see him."

• • •

A chance encounter with one of the most iconic guitar players of the past seven decades? It doesn't get any better than this. Aside from the sheer pleasure of the experience, this story conveys much about the reach and presence of Taylor Guitars and about the singular impact of the person—Bob Taylor— whose name adorns the headstock of every one of the hundreds of thousands of instruments that the company produces each year.[3]

By any standard—production volume, sales, reputation, innovation— Taylor Guitars has indeed been what master luthier Ren Ferguson calls a "game changer" within the acoustic guitar world. Since its founding in 1974 by two young southern Californians—Bob Taylor (then nineteen) and Kurt Listug (then twenty-two)—Taylor Guitars has gone from a bare-bones shop of three employees making a few instruments a month to a large operation of two factories, with a total of about 1,400 total employees (direct and indirect labor) producing hundreds of guitars every day.

In the process, the company has established a powerful position in this highly competitive industry. In acoustic guitar production output alone, Taylor has amply surpassed the two long-established giants in the industry, C.F. Martin & Co. and Gibson. According to Ferguson, Martin produces about four hundred acoustic guitars per day, while Gibson makes about one hundred, so that these two companies have a combined daily production of roughly five hundred guitars. By contrast, Taylor manufactures about seven hundred guitars per day in its two plants—one near San Diego in El Cajon, California, and the other across the border in Tecate, Mexico.[4]

Taylor's emergence as a game changer has not been without controversy, however, especially from those in the guitar industry who value the artisan handcraft that has traditionally gone into making the instrument. For context, in 1990 Taylor became the first guitar manufacturer to deploy a Fadal CNC (Computer Numerical Control) machine, which was described by one observer as "a computer controlled vertical milling machine that was capable of carving complex parts with an extremely high degree of precision."[5] As in any industry in which a newly created company inserts—and asserts—itself to gain significant market share, these critics view Taylor's focus on growth and its adoption of automated technologies as a threat to hand builders. By his own report, Bob Taylor's move to introduce the Fadal into guitar making was considered a "sacrilege." Guitar makers, he said, considered the CNC to be "the machine that eats men's bones and spits them into the sky!"[6] In what was likely a majority view among luthiers at that time, the automated fashioning of such components as bridges, necks, and fingerboards, while increasing output and being able to replicate these parts precisely ad infinitum, would come at enormous cost: the elimination of jobs and the de-skilling of the jobs that remained. Since that time, Taylor has continued to prize such innovation, and the critiques have also continued.

Has Taylor been not only a game changer but also, in some sense, a game killer—at least of the handcrafted guitar? This question is on my mind as I go to see Taylor's facilities for myself.

GETTING TO KNOW YOU

First Impressions of a Visit

On a crisp January afternoon, I drive into the Taylor Guitars industrial park, consisting of eight buildings spread over several acres. The company has been receptive to my entreaties for a visit, and so I'm scheduled for a guided tour of the production works and interviews with some key personnel. At a building marked "Visitor Center," I go in and am soon greeted by a genial man in his early forties, Chris Wellons, who is the vice president for manufacturing. For the next three hours, Wellons takes me around the plant, showing me the production process and talking about—what else?—Taylor Guitars.

As we exit the Visitors Center and cross an access drive on our way to the main factory, I notice that Bob Taylor himself is crossing the drive in the opposite direction, about fifty yards away. He is chatting with two men, and they do not notice us. I quickly register his attire: blue jeans and a black t-shirt—he looks like any other worker. Again, first impressions can be tricky, but I wonder if Taylor's informal dress says something about the relaxed vibe of the place. It *is* southern California, after all.

As we start our visit, I ask Chris Wellons what he does all day as the vice president for manufacturing. He says that he spends most of this time walking the factory floor, talking to workers, seeing their work, and making sure all is going okay. Chris makes a point of saying he tries get to know everyone by name and learn something about their background and personal and family life. He tells me, "It's important to our mission to have that kind of knowledge and information flow up and down the levels of the company."

In my first few minutes on site at the Taylor plant, I am starting to have an image of a company whose own self-image is as friendly and sunny as the San Diego skies. To be sure, any company subjected to an outsider's gaze will play up its strengths while playing down its shortcomings. But does the company's self-image—its "story" of itself—match reality?

MAKING SENSE OF TAYLOR GUITARS

Context and Contingency

But first things first—namely Taylor Guitars' origins and early development. How did this company get its start? On this topic, there has been much mythologizing. Much of the reporting tends to portray Taylor as a start-up, led almost singlehandedly by a gifted young luthier and a savvy business partner, that has had a seamless, rapid ascent. Terms such as "visionary leader" and "meteoric rise" seem to fit comfortably in the conventional view of Taylor Guitars.

A closer study yields a more nuanced account, however, and I dispute both quasi-myths about Taylor Guitars [7] The first is what I will term the "solitary-genius" myth: the view that the person whose name adorns the headstock, Bob Taylor (born 1955), is the very embodiment of all that the company is and stands for. While understandable, given Taylor's talent as a designer and builder, this view neglects the considerable help he had along the way.

The second myth is what I term the "meteoric rise": the claim that Taylor Guitars has been a juggernaut, going from success to success, since its founding in 1974. Again, this depiction simplifies the company's early development, which was far from smooth and rapid. Like many myths, these two views have the tantalizing ring of truth but do not hold up to serious scrutiny. What is missing in these accounts is the role of two often-neglected factors: context and contingency.

The solitary-genius myth relegates to the background the family and social context in which Bob Taylor was reared and encouraged to become a luthier. To put his contribution in proper perspective and ultimately to understand the company he cofounded, we must recognize that his success owes much to a felicitous mixture of nature—his natural endowments and proclivities as a craftsman—and nurture—the circumstances in which he grew up and matured as a young luthier—just as it did for many of the skilled luthiers portrayed in the previous chapter. Separating these two aspects—innate ability and the shaping influence of one's upbringing—is impossible; nonetheless, I conclude that Bob's formidable skills as guitar maker and Taylor Guitars' success as a company owe as much to contextual influences as to the founder's inborn talent.

To be sure, native ability played a strong role, and there is no denying that Taylor was blessed with natural ability as a designer and builder. As a child he took to making things, and by the time he finished high school, his main desire in life was to build guitars. As he grew older, he remained committed to that goal. Today, approaching fifty years since cofounding the company, he remains both the titular head and public face of Taylor Guitars.

Anyone who meets Bob Taylor can understand why he has remained "The Man" of the company for so long. Having met and interviewed him elsewhere a few days before my plant visit, I was first struck by his tall, friendly-yet-serious physical presence. In conversation he projects a combination of affability, modesty, engagement, and, perhaps above all, an ability to convey ideas in succinct, arresting ways, as in the epigraph to this chapter. As he and I settled into a long interview about his life and work, I felt immediately at ease, finding him open, thoughtful, and self-confident, yet generous in giving others credit for his success.

In his memoir, *Guitar Lessons,* and in our interview, Bob depicts himself as a natural DIY'er, who built and fixed most of his own toys.[8] That propensity owed much to the context in which he was raised, in a family that reinforced his innate tendencies. Taylor grew up in suburban San Diego, where his father was a Navy electrician and chief petty officer stationed at the huge US naval base nearby. With a dad earning a seaman's salary and a stay-at-home mom raising four kids, money was not plentiful, and so both parents made the most of the resources at hand. Taylor's father was skilled at woodworking—for example, he built and repaired much of the family's furniture—while his mother sewed and mended many of the kids' clothes. The parents naturally encouraged their children to make and repair their own toys and other personal possessions.

Beyond the necessity to make do with the limited material goods available, Taylor showed an early interest in how things worked—an interest that manifested itself in a willingness to take things apart to see for himself. He would then try—sometimes successfully, sometimes not—to put things back together again. He confesses, "I've broken nearly everything I've ever owned at one time or another, trying to figure out how it works."[9] Happily, I'm sure, for his parents, Bob's fearlessness went along with an ability to learn from mistakes. He describes one such learning experience when his parents gave him a folding traveling alarm clock. In typical fashion he disassembled the clock soon after, but then did a poor reassembly job, and the clock never worked properly after that. But he didn't regret the attempt; the clock's malfunction became a learning moment. He writes, "I learned how disappointed I was to have a clock that worked and then a clock that didn't. I also learned to take things apart more carefully in the future."[10]

In our conversation, Taylor recounted his growing interest in guitars and ultimately his decision to build one on his own.[11] He says that in his early teens, he became interested in music and the instruments—mainly guitars—that made the music he liked. Combining a growing interest in guitars with the curiosity to figure out how something was built, Bob set out, at age sixteen, to build a guitar himself. He already had a small-body Japanese guitar, and he used that as a starting model to build his own instrument. He ended up building three guitars, completely on his own, by the time he graduated high school two years later. What is striking in Taylor's account of his early beginnings as a luthier is his apparent readiness to do something without formal study, training, or supervision. He claims, for example, that he had never heard of Martin guitars, the iconic brand in the industry, when he started building his own instruments.

By the time he graduated high school in 1973 and had built those first three guitars, Bob had indeed heard of the Martin brand and even bought one of its D-18 models by selling his motorcycle. But he insists in our conversation that he never copied a Martin; rather, he was inspired by the company's level of craftsmanship: "I never made a guitar that was shaped like a D-18. That had no meaning to me. What had meaning to me was that the kerfing was on really nice, the braces fit nicely into the kerfing, the binding didn't have gaps on it, there were no kinks in the shape, and the bridge was polished nicely but it wasn't too shiny, the nut fit well."

What mattered for Taylor was not Martin's designs as much as its commitment to quality. That commitment to quality, he explains, was what he aspired to achieve: "The only thing that I copied from a Martin guitar was the quality of the work. I can take you back to those moments. . . . I looked at that Martin and said this is made well, but I never even asked myself the question of what shape it was—it never crossed my mind. I just thought that my Martin was made well. And so that's what I copied from my Martin—it was the high level of craftsmanship." Bob eventually sold that D-18 so that he could buy materials to make more guitars. He concludes, "So Martin came in and left my life in a one-year period, and what I walked away with from that was that their craftsmanship was really nice, and I wanted to make a guitar with that level of craftsmanship."

Taylor never faced the classic existential question of "now what?" at age eighteen when he graduated from high school, for he had his answer already: his life's goal was to build guitars, and that did not require going to college. Here again, context—family influences and an opportunity at hand—shaped the young man's future. The opportunity was the offer of an open spot in a local guitar shop—an experience that would constitute his higher education in guitar making. The shop, American Dream, was a combination guitar-making cooperative and retail store run by the Radding brothers: Sam, a skilled luthier who oversaw the cooperative, and his brother Gene, who managed the retail operation. One of its other young aspiring luthiers at that time, Tim Luranc, describes American Dream as "a typical hippie guitar shop, housed in the two front commercial units (1,500 sq. ft. each) of four. It was definitely *not* in the San Diego travel guide."[12]

American Dream provided developing young guitar makers both bench space and access to tools in exchange for making guitars under Sam's tutelage. Those guitars would then be sold by the store and the proceeds split between the luthiers who made them and the Radding brothers. During his senior year, Taylor had become friendly with Sam Radding, as well as some of the other local instrument makers who worked there. Liking both the ambiance and the learning opportunity that came with being surrounded by other luthiers, Taylor wanted to stay on. In turn, Sam, recognizing Taylor's talent and commitment to the craft, promised to keep him on once he had graduated.

Toward the end of his senior year, Taylor announced to his parents that he would not be going to college; instead, he wanted to remain at American Dream and build guitars, since that was his goal in life. His announcement was met with a mixed reaction from his parents. Bob recounts the experience: "I remember my dad was reading the paper on the living room couch and mom was puttering in the kitchen. My announcement upset her, and she said I could be a doctor or a lawyer of something like that; that I was smart enough to do those things. She said to my dad, 'Dick, tell him. Say something.' And dad folded the corner of his newspaper down and said, 'Ah, let the kid do what he wants.' And that was that. I had become a guitar maker."[13] Apparently, patriarchal authority held sway, and Bob remained at American Dream while further honing his lutherie skills.

So at age 18, Bob had skill, passion, and a general direction for his young life, but he could not have imagined where that direction would lead. What ultimately determined that direction was a lot of good fortune. Again, context is important in explaining the subsequent trajectory of both Bob Taylor himself and Taylor Guitars.

For Taylor, good fortune on his journey presented itself in three main ways: timing, place, and relationships. Taylor came of age during a period when the acoustic guitar was undergoing a cultural renaissance, as many popular performers were incorporating the unplugged sound into their music. A short list would include singer-songwriters such as James Taylor, Jackson Browne, Paul Simon, Joni Mitchell, John Denver, Harry Chapin, and Neil Young. Even groups typically thought of as belonging in the rock category—for example, Led Zeppelin; Crosby, Stills, and Nash; and even the Beatles—featured acoustic guitars. In the worlds of blues, bluegrass, and other forms of normally unplugged roots music, guitarists such as Ry Cooder, Taj Mahal,

Doc Watson, Tony Rice, John Fahey, Leo Kottke, and many others were developing creative ways of playing the instrument. Demand for acoustic guitars soared, especially among young men who discovered that being able to strum a few chords and sing on key raised their cool factor with young women. This demand stimulated, in turn, an incentive for guitar makers to supply more acoustic guitars to a hungry market.

This market signal not only spurred the dominant guitar companies, Martin and Gibson, to boost production of their popular models; it also stimulated individual luthiers and small shops to offer ever more variety in terms of body shapes, wood choices, and ornamental options. At that historical moment, for many young men the prospect of skipping college and proceeding to make guitars for a living seemed just as viable as pursuing a liberal arts degree. Bob Taylor, like many of his generational cohorts, did not have to swim upstream against the craft-building current; he could flow with it, in the process gaining from the knowledge and expertise of others.

Not only was Taylor born at the right time, but he was also born in the right place: the San Diego area. I have already underlined American Dream's importance in his development as a luthier, but that small shop did not operate alone in a sun-drenched, southern California vacuum. American Dream was, in fact, just one of several shops in a growing informal network of other young guitar makers who were glad to share knowledge and information. For example, two instrument makers—Greg Deering and Geoff Stelling—worked at American Dream for a time and then went on to found highly respected, successful banjo companies.[14] Other promising young luthiers emerging in the San Diego area in the early 1970s included David Russell Young, the brothers Larry and Kim Breedlove, and James Goodall, all of whom went on to successful lutherie careers. Looking back over his own career, Taylor clearly appreciates how important these early connections were for his skill development and innovative leanings. He has said, for example, "People often give me credit for inventing the bolt-on neck, but I didn't come up with it on my own. A lot of people like Sam Radding, David Russell Young, and James Goodall helped out either directly or indirectly. Like a lot of ideas that bubbled up back then in the San Diego guitar world, it was a group effort."[15]

Finally, the guitar maker had the good fortune to develop lasting relationships with other luthiers who gave him advice and tutelage in his early years as an independent builder. These relationships not only deepened his knowledge and skill in guitar making, but they also enabled him to establish a viable way to make a living at it. Foremost among these was a friendship that Taylor struck up at American Dream with another young San Diegan who was working there, Kurt Listug. Three years older than Bob, Listug had dropped out of San Diego State and enjoyed working on guitars, although he had never built one. What better way to learn to make a guitar than to work at American Dream?

As the two young men developed their friendship, it became apparent that their respective skill sets were different yet complementary. Whereas Taylor was quickly recognized as the most skilled guitar maker among his peers, Listug showed an aptitude for the business side of producing and selling guitars. Within a year of working together at American Dream, they decided in 1974 to form a partnership, along with a third luthier at the shop, Steve Schemmer. They would buy American Dream and create a company of their own.[16] As of this writing, that lasting and successful partnership has endured for almost fifty years, with no immediate end in sight, even though both Bob and Kurt are now of retirement age.

Two other relationships—both with established luthiers—proved important for the early development of Taylor Guitars. One was with Jean Larrivée, the Quebec-born luthier we met in the previous chapter. The two met at the 1977 summer meeting of the National Association of Music Merchants (NAMM) and, in Taylor's words, "We became instant friends."[17] His takeaway from his very first encounter with the decade-older Larrivée was a new approach to installing frets on the neck of the guitar. Standard industry practice at the time was to install frets in their slots on the neck *before* attaching the necks to the guitar body. This sequence often resulted in string buzz and other playing problems once the neck was installed, which then caused delay and repair costs even before the guitar was completed. Larrivée recommended the opposite sequence—installing frets *after* attaching the neck to the body—and demonstrated how to do so effectively using different hammer techniques and a softer type of fret wire.[18]

Jean Larrivée's readiness to give away expert know-how to a relative novice illustrates a key aspect of the luthier community discussed in Chapter 2: the willingness, even among competitors, to share information and suggestions for improvement. This generous reflex stems from a combination of commitment and socialization among guitar makers.[19] Although all luthiers would like to craft instruments that are considered unique or at least distinctive compared with their peers, the lutherie community is just that: a community of people who love and are committed to making stringed instruments—in this case, guitars—largely by hand. It goes without saying that luthiers appreciate the guitar as a beautiful object that can also create beautiful sounds. It is natural, then, that they are forever motivated to make a better guitar and therefore inclined to welcome tips and insights from fellow luthiers about how to improve the quality and sound of their instruments while producing them more efficiently.

The other side of that exchange results from the process of socialization into the craft. To become a luthier is to join a particular kind of community, one based on information sharing, cooperation, and reciprocity.[20] All guitar makers receive training and help along the way from more experienced and knowledgeable luthiers. Once established, most guitar makers feel inclined, and even obliged, to reciprocate by helping to train the next generation. Luthiers typically do not see themselves as competing against fellow guitar makers for market share; rather, they feel engaged in the common goal of building a better guitar. In my interview with him, master luthier Ren Ferguson makes this point about the guitar-making community, and he pointedly mentions Bob Taylor: "He's got an open door. He says 'Please come down and spend a day with us and see what we do. We'll give you all the resources you need.' I'm not going to build a Taylor guitar, but it might spark my imagination to do something on my end. And he does the same with me."[21]

Along with learning helpful building techniques from his elders in the trade, the twenty year old Bob Taylor also absorbed new lessons about organizing the production process as he sought to increase his output. Most valuable was the counsel of Augustino ("Tino") LoPrinzi, a luthier based in New Jersey who been building guitars since the late 1950s. Much as Jean Larrivée had done in helping a fledgling luthier learn the ropes, LoPrinzi befriended Bob and convinced him to change his approach to production.

Again following standard practice, Taylor was using the batch process—that is, the building of a batch, or set, of guitars together at the same time. This method requires that all guitars in the batch undergo each step in the building process as a group. Since no single guitar is completed until all guitars in the batch are completed, several days typically go by without a single finished guitar being produced. The batch method also means that any flaw in one of the building steps can cause delays and, in some cases, even failure of the whole batch. Tino LoPrinzi recommended that Bob abandon this method and switch to producing "one guitar at a time," which meant organizing the work as a kind of highly skilled assembly line, in which each instrument passes from step to step "on its own" and not in a batch. Taylor immediately understood the advantages of this approach and adopted it as the "backbone of the production at Taylor Guitars."[22]

Just as in the case of Jean Larrivée, Bob Taylor's relationship to LoPrinzi resembled that of pupil-to-master, and the young man eagerly soaked up the advice being freely given. For all his innate talent, Taylor benefitted greatly from such early relationships, and so the oft-painted mythic portrait him as a solitary genius needs replacing with a more complex, nuanced view that considers the full context of when, where, and how he developed as a guitar maker and producer.

The same is true of how Taylor Guitars grew as a company, a history that is often portrayed as a meteoric rise: steady, relentless growth from the outset. Yet even a cursory examination of the company's first decade reveals a much different trajectory. An authoritative statement comes from the fellow luthier mentioned above, Tim Luranc, who knew and worked with Bob and Kurt from the beginning:

> They tried their best to keep the company going. They would hire people and then lay them off through those next ten years. Bob was married to Cindy, and she had a school teaching job, so she was able to support them. Kurt lived at home [with his parents] for a while. Those guys literally were broke for ten years. People think this was an easy climb to fame, but they had nothing. They were giving themselves $15 a week for gas. They didn't even take any pay—many of the months they took no pay. It was a labor of love. They had a vision and a dream, and they stuck to it. . . . I just didn't see how they would ever make it.[23]

Taylor Guitars' growth and success, then, was far from inevitable or predictable in 1974; a long period of struggle to survive preceded the company's eventual rise. Far from meteoric, the company's development was contingent on the company's making changes in how it produced and marketed its instruments. From its beginning Taylor engaged in a protracted, uneven, but essential period of trial and error that took years to produce good results. The learning was long and slow.

On the production side, I have already underlined the counsel Taylor received from fellow luthiers such as Larrivée and LoPrinzi, which helped streamline, cut costs, and scale up the small company's output. Just as important was the learning that took place on the marketing side. A key moment came in 1979 with the decision to cut ties with a distribution company, Rothchild Musical Instruments (RMI), that, in Taylor's view, was doing a poor job of promoting and distributing their guitars. Ending their relationship with RMI meant that the fledgling guitar maker had to do its own marketing and sales—in short, do whatever it took to survive. This decision also required laying off the company's eleven employees, thereby paring Taylor Guitars

Bob Taylor and Kurt Listug in 1985. Courtesy Taylor Guitars.

down to its three owners. By their calculation, whereas the eleven employees had been building sixteen guitars a week, Taylor Listug, and Schemmer could make half that number—eight instruments—in the same period. That projection proved too optimistic. During the following year, 1980, Taylor produced just a hundred guitars. The company survived, but barely.[24]

With RMI gone by 1980, Kurt Listug took on the roles of publicist and salesman. Hitting the road, he tirelessly visited dealers, carrying sample instruments in his station wagon and making his pitch. Slowly his efforts began to pay off. By the mid-1980s, sales were steadily improving, and the company was producing about ten guitars per *day*—a big jump from the two guitars per *week* just five years earlier. Taylor guitars were now appearing in the hands of professional guitarists such as Chris Proctor and Dan Crary. While not yet a household name in the guitar world, Taylor Guitars was on the rise. By 1990, the company, having moved to a larger factory, was producing more than two thousand guitars per year with a work force of forty employees.

Far from a vigorous start, then, the new company struggled for over a decade—from its formation in1974 until the mid-1980s—to improve its production processes and reach a visible position in a competitive marketplace. Taylor's rise to becoming the largest producer in the guitar industry came only after lean times and a strenuous learning curve.

STRATEGIC VISION:
GROWTH THROUGH INNOVATION, SUSTAINABILITY, AND CONTINUITY

Taylor Guitars today not only holds a place as the largest producer among North American guitar makers, but it also enjoys a reputation for quality—precision fit and finish, easy playability, and tonally balanced sound across a dizzying array of models, options, and price points in both its acoustic and hollow-body electric lines.[25] How has Taylor Guitars become a game changer within the guitar world?

At issue is the company's strategy for making and selling its instruments in an established, competitive market of producers. It is no revelation that every guitar maker—from the independent luthier to the large manufacturer—

tries, in some way, to distinguish its brand from that of other makers. In my interviews with guitar makers, I typically start with an icebreaker question designed to draw them out on this topic: How do you consider your instruments, including perhaps the way you make them, distinctive compared with other makers? Without exception, my interviewees launched into replies that echo the boilerplate in their print and online promotional materials. Guitar makers, as all producers in competitive markets, must engage not only in making their wares, but also in presenting them to the public in enticing fashion.

My research leads me to conclude that Taylor Guitars has created and consistently projects a story of its distinctiveness that is more multifaceted and comprehensive than that of any other guitar maker that I studied. Whereas some makers define their distinctiveness as being a custom shop or an enterprise with a long tradition of excellence, Taylor has fashioned a self-narrative with a strong strategic vision. Though not stated as such on the company's website or its own publications such as *Wood & Steel*, this vision is conveyed implicitly, and it comes through clearly in conversations with Bob Taylor and other top employees. Succinctly stated, this vision consists of growth through innovation, sustainability, and continuity.

GROWTH

Since 1990, Taylor Guitars has grown in output and sales like no other guitar maker, and there is no question that growth is the ultimate driver for the company. A few days before my first visit to the plant, Bob Taylor makes this clear when I interview him: "I believe in the power of manufacturing." Whereas the conventional economic view is that demand creates supply—i.e., manufacturers respond to what consumers want by increasing their production of it—Taylor turns the equation around. In effect, build it—something that people will see as cool, useful, and well-made—and they will come. In our interview, Taylor goes on to say, "Cellphones? I remember the first time they started putting email on a phone. People said, I don't want my email with me, and now you can't imagine a phone without it."

The power of manufacturing, for Taylor, lies in the ability to create new products that people may not have even conceived of, but that, once created, become things that people desire. The implied mantra of Taylor Guitars might be, "to stop growing is to stagnate, and so grow we must."

I witness a concrete example of this imperative in my two visits, a year apart, to Taylor's manufacturing facilities. Growth was indeed taking place in its satellite plant just over the US-Mexico border in the small town of Tecate, about forty miles from the main factory in El Cajon. First built in 2000, the Mexican plant produces Taylor's less expensive line of guitars as well as all of its cases and gigbags.[26] During recent years, demand had grown to the point that Taylor needed to expand its production space, and so it had purchased a much larger (116,000-square-foot) facility across town from the original plant. During my first visit, in January 2015, production manager Pat Wilson tells me that all production from the original plant will be transferred to the new plant during the course of that year. The transfer had already begun; guitar necks and bodies were being shipped from the older plant to the new one to

Pat Wilson (right), production manager, and a coworker at the Taylor plant under construction in Tecate, Mexico, January 2015. Photo by author.

be assembled and finished. But much of the huge space was still unoccupied (see photo). A year later, the move is complete. The huge space is now filled with people, materials, equipment, and machines, and the new plant is up and running.

In justifying this growth imperative, Bob Taylor claims that his company has supplied innovative, competitively priced guitars, which in turn has created new sources of demand among guitar players. To demonstrate the point—and to reinforce James Burton's story about Taylor Guitars—he asks,

> Would music be different today if we erased 40 years of Taylor Guitars? I think it would be. When I started playing guitars, there were acoustic guitar players and electric guitar players. The two weren't the same, and you didn't play the instruments the same way. And now it's kind of melded. People have capos on their electrics and strum with a pick, and people put effects on their acoustics and play lead on it. And it's gotten to where you play both of them a little bit more alike. A lot of that has to do with the first 12 years we were in business, we sold to electric guitar players. Acoustic players didn't want our guitars, because they already had acoustic guitars. But electric guitar players wanted our necks. Their confession to us was: I always wanted to play acoustic but I never could, but your guitar is so easy to play, it reminds me of my electric. And so I think we helped to blend those two talent pools.

How do you "grow" a guitar company and make growth your perpetual driver? Bob Taylor is quick to insist that growth is not just a question of quantitative output. Just as much, it's the *quality* of that output that matters. In reflecting on the company's early years in the 1970s, he claims to have desired to always improve both the quality of its instruments and the number of guitars produced: "I was usually dissatisfied with our final product and would work on my techniques or my tools to improve the quality. I could see clearly what could be done better on the guitars. I also had a natural desire to produce a substantial quantity of guitars. I've always felt that quantity was as important as quality."[27]

Improving quality is not just a question of the technical challenges of fashioning precise-fit components and then assembling them, in the process using as much automated technology as possible. There is also the human factor. Quality of the final product, Taylor notes, depends crucially on the company's relationship with its work force, and he claims "We've been able to grow our company and grow our quality, all at the same time. That's very purposeful, and that means you have to learn. We had to learn how to take care of people. . . ."

I saw a symbolic demonstration of this concern when I began my factory tour with Chris Wellons. As we headed toward the main plant, Chris and I passed down a corridor featuring a photo gallery along the wall. Hanging there were rows of about fifty 8"x 10" color pictures of employees who have worked at Taylor for at least ten years. Wellons informed me that these are arranged by descending seniority, starting with the most senior worker in the upper left corner. Then one reads the seniority story in book style, from left to right, then down to the next row, and so on. Is this a typical PR–style display of employee appreciation that one might find in any factory? Perhaps. But even if so, so what? Better to express public recognition than not, and at least Taylor Guitars is making the effort. Moreover, I was struck by the number of photos on the wall; at a minimum, this would seem to speak well for the company's ability to retain its workers.

But aside from putting their pictures on the wall, how do you "take care of people?" Bob Taylor believes the key is building mutual trust and personal relationships with employees. Mutual trust, he claims, comes from keeping one's word as an employer: "Kurt and I have always had the philosophy that when we ask employees to do stuff when there's a pinch, once we recover, we say, hey, we've recovered, you guys sacrificed when things were tough, let's share some of this with you. Because if you trust us in the good time, you'll trust us in the bad time. You've got to trust them all the time."

Trust, Taylor claims, is a by-product of making sure your employees are happy, and that entails developing personal relationships: "When we know their names when we walk through the factory, when we train them how to do their jobs so that they're successful, when we share money with them, when we treat them with respect, fill them in—all those things make them happy. There is no single employee at Taylor who doesn't want a joke, a hand on their shoulder, to feel comfortable around me."

Taylor also notes, "When I give people tours of the factory, the number one comment I always get is: 'Your employees are so engaged, and you seem to know every one of them.' And when I'm around, people say 'I notice that your employees are just as comfortable with you around as they are when you're not.' They say this doesn't happen at other places." Such claims, while I could not independently verify them, indicate that Taylor Guitars values the importance not only of training workers in their jobs, but also of making them feel part of a team effort—all of which serves to maintain and even improve the quality of its instruments even as it pushes to expand overall production.

Must growth go on forever? When I ask Bob Taylor this question, he replies with an emphatic yes, with a rationale that has both a market-driven and a social component. He explains that in a competitive capitalist context, growth means maintaining and increasing the company's market share: "Yes, we'll keep growing. We're always expanding square footage, I always expand my production, I always make more guitars. I tell our people: We can't have market share by advertising; we get market share by building. You can have "mind share" by advertising or marketing, but you can't have market share unless there is a guitar that someone gets to buy. So market share comes with building things." But growth, in Taylor's view, is not just about the financial

Bob Taylor and Kurt Listug today. Courtesy Taylor Guitars.

side of market share and profits; growth also provides social benefits in the form of job creation. He says: "What do we like about bigger? Well, I think making a job is as honorable as making a guitar, especially if it's a good job and we're making a good guitar. I love that."

The question remains: *How* does a company ensure that growth becomes continuous and even perpetual? Taylor Guitars' strategic vision is that growth depends on achieving and balancing of three essential factors: innovation, sustainability, and continuity.

INNOVATION

To innovate is to depart from accepted practice, the standard pattern of things, and to achieve something not done before. That can be risky, of course, and innovation implies the willingness to accept risk. Those qualities were emergent in the young Bob Taylor when he made and fixed his own toys and later began building instruments. The desire to innovate—in the parlance of the 1960s, to do his own thing—was central to his identity by the time he graduated high school and began working at American Dream. A fellow luthier who has known and liked Bob for many decades describes him, tongue firmly in cheek, as a young man: "Let's go back to our high school experiences. Bob was the guy that was taking industrial arts, maybe auto shop, or Future Farmers, and you were taking college prep. And you didn't quite understand them, they were not in your social thing. Bob was making stuff for science fairs and industrial exhibitions, and he had white adhesive tape on his glasses, his pants were too short, and he had on a too tight white shirt. That's who he was. And he ate, drank, and slept mechanical. I used to tease him, and he said, 'It could have been anything, making something.' He is very gifted mechanically."[28]

Bob's desire to build a better guitar carried over in the formation of Taylor Guitars and its subsequent development. On its website the company continues to promote its claim to be an innovator. In so doing, Taylor is unabashed in its celebration of automated technologies: "Renowned for blending modern, innovative manufacturing techniques with a master craftsman's attention to detail, Taylor guitars are widely considered among the best-sounding and easiest to play in the world. The company was a pioneer in the use of computer mills, lasers and other high-tech tools and proprietary machinery, and today Bob Taylor is widely recognized throughout the musical instrument industry as the visionary acoustic guitar manufacturer."[29]

This description references two interrelated yet distinct dimensions of Taylor Guitars' conception of innovation. One dimension is that of innovation in the guitar's components, all designed to make Taylor guitars, according to the website, "among the best sounding and easiest to play in the world." A second dimension is innovation in the production process to increase efficiency and consistency.

Perhaps the most noted of the innovations in the guitar's components are to the instrument's neck, specifically to its "profile" (or thickness) as well as to the neck-body joint. My lunchtime encounter with James Burton in Sharon's Café brought direct testimony from one of the virtuosos about how much electric guitar players appreciate the slim design of Taylor necks, which makes them more playable compared with the thicker necks of traditional Martins, Gibsons, and other acoustic brands.

As for the neck-body joint—that is, the way the neck is joined to the box of the guitar—I had occasion to see this innovation in my plant visit with my guide, Chris Wellons. He explains—patiently, to this nonluthier—that the traditional design of this joint is a dovetail joint—essentially a variant of a centuries-old mortise and tenon joint by which an extruding or projecting edge in one piece of wood (the tongue or tenon) is fitted into a cavity (mortise) in another piece of wood, then glued securely. Such a design works well when joining pieces of wood that are not subject to tension on the joint itself; for example, dovetails are widely used in joining the sides of wooden boxes, drawers, and the like. In the case of guitars, the tenon/tongue (the dove's tail) extends from one end of the neck, which is slotted in and then glued into a mortise/cavity in the side of the body.

Though still widely used in all types of acoustic guitars from nylon-string classical guitars to steel-string acoustics, the dovetail method is problematic, Wellons says, precisely because the strings under tension exert much pulling force on that joint. Over time, this pressure can distort both the neck and the body and render the instrument virtually unplayable. Eventually, many guitars need to undergo a neck reset, a process that involves removing the neck, trimming the wood to adjust the neck angle, then regluing the neck to the body.

Such a repair is exacting (and therefore easily botched), time-consuming, and costly.[30]

Chris then proceeds to show me Taylor's innovation, which is to replace the traditional dovetail joint with a bolt-on neck, requiring three bolts and no glue.[31] Since its introduction in 1975, Taylor's bolt-on neck design has been further refined, and even patented, allowing the company to minimize and even eliminate other problems such as sinkage and cracks in the top.[32]

As for the infamous neck reset, this operation has become more of a quick, inexpensive adjustment rather than a repair. Wellons tells me that resetting a Taylor neck is so easy that it has even become a kind of public performance piece for the company: "We do a road show in guitar shops. We tell people to bring in your Taylor guitar, because we like to see their guitars—how are they performing and how are they holding up. And it gives us a chance to unbolt that neck, give it to the customer to hold, put in some shims, put the neck

Chris Wellons, vice president of manufacturing, Taylor Guitars, demonstrating bolt-on neck. Photo by author.

back on, bolt it back together, and string that guitar up in ten minutes. We hand the customer back a fresh, brand-new playing and feeling instrument. It wows everybody. The whole crowd will go crazy."

A second area of innovation in components for Taylor has been in onboard electronics. Seeking to put more control in the guitarist's hands in terms of not only volume but also tone, the company has created the Expression System pickup that is now standard on all acoustic models above its entry-level Academy Series. Three small knobs on the player's side of the guitar near the point where the neck and body join enable one to adjust treble and bass boost as well as overall volume.

Moreover, Taylor has ventured into electric guitar territory with a line of hybrid guitars that combine aspects of both the acoustic guitar (a semi-hollow body) and the electric guitar's sonic effects. Taylor's website describes its T5z guitar this way: ""Crafted as a semi-hollowbody electric guitar, the T5z merges two worlds of tone into a single package. Three pickups give the T5z a wide range of tonal possibilities: a magnetic acoustic body sensor, a concealed neck humbucker and a visible bridge humbucker, controlled with five-way switching that enables everything from searing, high-gain electric leads and warm, rounded acoustic textures."[33]

One of the hallowed concepts in the lexicon of most acoustic guitar makers is an appeal to tradition, with the Platonic ideal being a 1930s Martin or Gibson. In that sense, Taylor defers not at all to that ideal, at least rhetorically, but rather strives to project a "modern" image based on continual improvements in existing products and creation of new ones.[34]

Finally, a third example of Taylor's penchant for innovation concerns bracing the box of the guitar. Other than perhaps the type and quality of wood that a builder uses, the type of bracing glued to the underside of the top (or soundboard) is generally considered most crucial in determining a guitar's sound. At issue is the tradeoff between stiffness and flexibility in the top, and the key to gauging and managing that tradeoff lies in the braces. Some kind of bracing is required in the first place to reinforce the soundboard's ability to withstand string tension; without bracing a guitar's relatively thin board would quickly crack and come apart. Beyond this basic function, bracing also provides a certain stiffness to the top that enhances its ability to produce sustain when the strings are plucked. Too much stiffness, however, limits the top's flexibility and therefore its capacity to produce volume or loudness. How to shape and configure the braces so as to optimize both a guitar's sustain and its volume?

For the past century at least, luthiers have embraced a complex soundboard bracing that requires a highly skilled, three-step process that can be captured in one phrase: scalloped X-braces, shifted forward." (Being able to rattle off that phrase will gain you instant "street cred" in any guitar shop or group of guitar geeks!) One first scallops the braces—that is, selectively cuts gentle scoops out of the two pieces of wood that are the main braces—thereby slightly reducing stiffness in the top and rendering it more flexible. Then these braces are crossed in an "X" pattern.[35] Finally, conventional wisdom dictates that this X-brace should be positioned closer to the sound hole than braces typically have been. This forward shifting of the X-brace is also believed to enhance the top's flexibility and therefore the guitar's volume. All these operations were performed on the major Martin Guitar models of the 1930s, the so-called Golden Age of acoustic guitars; however, only the X-shaped brace was retained after World War II as the major producers, Martin and Gibson, turned to heavier bracing to accommodate the use of heavier gauge steel strings.[36]

In its latest attempt to cast off tradition and embrace innovation, Taylor Guitars has chosen a new letter for the alphabet of bracing, at least in its middle- and higher-end offerings, by introducing V-Class bracing. As the name implies, V-bracing rranges two long braces in a V shape, with the bottom of the V being near the bottom (wider) end of the body, while the two sides of the V extend upward, past the sound hole to terminate near the fretboard. The luthier who designed this V-bracing, Andy Powers (see below), claims that the linearity that the V-braces provide up the length of the soundboard reinforces the top's stiffness and therefore its sustain, while the larger, unbraced regions on either side of the V enhance volume. The result, Powers asserts, is improved sustain, volume, and even intonation. Taylor's website features slightly agog reactions from musicians such as Zac Brown: "There's some kind of wizardry going on. There's definitely some kind of magic." Perhaps so, perhaps not—time and nonsponsored guitarists will tell. What is for sure is that V-Class bracing is just the latest in a series of specific innovations of the guitar that Taylor has introduced.

Beyond these specific innovations in various guitar components, there is a more general dimension to the company's drive to innovate: its effort to achieve greater efficiency and consistency—i.e., greater scale and replicability—in the manufacturing process itself. On our plant tour, my guide Chris Wellons shows me two examples of such innovations. We first come to a station which entails gluing several braces—cut strips of spruce wood—to the top and back of the guitar. Traditionally, this has been a time-consuming process using flexible rods to hold the braces in place while the glue dries. Taylor has replaced this with a vacuum device that sucks a flexible cover over the braces to hold them in place while they dry. This process speeds drying while eliminating the need to position and fix the series of rods.

A second example is the finishing process. Toward the end of our tour, Chris and I come to the station at which the guitar's glossy finish is applied. Conventionally, the time-consuming aspect of this final touch has been the drying of the finish. Typically, the lacquered guitars were literally hung out to dry—put in racks to allow for the air to do its evaporative work. This step alone would typically take several hours. Wellons points out a device designed by Taylor that can dry the instruments in seconds using UV light. First, the guitar, with fresh finish applied, is placed in the device. Then the guitar is revolved 180 degrees behind a shield and hit with three or four UV lights of differing intensity. Elapsed time for complete drying: thirteen seconds.

REFLECTIONS ON THE TECHNOLOGY QUESTION

As Chris Wellons and I finish our tour, we say our goodbyes for the day. Overall, this visit has caused me to reflect on how Taylor's drive for efficiency and consistency has incorporated high-tech tools, especially computer-driven, automated machinery, throughout the production process. This drive goes back to the early 1990s, after the company's initial fifteen years of building largely handcrafted guitars—with assists, of course, from erstwhile high-tech tools such as saws, drills, and lathes. As mentioned earlier, Taylor has come in for vigorous criticism from those who still prize hand-built instruments. Automation through digital technologies, so goes the classic critique, both destroys jobs through labor saving devices and removes much of the true skill from the jobs than remain. One such critique comes from a local skilled luthier who testifies,

I do indeed feel the CNC innovation lowered the skill level needed to craft a guitar. That doesn't mean the quality of the finished product suffered as precise replication of parts does improve the quality of the guitar, but there is little skill required to produce and assemble those parts like there was in the "old days." I do enjoy using the skill set I developed to reset a Martin dovetail neck. . . . It's pretty cool to steam off a Martin neck and think that the last guy to see that joint was doing it in 1944. Unbolting a Taylor and swapping shims is not exactly romantic, just a mindless task that requires only minimal training.[37]

To this type of criticism, Taylor Guitars has three retorts. The first is that employing a CNC machine is first and foremost a question of design. Bob Taylor expressed it this way in our conversation: "Yes, CNC will bring in repetition, but it also brings in design. Any time you design anything, as a designer you ask yourself: Can I make it? You only design something that you can achieve to make. The relationship between machine and the human mind is symbiotic, because sometimes you'll say to yourself: I have a laser machine, which means I can make that brace I've never made before. I'm going to develop that idea, because now I know I can make it. We make parts now that you can't make by hand, so a CNC allows us to design those parts." In her penetrating study of artisan lutherie, Kathryn Marie Dudley concisely paraphrases Taylor's view: "The challenge guitar makers confront . . . is to create the best design and produce the best guitars possible given the tools at their disposal. . . . Authentic human making, in this view, involves using the tools and manufacturing techniques that best translate a creative vision into a material reality."[38]

Taylor Guitars also insists that its use of CNC machines does not displace workers. When I asked Wellons about the labor issue, he responded, "I tell everyone this: we employ robotics and automation every chance we get. One thing we don't do is: no one loses a job to that. What that's allowed us to do is keep our overhead and fixed costs down and continue to expand as a business and remain profitable. Turnover's expensive, so is training. We want our workers to be productive and happy."[39]

Finally, Bob Taylor has a third retort, not stated as such, which could be summarized as: the proof is in the pudding. Once denounced as taking the skill out of guitar making, the CNC is now a common tool in the workshops of such highly respected high-end makers such as Collings, Santa Cruz, and Bourgeois. Moreover, Taylor has freely offered technical help to other makers.

Ren Ferguson, for example, reflecting on his tenure at Gibson during the 1990s, remarks on a cooperative effort among Taylor, Martin, Gibson, Collings, Santa Cruz, and Larrivée: "We all met regularly at conventions and brainstormed—how do we do this, how can we do things better? Bob's definitely a driver in the industry. He's got an open door. Please come down and spend a day with us and see what we do, we'll give you all the resources you need."[40]

Bob Taylor himself makes no secret of his determination, even as a teen-aged neophyte guitar maker, to forge his own path, make his own mistakes, and, above all, make guitars that are original. One could conclude that that mindset put Bob himself, along with the company he cofounded, permanently in search of ways of build a better guitar, i.e., to innovate. Recalling to me his early admiration for Martin guitars solely for their craftmanship and not their shape or sound, Bob stresses this "my way" aspect of his approach that is essential to Taylor Guitars' self-identity as an innovator: "Taylor guitars are naturally born in a vacuum of guitar knowledge. So our shapes are unique, our trade dress is unique, our tone is unique. Most people who start acoustic guitar companies end up copying some of the great old guitars such as Martins and Gibsons. But we don't—we make Taylor guitars, and nothing we make is anything like any other guitar brand. We made our own brand. Part of that is because that's just the way it happened. I didn't know enough to copy anything."

SUSTAINABILITY

Growth, for Taylor Guitars, requires not only perpetual innovation, but also an unending supply of raw materials, especially the principal woods that comprise the guitar's top, back, sides, and neck. Ecologists are not the only ones who worry about the exhaustibility of nature's bounty. Manufacturers who utilize natural resources do as well, and any conversation with a Taylor executive or production manager soon turns to the company's efforts to ensure continuous stocks of essential woods, notably spruce, ebony, mahogany, and rosewood. For Taylor, this imperative implies not only securing but also, in some cases, literally cultivating and harvesting sustainable sources of wood materials. As its website states: "In addition to its forward-thinking approach to guitar design and manufacturing, Taylor has applied that same approach to its wood sourcing and environmental sustainability initiatives. Taylor is dedicated to the pursuit of best practices in forest management, new models of reforestation, and bringing ethically harvested tonewoods to market."[41]

In a twist on the usual environmental critique that incessant growth equals environmental plunder and destruction, Taylor Guitars views its growth as being compatible with, and even promotive of, environmental preservation. Bob Taylor states: "I feel that making guitars that please the environment as much as the player is of utmost importance."[42] He insists that Taylor's size and need for large sources of wood is not necessarily detrimental to the environment. In fact, the company's scale of operations, he says, gives it the capacity to establish and engage in good resource management practices: "If I was making one third the number of guitars that we're making right now, I wouldn't be able to start a forestry operation that I could commit to for a hundred years like we're doing in Hawaii. I wouldn't have the money."

Bob proceeds to describe several other environmental sustainability initiatives, notably the one cited most frequently in the company's publications and website: the Ebony Project. In the West African nation of Cameroon, Taylor has partnered with a Spanish company, Madinter Trade, to protect and replenish the ebony trees that provide the wood for the guitar's fretboard and bridges. Taylor's work in Cameroon is three-pronged. First, the company has built its own sawmill in Cameroon that turns ebony logs into semifinished items such as fretboards and bridges that will then be shipped to Taylor's headquarters for final finishing and installation. Being an owner, and not just an extractor, is a win-win proposition, according to Bob, because it provides jobs for local workers while reducing shipping and other costs for the company. Moreover, Taylor is engaging in reforestation by planting new ebony seedlings.

Finally, the largest impact of the company's operations in Cameroon has been to reduce its extractive footprint by extending the variety of ebony that it uses. Historically, piano, violin, and guitar makers have used only the pure black variety of ebony for keys, fretboards, and bridges. This is a preference that results in wasteful and ecologically destructive logging practices, since the determination of whether an ebony tree's interior is totally black or marbled (some mix of black, brown, and olive-colored wood) can be only when once the tree is cut down. Since only a minority of ebony trees are pure black, this means that most of the less-valued marbled trees are left to rot in the forest. Taylor is now using all varieties of ebony, whether black or marbled.[43]

Other examples of the company's sustainability efforts include involvement in two "green" coalitions to preserve wood species. One of these, Musicwood, was a Greenpeace-initiated campaign to reduce clear-cutting of Sitka spruce on Native American–controlled land in the Tongass National Forest in southern Alaska. Greenpeace enlisted Taylor and several other major guitar companies, all heavy consumers of Sitka spruce, to help persuade Sealaska, the corporation that managed the land, to replant seedlings and engage in more sustainable logging practices. Despite their efforts, the coalition failed to reach an agreement with Sealaska to change their logging practices.[44]

A more successful coalition that Taylor has joined is with Greenwood, a forest-preservation organization based in Maine. Greenwood works in Honduras to protect forests that provide, among other things, mahogany, a principal wood used in guitars. Bob links his work with this organization to the purposeful design of Taylor's guitar necks, which can be made from a single piece of mahogany, or what he terms "wood from primitive sources." He explains, "It's wood that's not cut on a fancy sawmill that's operated by an experienced sawyer. Why? Because to get wood to a sawmill you have to have a truck and a road and access to the forest. That's 'modern' logging. But we need to go primitive. You've got to be able to go into a roadless area with mules and people, cut down a tree, and pull that thing out like *Gulliver's Travels* with primitive means. Roads bring in people, more development, ruin forests. Roadless forestry in Honduras is something we wanted to develop. The whole thing—keeping forests roadless and using easy sawing methods—this was a concept that fit together like a jigsaw puzzle."

CONTINUITY

Sustainability of another kind has been on the mind of Bob Taylor and Kurt Listug during the past decade, namely continuity—not only of Taylor's leadership but of the nature of the company more generally. Regarding the first of these, leadership, around 2010 the two owners recognized that the company they had cofounded thirty-five years earlier would face a succession issue sometime in the not-distant future, since both Taylor (born in 1955) and Listug (born in 1952) were nearing retirement age, and neither man had an heir apparent in the wings. Unlike C. F. Martin & Co., which has had a family successor come along each generation for over 150 years, Bob and his wife, Cindy, have two daughters, neither of whom showed an interest in following their dad into guitar making or the family business. The same lack of a successor was true for Kurt Listug, as well. As noted in the previous chapter, many in the reinventors generation also confront this challenge; as Dana Bourgeois told me in our interview: "the challenge for me and companies like Santa Cruz, Collings, and others is how to outlive their founder."

Taylor makes it clear in our interview that neither he nor his partner Kurt foresee themselves heading to the golf course any time soon: "I'm not thinking of retiring—I won't retire. It means too much to me. I'll come down, it's my baby crib . . . what we do here is fun, I meet interesting people. And Kurt feels the same way. We love the people, we love the relationships, we love the business, the company's strong. These are joyful years for us. There's no good reason to get out." And yet . . . although Bob plans to "keep a hand in," at least for several years, he and Kurt have taken steps to prepare the way.

Above all, Bob Taylor wanted to ensure continuity by choosing the right person to eventually lead the company. Bob was forthright in desiring a successor who was both a master luthier and a guitar-playing musician. On the one hand, he wanted someone who could design and build guitars by hand, while also embracing the technological tools such as CNC machines that can reproduce original designs precisely. On the other hand, the successor needed to be savvy musically, able not only to play guitar competently but also to understand and respond to what guitar players of many styles wanted out of their instrument. One authoritative source reports Taylor saying that he actually wrote down on paper a request addressed to the Almighty: "Dear God, I need one guitar builder. He needs to be a way better builder than I am. He needs to be self-taught. He needs to know guitar history way deep. He's got to be a pro player. . . . He has to have twenty years of experience. He has to be less than thirty years old. And he has to be from San Diego, because we don't build East Coast guitars."[45]

The Lord apparently answered Bob's prayer in the person of Andy Powers, a young California-born guitar maker who was hired in 2011 to take over product development. In virtually all respects, Powers fits the particulars of Taylor's wish list. Like the founder, Powers came under the early tutelage of his father, a professional carpenter, who taught his young son to work with wood. The boy took to his dad's teachings, first building ukuleles and later, as a teenager, archtop and flattop guitars. His family also fostered his musical interest and skills; there were acoustic instruments around the house, and jam sessions with friends and family were a frequent occurrence. Andy became a fine guitarist, eventually graduating from the University of California, San Diego with a degree in guitar performance. By his mid-twenties, he had reached a professional level as both a guitar builder and player.

No wonder, then, that Andy Powers's personal background made him attractive to Bob as a possible successor. There is finally the element of personal chemistry between the two men that ultimately moved Taylor to designate Powers as his heir apparent. When I talked with Chris Wellons later, he commented on this personal relationship: "It's also who Andy Powers is to Bob. Maybe you could say in a sense that Andy is the son Bob never had. He's handed those reins of guitar building over to Andy. He says, 'Andy, you are the master builder.' And look who's signing our label—it's now Andy who's got his name on the label."

In the years following his joining Taylor in 2011, Powers introduced several important changes in the company's line of offerings, including a new guitar body shape (the Grand Pacific), a line of entry-level guitars (Academy Series), and a small-body bass (GS Mini Bass). As mentioned earlier, his most celebrated innovation was the development of the V-Class internal bracing system. In late 2019 Powers was named a third ownership partner. The stage appeared set for the post-Taylor era, with Andy Powers as the company's chief creative person and public face. Powers's prominence as Taylor Guitars' leader into the coming years kept rising into the next decade. By 2022 he bore three official titles: master designer, CEO, and president.

How has this transition from solo luthier to chief operations officer and ownership partner of the largest guitar company been for Andy Powers himself? Some months after my factory visit to the Taylor plant, I discussed this and other issues with him directly. Andy was frank and articulate in talking about the change in his career plans. He admits that the offer to work for Taylor made for a left turn in his life; he had previously envisioned that his career, post-college, would be as an independent guitar maker. He realized, though, that working for Taylor would mean expanding his reach and impact, which is important to him:

My whole intent and purpose is to bring more music into the world. Working alone, there were maybe a dozen musicians I could make really happy in a year, because I put a lot of time and effort into every one of those instruments that I build. In this context [at Taylor Guitars], we can provide instruments for thousands of people around the world, we can provide for a thousand employees to put bread on the table, and we can provide livelihoods for the people who supply the material. There are a lot of people who get to benefit from these instruments and the music that comes from it. It's a much better way to help more people.[46]

This transition has had its challenges for Powers, notably adjusting to the scale and speed of Taylor's operations. Designing and building a single guitar is one thing, but working at Taylor requires building a *process* to make many guitars. He comments, "You have to think about a process to build just this

Andy Powers, Taylor Guitars' master guitar designer, CEO, and president.
Courtesy Taylor Guitars.

one part, and then you have to create a process for assembling things such that a single person could do it several hundred times a day and not get wrist pain. That means you've got to be very clever about how you design that job. So, for me, the challenge meant getting up to speed about how you're going to do things on a much bigger and quicker scale."

To make this transition Powers thinks of the process in terms of translation from old methods to new. When he builds or designs a new guitar, he does so, he says, "in the language of an eighteenth-century craftsman, using chisels, hand planes, and other hand tools." But then he proceeds, in his words, to "translate that design into a modern language of a computer model, of digital drafting plans," and finally he works with engineers and machinists to design the necessary tooling. He concludes by expressing admiration for Bob Taylor's ability to make this translation: "Bob can figure out right away how to make something in large numbers. He's very good at it." In just a few years, Andy Powers has come a long way, from solo guitar maker to master designer and engineer—just as Bob Taylor did several decades before.

The term "translation" is also apt for the most recent step by Taylor Guitars to assure its survival going forward: the company's announcement on January 11, 2021, to transfer ownership to the company's employees via an Employee Stock Ownership Plan (ESOP). This plan translates, for the three owners, into continuity and corporate independence. According to a company press release, "Taylor's new ownership structure will support the continuity of Taylor's established leadership, enable the company to remain independent, and preserve its creative culture for many years to come."[47] The practical effect in the immediate term is minimal; according to the local newspaper, the ownership transfer will result in no changes in management structure, operations policies, or practices.[48] Taylor, Listug, and Powers continue their duties into the immediate future. Legally speaking, however, the ESOP transfers ownership of Taylor Guitars to its employees—in both El Cajon and Tecate—via a pension plan through which retirement benefits are linked to the company's future equity value. The goal of this complex arrangement is to safeguard the company's future independence.[49]

Taylor's vice president for manufacturing, Chris Wellons, links the new ESOP arrangement to the way Bob Taylor and Kurt Listug have conceived of their company throughout the past five decades—a view that could be stated succinctly as "If it ain't broke, don't mess with it." Chris says, "If you took a selfish perspective, Bob and Kurt could go out and sell this business to whomever they want, at whatever valuation they want to attach to it. They could have sold it, handed the keys to a new owner—whether it's a financial co., a bank-owned thing, some company that just wants to come in and squeeze every bit of profitability they could out of us and then leave." Wellons goes on to reflect on what other companies have done: "How many times has Fender or Guitar Center changed hands just because they got sold to some financial company or they got bought back or they got traded? Bob and Kurt could have done that, and they probably would have made a lot more money than what they're making with this arrangement. But they didn't want that to happen to Taylor Guitars. They've built this company for the past nearly fifty years. This is their baby, they don't want to let that go. They wanted to make sure it stayed Taylor Guitars long, long, into the future."[50]

CONCLUSION

Few people in the guitar industry—from suppliers to makers to sellers—would dispute Ren Ferguson's claim at the heading of this chapter that Bob Taylor—along with the company he cofounded—has been a "game changer." One can say with some confidence that in 1974, the nineteen-year-old Bob Taylor and his new partner Kurt Listug, did not view themselves in such august terms. In founding Taylor Guitars that year, they knew two things for sure: they loved making guitars, and they wanted to make a living at it. Making good guitars and putting food on the table—such were their modest goals at the time, hardly game-changing intentions. Reflecting on that period, Taylor recounts, "There was no vision. The vision was to make guitars for a living. It really didn't expand beyond being able to sell a guitar that I was working on, and hopefully make another guitar that we could sell, too."[51]

Nevertheless, a combination of woodcraft talent, technological savvy, business sense, and sheer persistence got them through a decade-long series of ups and downs, such that by 1990 Taylor Guitars was becoming recognized within the industry as a growing producer of precision-built, reasonably priced instruments. In the decades since, the company has, in fact, gradually developed a clear strategic vision that I have summarized as growth through innovation, sustainability, and continuity.

Numbers—in terms of units produced and total sales—tell the basic tale of growth. In 2019, Taylor was the largest producer of primarily acoustic guitars, surpassing the oldest and most storied of guitar companies, C. F. Martin & Co.[52] As we have seen, that growth was made possible on the production side by a series of innovations both small and large. Small innovations include the redesign of various components of the guitar, most notably the neck, as well as the almost universal installation of electric pickups for amplification. Innovation of a larger, more general kind has been the widespread adoption of CNC machines to manufacture, with precision and replicability, most of the guitar's components, including bridges, nuts, fretboards, necks, and the tone woods that comprise the body.

Critics have claimed that Taylor has de-skilled much of the traditionally handcrafted work that has historically gone into making the best guitars—work that can now be done by semiskilled machine operators. To which Taylor gives three replies. First, the skill involved in guitar making—given the growth and scale that the company seeks—has not disappeared; rather, it has moved from the individual crafter to the innovation just mentioned: computer-assisted design and manufacture. The payoff comes in precision-made components and fittings, lower costs, and a wide range of body styles, wood choices, and price points. Moreover, Taylor claims that workers are not displaced by machines. "No one loses a job" to robotics and automation, says Chris Wellons. Finally, Taylor can also claim to have led the pack in the use of computer-driven technology, which is now employed widely throughout the industry, even by high-end makers.

Growth for Taylor is not only a question of producing, in the here and now, an average of about seven hundred guitars per day in its US and Mexican factories; growth is also about the long term in terms of securing sustainable wood supplies and ensuring continuity of the two founders' vision for the company. This chapter has noted Taylor's efforts to source its wood in environmentally responsible ways as well as to preserve the company's operational and financial autonomy transition in the coming years.

Taylor's rise to its place as the largest acoustic guitar manufacturer has not come without criticism. Skeptics will likely continue to question whether

Taylor's emphasis on computer-based production has come at the expense of a long tradition of building guitars by hand. Criticism has also been voiced by some of the company's eight hundred dealers, who have complained that Taylor's push for growth extends to undue pressure on dealers to continually increase their orders of Taylor products. During my research, for example, I talked with two established guitar shop owners in different cities who once carried new Taylor guitars but do so no longer. Why not? According to both owners, the company became too demanding in terms of how many guitars they were expected to purchase from Taylor. These owners claim that Taylor gave them a quota of how many guitars they had to buy to remain a dealer, and when the owners failed to sell all of their quota and did not order more guitars, they were let go as Taylor dealers. I asked Chris Wellons about this claim, and he responded, "We don't say to dealers: this is the mandate, you must buy 30 percent more next year, or you're not going to be our dealer. We have said, in recent years, that this is the minimum qualifying order, and if you're not going to order that number of guitars, we need to look elsewhere for a dealer who can support our brand at that level." Wellons does make the point that working with dealers is a critical balancing act between, on the one hand, maintaining cordial relationships while, on the other hand, setting sales goals that dealers are expected to meet. Growth does have its pushy side.

What cannot be questioned, though, is the overall durability and success of the partnership between Bob Taylor and Kurt Listug, which began in 1974 with the purchase of American Dream. Each man is quick to give credit to the other. Taylor dedicates his 2011 memoir, *Guitar Lessons* "to my partner Kurt Listug, whose contributions to the success of Taylor Guitars are equal in every way to mine." He has also said that "the real reason for Taylor's success is the quality of my relationship with Kurt. We really need each other to make this company happen."[53] Listug as well notes the ways the two men balance each other: "I discovered early on that even though I loved guitars, I wasn't cut out to be a luthier. It turned out that I was as good at managing a business as Bob was at building guitars. It was extremely fortunate for both of us that our skills and interests complemented each other so well."[54] Harmony of skills, in the case of these two cofounders of Taylor Guitars, has indeed gone a long way. No doubt James Burton and many other guitar players would agree.

Chapter 4

GLOBALIZERS

The Rise of Imports

Author: Do you worry about imports?

Well-Known American Guitar Maker: I've been making guitars for 50 years. It's all about brand name recognition. If someone invests their money and buys one of my guitars, they do so because it's a good value. They know that if they keep it, they'll never lose on it; it's a quality item. If they buy a Chinese-made guitar, the minute they take it out of the shop, it's not worth anything. Those brands never get big names. . . . There's a stigma attached to "Made in China," unfortunately.

—*AUTHOR INTERVIEW, JANUARY 29, 2016*

With a changed political climate resulting in an increase of foreign investment, the last few years have seen a dramatic increase in guitars made in China. Once the exclusive domain of ultra-low-end instruments, Chinese factories are beginning to make the kinds of mid-level instruments previously obtained from plants in Japan, Korea, and Taiwan.

—*TEJA GERKEN, ET AL., ACOUSTIC GUITAR, 2003, P. 362*

To this point we have examined two of three major transformations in the acoustic guitar making industry that were identified in the Introduction via our imaginary stroll through three guitar stores separated by time and distance. To recall briefly, the first transformation, discussed in Chapter 2, has been the development of the new lutherie movement, while the second, examined in the previous chapter, has been the rise of the "game changer," Taylor Guitars. This chapter analyzes the third transformation: the proliferation of acoustic guitars made abroad. As we saw, today's Guitar Works, not to mention the online "store" accessible on my computer, carry a veritable flotilla of imported steel-string instruments, virtually none of which were being made six decades ago. The growing presence of such guitars testifies to what I am terming the instrument's "globalization": American-style acoustic guitars being made all over the world.

This is hardly surprising. This observation might well induce a yawn, and the skeptic might ask: What else is new about the story of manufacturing in recent decades? Haven't we seen this scenario before—East Asian production prowess in scores of industries including motor vehicles (automobiles, motorcycles), electronics (radios, phones, you name it), clothing, kitchen products, and the list goes on? Why should the guitar making industry be any different?

The skeptic's question is both fair and challenging, and the task of this chapter is to address it. I do so by posing two further questions that get to the heart of the matter concerning imports, and these questions frame the rest of this chapter. First, how has this rise of imports happened? Second, so what? That is, what difference has it made in the American world of guitar making?[1]

HOW HAS THE RISE OF IMPORTS HAPPENED?

First Japan

The story of imported acoustic guitars begins—as it did with many products manufactured in Asia during the past six decades—in Japan in the early 1960s. The main reasons for the country's early advantage in production for global markets are basically twofold: on the one hand, despite its defeat in World War II, Japan already had a strong industrial heritage and experience to draw upon, and, on the other, the country's labor costs were much lower than those in the United States and western Europe. Throughout the 1960s and 1970s, Japanese guitar makers had the export sector largely to themselves. During that period, the People's Republic of China under Chairman Mao remained isolated—both from the West and even its erstwhile ally, the USSR—and consumed by its own internal conflicts and economic challenges (see below). During those same decades, other Asian countries that later developed guitar-making capacity—South Korea, Taiwan, and Indonesia—were only slowly beginning to industrialize and produce for export.

It is unclear when the first shipment of acoustic guitars made in Japan guitars arrived on these shores, or which company produced them, but one thing is clear: by the end of the 1960s, Japanese guitars—both acoustic and electric varieties—were gaining a presence in American music stores and in the hands of popular performers. This growing presence was not without its hiccups, however, for Japanese instrument production threatened American producers in two ways. The first, of course, was price competition in the lower-price segment of the market. American producers in that segment—longtime producers such as Kay and Harmony—suffered in direct proportion to growing Japanese competition, and both eventually ceased production. The second threat was design infringement by Japanese makers turning out copy-cat models of well-established American-made models. In 1977, for example, Gibson's parent company, Norlin Industries, sued the Elger Company, the American importing facility for Japanese-made Ibanez guitars for copying its headstock design.[2] Suffice it to say, the burgeoning presence of Japanese-made guitars was not welcomed with open arms by American producers.

Nonetheless, the Japanese makers had staked their claim to the American guitar market. There is perhaps no better visual evidence than performance at the Woodstock festival in August 1969. Brandishing his acoustic guitar, Country Joe McDonald took the stage before half a million young people to sing his forever-infamous "F—k Cheer" followed by his satirical anti-Vietnam War sing-along, "I-Feel-Like-I'm-Fixin'-To-Die-Rag." The guitar hanging around his neck was . . . a Yamaha.[3]

Founded in the late nineteenth century, Yamaha is one of four Japanese guitar makers—along with Takamine, Ibanez, and Alvarez—that became global companies in the 1960s, and all four have remained prominent in the US market ever since. What makes this group distinctive? A likely answer, based on stereo-types, might be that these guitar makers are distinctive only in their similarity to one another. Alas, the stereotype of global Japanese companies—think Nissan, Toyota, and Honda—is that they are more or less alike in terms of their technical prowess, production and marketing strategies, and hierarchical corporate cultures. To use the old cliché: Japanese corporations appear, to many in the West, to be cut from the same (homogenous) cultural cloth.

Such a stereotype misses the reality of Japanese guitar making. On the contrary, this sector is striking in its diversity, for there is little similarity among these four guitar producers in terms of their ownership, corporate structure, or production and marketing strategy. Only Takamine, for example, is truly an acoustic guitar producer. From the outset, Takamine, founded in 1962 and so named for the nine-thousand-foot-high mountain in central Japan near the company's first workshop, focused on building high-quality acoustic guitars.

Since that time, Takamine has remained true to that central mission, which it states clearly and only slightly hyperbolically on its website: "For more than half a century, Takamine has proudly dedicated itself to the art of fine guitar craftsmanship. Its longstanding devotion to innovation and continual improvement has placed it among the world's premier acoustic guitar makers, with truly fine instruments that are the first choice of performing guitarists worldwide."[4] Keeping its focus on acoustic guitars means that Takamine has rejected the diversification path taken by many lutherie companies to make not only electric guitars, but also other instruments such as mandolins, banjos, and violins.

Takamine's focus on acoustics does not mean, however, that it has neglected the guitarist's frequent wish to amplify the instrument via electronics. In fact, Takamine claims to have been among the first companies to build an acoustic-electric guitar—a fully acoustic instrument that incorporates onboard electronics such as a pickup, pre-amp, and other volume and tone enhancers. Today most of its guitars, à la Taylor Guitars, feature some type of built-in electric amplification. This emphasis has paid dividends in terms of the brand's visibility. For example, Takamine guitars are popular with rock and country stars—including Bruce Springsteen, Glenn Frey, Garth Brooks, Kenny Chesney, Toby Keith, Nancy Wilson, and Don Henley—who want an acoustic sound in their music.[5]

A second Japanese guitar maker with a global footprint, Ibanez, founded in 1957, has pursued a different production strategy from Takamine's in two key respects. First, unlike Takamine, Ibanez has branched out well beyond acoustic guitars to produce a wide range of instruments, including electric guitars and an assortment of mandolins, banjos, and basses. Moreover, although Ibanez still produces acoustic guitars, the company's bread and butter is their electric instruments. For example, a brief visit to Ibanez's website features a daunting variety of electric guitars, including twenty-three signature models—including Steve Vai and Joe Satriani—and ten different series models (AZ, RG, AX, etc.), each of which offers several variations in terms of wood, color, electronics, and the like. By contrast, the company's acoustic guitar offerings appear meager in number and variety.

A third well-known Japanese company, Alvarez, contrasts with the other three main Japanese guitar makers in one unusual way: it is not really a Japanese company at all! Today, the Alvarez brand is a division of a major American music instruments distributor, St. Louis Music (SLM). There is an important Japanese lutherie connection, however, and this is key to the brand's image and its commercial success. The connection goes back to the late 1960s, when SLM's then owner, Gene Kornblum, established a partnership with Kazuo Yairi, a master Japanese luthier, whereby Yairi, on behalf of SLM, would develop acoustic guitar production in Japan for export to the United States and elsewhere.

This arrangement essentially became a two-tier production-for-export system. On the one hand, Yairi continued to build his handcrafted, high-quality, high-priced guitars in his own shop in Japan and export them under its own label, Alvarez Yairi. On the other hand, the two partners also established facilities elsewhere in Japan and eventually other countries to make mass-produced, lower priced instruments. This arrangement has benefitted both partners in that Kazuo Yairi's instruments (and therefore Alvarez as a brand) gained international visibility and prestige, and St. Louis Music has been able to market guitars at a wide range of price points.[6]

Finally, within this group of four guitar makers, Yamaha is easily the best-known brand. Yamaha, of course, is known for its guitars (acoustic and electric), but also for much more, as it is a fully diversified corporation. Beyond the music world, Yamaha has myriad recreation products for land (motorcycles, ATVs, snowmobiles) and water (boats, outboard motors, WaveRunners, swimming pools), not to mention sports equipment (golf, archery, and tennis gear). Within the music world itself, Yamaha—like Ibanez—produces nearly every conceivable type of music-related item, including pianos, keyboards, strings, brass and woodwind instruments, drums, amps, and the list goes on.

Given Yamaha's long history, dating from the late nineteenth century, as one of Japan's most prolific instrument makers, one might assume that Yamaha guitars are made in Japan. That would be incorrect, as I discovered through a recent personal experience. In a benefit silent auction, I won a bid on a new, well-finished, easy-playing Yamaha acoustic guitar, which has a street price of about $250. Getting the guitar home and examining its interior, I was surprised to read the label: Made in China.

And Now China

As someone interested in the provenance of guitars, I was already aware that certain American brands such as Blueridge and Johnson were produced in China. I also knew that acoustic guitars with a well-known American pedigree—Recording King, Washburn, Epiphone, and even Fender—were now being built in Chinese factories. I did not realize, however, that even famous Japanese-origin guitars such as Yamaha were also being made in China.

I should not have been surprised by this, of course. Migration—of people, but also of production sites—is an inherent component of a capitalist economy, not only within a single nation, but also across the globe. Stated succinctly but not overly simplistically, the pursuit of profit is the driving force behind capitalism, and a key determinant of the profit margin is the cost of labor. So my Chinese-made Japanese guitar is just another example of capitalist manufacturers seeking out lower-wage locations in which to manufacture their products. At some point in recent decades, Yamaha, taking advantage of China's lower-cost labor, migrated its acoustic guitar production from the home country to China.

Of course, none of this migration would have occurred without China's opening to the West during the 1970s. The first dramatic step was the country's establishing of diplomatic relations with the United States—a pivotal turn in China's foreign policy that was capped by Nixon's 1972 visit to China. Diplomacy facilitated economic opening, and the next step came with China's welcoming of foreign investment by Mao's successor, Deng Xiaoping. Deng's Four Modernizations program, launched in 1977, stressed modernization in the areas of agriculture, industry, defense, and science technology—all of which required some level of cooperation, technology transfer, and foreign investment with the U.S., Europe, and Japan, among others. That initiative paved the way for China's impressive advances in many export-oriented sectors, including musical instrument production.[7]

In the manufacture and export of guitars specifically, China advanced swiftly. During the 1990s, China's total exports of guitars—both acoustic and electric—rose steadily to about two million units per year.[8] Between 2000 and 2010, that number increased year over year to eleven million units. Since that time, the export volume of Chinese-made guitars has stabilized, varying between ten million and twelve million units annually. Stated differently, during the past two decades, China's total guitar exports have more than quintupled.

Where do those guitars go once they leave China and head out in the world? The answer is, of course, everywhere, but especially to the United States. For example, in 2015, China exported ten million guitars (acoustic and electric combined), and about 2.5 million of those arrived in the United States. This number was far more than any other country imported; the second largest importer of Chinese guitars was Germany with only one-fifth that number (500,000), followed by Brazil, the United Kingdom, and Malaysia.

Another way to judge China's preponderance in the US import market is to ask the question from the US viewpoint: How do other guitar-exporting countries compare with China in the US market? The simple answer is poorly. Looking only at acoustic guitar imports, no other country comes close. Between 2015 and 2019, the United States imported between 1.5 and 1.8 million acoustic guitars annually. Chinese-made guitars accounted for about 70% of that total, with Mexico and Indonesia splitting most of the remainder of the import market. Japan has largely dropped from sight as the generator of guitar exports to the United States. As mentioned, the large instrument companies such as Yamaha have outsourced much of their production to China and, increasingly, to Indonesia.

Just as there many ways to make a quiche, sing a song, skin a cat, etc., there are also many ways to produce a guitar in one country and export it to another. The business of producing for export, as just one aspect of global capitalism, is multifaceted and never static. Nowhere is this truer than in China where one finds a variety of ownership and production arrangements that have developed since the country's economic opening; moreover, these arrangements often change over time. In my research, I have been struck by two contrasting companies—Saga Music and Eastman Music—that illustrate this variety. Saga, for example, is an American-owned importer and distributor of musical instruments with extensive ties and interactions with Chinese manufacturers. By contrast, Eastman is a Chinese-origin manufacturer that is now global in both its production and distributional. A profile of each company will demonstrate the range of diversity in how companies make and export musical instruments from China to the rest of the world, and especially to the United States.

The Saga of Saga: Riding the Camels Around

Among the pioneer American importers of East Asian musical instruments into the United States is Saga Music, based in South San Francisco, California. As the company's website declares, "For over four decades, Saga has sought out individual craftsmen as well as established factories to provide the very best handcrafted instruments possible at the best price available on the world market. . . . So when you order instruments, parts, or accessories from Saga Musical Instruments, you know you're going to the source—*your source* for the finest quality instruments from a host of established, proven worldwide manufacturing sources."[9]

From modest beginnings in the 1970s, Saga has developed into a company with an impressive array of music-product offerings. Even a cursory inspection of its website reveals Saga to be an importer of a wide variety of acoustic instruments. Probably best known for its line of Blueridge guitars and Kentucky mandolins, Saga also carries seven other guitar brands, with each brand offering several models. The company also imports various brands of banjos, mandolins, ukuleles, and violins, and it carries a selection of accessories including cases, bows, and strings. It is fair to say that Saga provides the consumer with a large choice of instruments and models at price points ranging from low to high.[10] All of these instruments are now made in China, although this was not always the company's principal source of products. In fact, the case of Saga demonstrates the peripatetic tendency of instrument production to migrate from one site to another based on economic (especially labor cost) considerations.

Saga has its origins in the life and career of Richard Keldsen (born 1945), who established the company in the mid-1970s and still heads it today. In several conversations, Keldsen told me how he built an instrument-importing business essentially from scratch. This process has eventually engaged Saga in virtually every aspect of that business, including the design, production, importation, and distribution of the instruments just mentioned. I also learned that, for Richard, this business is not just a way to make a living—it's a way to make a life. His work, he says, has also provided an enjoyable, engaging way to travel and discover other cultures. My impression is that Richard Keldsen is as much a natural-born cultural anthropologist as he is an entrepreneur.[11]

Growing up in Michigan's Upper Peninsula, Keldsen attended Michigan State University, graduating in 1967. After college, he, like many of his young peers during the 1960s, joined the Peace Corps and served three years in the Philippines, during which time he also traveled to Hong Kong, Thailand, and Nepal. This experience merely whetted his appetite for future travel and living abroad. After his Peace Corps service, Keldsen settled in the San Francisco area and became involved in selling musical instruments, mainly banjos, eventually becoming the owner, from 1973 to 1981, of a string of stores offering instruments and lessons called the Fifth String.

During this period, Keldsen began returning to Asia, first to Japan in 1975 with the aim of importing banjo assembly kits. While on this initial trip, he became friendly with a Japanese businessman, Tsutomu "Tom" Hosokawa, who had connections with many small instrument factories and workshops in the Gifu-Nagano region of central Japan. The two men worked out an arrangement whereby Hosokawa worked with these local factories and workshops to produce the components of the banjo kits, which he then shipped to Richard in San Francisco. Keldsen says, "I knew that selling the kits only in my stores would not support an importing business, so I placed a couple of small advertisements in a couple of banjo related publications. That was the beginning of Saga Musical Instruments." This arrangement proved so successful that by the early 1980s the two men had gone beyond banjo kits and entry-level instruments and had established lines of Saga brands including

Kentucky Mandolins, Gold Star Banjos, and Cremona Violins. I asked Keldsen how he came up with the name, Saga, and he said with a smile, "I'm a Dane, and it's a Scandinavian word. It's short, the letters are balanced, it's easy to remember, and it doesn't mean anything negative in another language."

Keldsen places the experience of his first Asian partnership in its historical context, which was a period of major disruptions in the mass-produced, lower-price segment of the American instrument market, mainly because of the growing influx of imports. He mentions, for example, the Chicago-based music company, Harmony, which went bankrupt in the mid-1970s, whereas just a few years before that, Harmony's advertising catalogue proclaimed that the company's Chicago factory produced more guitars than the rest of the world combined. Keldsen's conclusion: by the mid-1970s Japanese imports had taken the bottom out of lower-end producers such as Harmony and Kay.

Japan's manufacturing and exporting success, he says, was not just a question of lower wage costs compared to, say, Chicago. Japan's success also owed to aspects of Japan's industrial infrastructure and culture. Keldsen points out, for example, that the West's image of Japan's economic rise in the 1960s and 1970s was that of a monolithic industrial structure, with many large factories. On the contrary, he says, Japan's economy was "a bunch of really small guys," that is, many small-scale small suppliers. Barriers to entry in manufacturing were low. He comments, "If you wanted to start a guitar factory, for example, you could buy semi-finished necks from a guy in the next town, you could buy bodies from somebody else making those, you could even buy components such as bridges and nuts. You could become just a guitar assembler, and you could compete, you could export. There was a growing market for those products."

Keldsen also found Japan's work culture congenial and efficient. He began to study the Japanese language and, by his modest admission, "I got pretty good at it." Having traveled back and forth to Japan during the latter half of the 1970s, Richard told his partner Hosokawa that he wanted to get to know Japan even better by working for a month or two in one of Hosokawa's factories. To which Hosokawa replied: How about two factories? So in 1980 Keldsen embarked on his Japanese work experience.

In the first factory, which made guitars, he was assigned to operate an automated side-bending machine. "From the cultural aspect and from every aspect, it was just a blast. Within the first twenty minutes, I was part of the team." That very first day, he reports: "At 10 a.m., a bell rings—it was the bell for everyone to take a break, but I didn't know that. So I just kept working. And so did everyone else. No one wanted to be the first to stop. Finally, a guy comes over to me and says, 'You've been working so hard, you should take a break.' So he's basically pleading with me to stop. It was that way every day. No one wanted to go first, and it was never when the damn bell went off. It was always several minutes later, and they all did it together."

The big transition in Asian guitar making began during the early 1980s, as Japan's low-cost advantage eroded as a result of new job opportunities in other sectors (e.g., electronics), labor shortages, and higher wage costs. Those costs created production and export opportunities elsewhere in East Asia—in Taiwan and Korea initially, and then later China—and both Japanese and American companies began seeking out such opportunities. Yamaha, for example, established a factory in Taiwan to make its lower-end instruments. Richard Keldsen, as well, saw new prospects for Saga in these countries. "As soon as this started happening," he says, "I was on a plane."

Because of Keldsen's extensive travel and cultural interest in the region, along with his knowledge of Asian-style production, Saga was among the first American-owned music instrument companies to establish manufacturing/importing relationships with Asian suppliers besides Japan. This meant widening both his sources of supply and the range of instruments he could import for his Fifth String music stores. Two good examples are violins from China and guitars from Taiwan (and later China).

Richard recalls the first time he became aware of China's emergence as an exporting force to be reckoned with. The year was 1981, at the Frankfurt Music Fair, where Saga Japan had an exhibit booth, and so did a group of Chinese violin makers. This was the first time Keldsen had ever seen a Chinese presence at a major trade show. "There was a group of Chinese men, all with bad haircuts and wearing Mao jackets," he recalls. But the Chinese had violins to sell, so he ended up ordering two hundred violins at $16.23 each (including case and bow). "I figured this would get me a visa to visit China," he says.

Keldsen also told the Chinese group that he would like to visit their violin-making factory, and four weeks later, he flew to Shanghai. He says that he is the first American in the musical instrument business to become directly involved in China. Thus was born Saga's line of Cremona violins and a relationship with the original Chinese supplier that has lasted to the present. The whole experience was transformative. After visiting China and assessing the instrument-importing possibilities, Keldsen decided to sell his Fifth String stores in San Francisco and engage strictly in the import business.

Alongside his developing relationships with Chinese instrument makers during the 1980s, Richard also began sourcing, from Taiwan, Saga's signature brand of acoustic guitars—the Blueridge line. Throughout the 1980s, those guitars were made in Taiwan through an arrangement between Saga and a Taiwanese instrument maker with experience in Japan, who agreed to produce guitars for Saga under the Blueridge name. This arrangement worked well, and Blueridge gradually built a name, especially within the bluegrass community.[12]

By the 1990s, however, Taiwan, like Japan before it, was developing labor shortages and consequently rising labor costs. According to Richard, Taiwan's growth provided many other job opportunities such that "people didn't want to work in factories anymore." The Taiwanese guitar maker building Blueridge guitars began losing money and eventually closed the factory. Then the partners considered a promising alternative: to build a guitar factory in China and relocate production there to take advantage of that country's lower labor costs. There were other good reasons to do so, Richard says, including his own experience of working in China since the early 1980s. Moreover, the Taiwanese group, though Chinese by ethnicity, had little experience in the People's Republic yet wanted to get a manufacturing foothold there. So the group decided to move its guitar production from Taiwan to China, with Keldsen facilitating the move through his contacts there.

The Taiwanese supplier built a new factory in Guangdong Province, near the city of Guangzhou (formerly Canton), and, since 1995, has produced Blueridge guitars there. In Keldsen's view, the move from Taiwan to Guangdong gave the Blueridge line a "rebirth." The new factory, built to the most up-to-date specifications, has enabled Blueridge to offer a total of sixty-six different models ranging in price from $600 to $3,500. If timing is everything, Saga's relocation of its Blueridge guitars from Taiwan to mainland China in the mid-1990s was near perfect, as this move coincided with a period of noticeable improvement in the quality of Chinese-made instruments. As the observer quoted at the outset of this chapter commented in the early 2000s: "Generally made to the specifications of large American or European parent companies, [Chinese] guitars are reaching a level of quality that would have been unthinkable a few years ago."[13] (See photo next page.)

Although the Blueridge factory in China remains owned by his Taiwanese partner, Keldsen sees himself serving as a bridge linking three sets of partners: Chinese, Taiwanese, and American. The bridge metaphor applies equally well to Keldsen's personality and his company's basic modus operandi.

First, it's clear that Richard finds working in Asia to be—how else to put it?—fun. He elaborates:

> The driving force for me was never lower labor costs. I just found it was easier to do things in Asia, and more fun, than it was here. Here in the US, at every factory I went to it would be: How many do you want? You'd have a conversation like that. But in Asia, it was never that conversation. You talk about the instruments, you develop a relationship, go have a few beers, and let's get started. It was that simple. I was comfortable enough with Asian culture, and they were willing to spend time to talk about it. Quantity was never a topic of conversation. It was a different style, and more fun. You could go out and ride the camels around.

He concludes on his personal affinity for connecting with other peoples and cultures by saying: "My advantage was that I didn't mind going to Asia and getting to know people. I love the minutiae of production. And then I love to travel and discover new cultures, getting to know their history. The music aspect made it just that much more interesting."

Moreover, Saga as a company conceives its mode of operation to be that of linking and coordinating the various stages of instrument production. This process starts with getting to know the suppliers intimately. Keldsen comments: "We're an importer, yes, but we're more than that. You don't just walk into a factory and say 'I'll take 10 of those and 10 of those. We don't start doing business with somebody unless we've really established some kind of relationship and understand what they do best—and what their strengths and weaknesses are. We want to understand the character of the owner."

From that initial relationship, Saga inevitably becomes involved in various aspects of the production process, including design. Of the Blueridge factory built in China by his Taiwanese partner in the mid-1990s, Keldsen says, "We told our partner, 'Let's do it the best way possible.' So all new machines, all state-of-the-art stuff. Then we started doing design ideas with them, how to make those guitars as close as possible to the 'golden age' guitars of the 1930s." The same dynamic has occurred with other instruments Saga carries, such as violins. Richard says, "Starting with Chinese-made violins in 1981, we quickly became the biggest importer of violins. But we weren't just putting in orders. We were supplying ebony and working with their factories on design."

The onset of Covid in early 2020 disrupted everyone in the guitar industry, and Saga has been no exception. Keldsen was unable to go to China, or Japan for that matter, for at least the first three years of the pandemic, and Saga had to deal with the challenges of importing instruments from a China under virtual lockdown. As Richard puts it, in a June 2022 phone conversation, "getting product is the big dilemma." Beyond these logistical difficulties, Saga's operations in China have faced labor shortages. He comments that there

The Saga Bluegrass Band, at 2019 NAMM Show, Anaheim, California.
Richard Keldsen on right in cowboy hat (photo by author).

used to be "a seemingly unending source of labor from the interior parts of China where prosperity hadn't reached out. But as China has developed, the prosperity has spread." This has meant, he says, that "established factories along the Chinese coast are feeling that crunch and have trouble being able to find workers. It also has meant that many of the workers who went back to the hinterland are starting their own businesses."

Yet faced with such challenges—travel restrictions, supply-chain bottlenecks, and labor shortages—Richard Keldsen exudes no pessimism. Rather, buoyed by an inherent optimism of spirit, a robust sellers' market, and the confidence derived from having built an operation from scratch that has endured since the early 1970s, Richard remains hopeful that Saga will endure into the future.

Home-Grown in China (and America): Eastman Guitars

In an actual, not imaginary, visit to Guitar Works recently, I added another element to my understanding of the guitar's globalization when I spotted a nice-looking acoustic guitar with a headstock name I knew nothing about: Eastman. I asked the store manager Larry Brown what he knew about the maker, and he said, "I must say I'm impressed—Eastman makes fine acoustic guitars, especially for the price. They're a great value." Whereupon I responded, "I'll take a wild guess: those are all made in China." Larry then said: "Correct, but it's not what you're probably thinking—that they're made for an American-owned company. That's not the case—Eastman is a Chinese company."

That news caught me up short; I did not know that a Chinese-owned instrument maker had a visible and growing presence in the world instrument market. I knew, of course, that in the world of pianos, Japanese companies such as Suzuki, Kawai, and, yes, Yamaha had established excellent reputations, rivaling Steinway and other elite brands. But I knew of no Chinese company that had that kind of status, especially in guitar production.

Up to that moment, I believed that virtually all guitar producers in China are what is termed an "Original Equipment Manufacturer," or OEM. These are Chinese-owned companies, anonymous to the outside world, that mass-produce guitars under contract for foreign companies whose own name or brand is put on the headstock. All Fender acoustic guitars, for example, are made in this fashion: in China, by an unidentified Chinese guitar producer, whose final step is to affix the decal of the all-American brand Fender to the headstock. Many other brands with American-sounding names, such as Dean, Johnson, Recording King, Teton, Walden, and Washburn, have their guitars produced in this fashion.[14] All of Saga's many instruments are manufactured in this way as well.

But an actual Chinese company that makes and markets its own guitars (albeit with a an American-sounding name like Eastman)? That got my attention. Naturally, in the revered tradition of direct observational research, I felt an obligation to test the product myself. I proceeded to rent from Guitar Works two different Eastman acoustic guitars—a dreadnought and a grand auditorium model—in successive weeks. I come away from my research testing as impressed with these guitars as Larry, the Guitar Works store manager, was. Both guitars had immaculate "fit and finish"—no spots of wayward glue or poorly fitted joints or blemishes of any kind. Functionally speaking, both instruments were light, responsive, tonally balanced, and projected well (they were loud!). With a retail price of just $350–$400, I do consider these guitars a true value.[15]

The next step was to find out more about Eastman Music itself. I learned that its story is more complicated than its being simply a "Chinese company," but Eastman stands as another example of how acoustic guitar production has become globalized. The company's story starts with its founder and still present owner, Qian Ni (pronounced "chin nee"). Born and raised in China, Qian was a serious flutist who came to the United States in the late 1980s to study music at Boston University's School of Music. Upon arrival, by his own admission, he spoke little English. But he persevered, learned the language, and earned a master's degree in flute performance.

Following graduation Qian sought a position, without success, in an American symphony orchestra. But in the spring of 1989, as Qian's temporary work visa was about to expire, and he was preparing to return home to China, massive political protests broke out in Beijing's Tiananmen Square. Following the Chinese government's June 4 crackdown on the protests, the U.S. government responded by granting visa extensions to all Chinese citizens then residing in this country, and so Qian was allowed to remain in this country indefinitely.

Three years later, in 1992 Qian returned home to Beijing and established his own music company, Eastman Music, with the long-term goal of distributing and making musical instruments and accessories, not only in China but also in his adopted country of the United States. Over the next decade, he also became an American citizen and a truly bi-national person. In the pre-Covid years since Eastman became firmly established, Qian has divided his time roughly equally between China and the United States.

In colloquial English honed over thirty years of living and working in this country, Qian recently explained to me Eastman's general strategy, which is to bring to the marketplace a range of instruments at various price points.[16] This approach is, to say the least, an ambitious one for any music company, but Eastman is carrying it out. The company can rightly assert that Qian "never imagined that over the course of twenty-five years, the company would grow from a small business operated out of the back of his car into a global maker of musical instruments."[17] Beginning in the 1990s, Qian—working together with his father—was distributing China-made strings for violin, viola, and bass. In the years since, he has proceeded to expand Eastman Music with a rare combination of diversification, acquisition, and, most recently, Chinese-American collaboration, all the while emphasizing craft-style production based in China.

The basic strategy is two-pronged, based on owning production facilities in both China and the United States. First, all Eastman instruments bearing the company name—a long list that includes not only acoustic guitars, but also electric guitars, mandolins, violins, violas, cellos, basses, woodwinds, and brasswinds—are produced in the company's own shops and factories in China. According to the company's website, "All of our guitars and mandolins are built in our workshops in Beijing by an expert team of luthiers and craftspeople."[18] The Eastman guitars that I research-tested at Guitar Works were made in one of those Beijing workshops.

The second prong of Qian's strategy is U.S.-focused, based on acquiring and managing established American companies. One prominent example is Wm. S. Haynes, a Boston-based flute-maker established in 1888 and bought by Eastman in 2004. Another one is S. E. Shires, another Massachusetts-based producer of custom brass instruments, such as trumpets and trombones. Founded in 1995, S. E. Shires joined the Eastman business portfolio in 2014. In both cases, Eastman has maintained these companies' continuity as American-based instrument makers, while also creating a "Q Series" of these brands featuring Eastman's Chinese-made instruments that have a lower retail price than the made-in-America Haynes and Shires products.

The most recent, and still emerging, element of Eastman's guitar operations is its 2019 majority acquisition of a respected American acoustic guitar maker, Bourgeois Guitars in Lewiston, Maine. Founder and sole owner of the company since 1977, Dana Bourgeois is considered one of the leading "reinventors" of the acoustic guitar during the past few decades. Under his leadership, Bourgeois Guitars has earned a reputation for "boutique" level quality, with its new guitars retailing for $4,500 and up. In this new arrangement, Dana retains a minority ownership share and still runs the company, producing all his erstwhile products in his Lewiston shop.

Eastman's acquisition of Bourgeois Guitars also comes with an interesting twist: a manufacturing collaboration. Having worked in the past with luthiers such as Eric Schoenberg, Bourgeois began a conversation with Qian Ni whereby the two companies would jointly build a mid-range guitar that would retail between $2,500 and $3,000. This conversation eventually produced what Bourgeois terms a partnership "not because it is a partnership in the legal sense, but because it feels like one."[19]

Each company saw economic opportunity in such a partnership. For his part, Dana Bourgeois was seeking to widen his market reach by offering a line of lower-price guitars that would still carry the name, quality, and cachet of the Bourgeois label. Dana freely admits that, given his production standards and operating costs, his company could not profitably make new guitars that sell for less than $4,000. In his view, a lower-price instrument co-built by Bourgeois and Eastman would find new buyers, not only in the American market but also in the growing Chinese domestic guitar market, where Eastman is a well-known brand. As the Bourgeois website states: "After extensive study, we've concluded that partnership with a proven international distribution and manufacturing company offers significant strategic opportunities that cannot otherwise be grown from within."[20]

For Qian and Eastman, an acquisition cum coproduction arrangement with Bourgeois would, in effect, achieve for Eastman the opposite of what Bourgeois is seeking: an entrée to a higher-price segment of the American market, since Eastman's guitars retail for between $300 and $1,500. Echoing the anonymous luthier quoted at the heading of this chapter, Bourgeois himself recognizes the image problem of Chinese-made guitars: "The mid-range market is huge—it's much bigger than the boutique market. The problem is that it's hard to break the price ceiling with a Chinese-made instrument, no matter how good the instrument is. People aren't yet willing to pay beyond a certain amount because it's Chinese."[21]

What has resulted from their conversations is the creation of a new series of acoustic guitars—labeled the Touchstone series—based on a division of labor in the building process. Bourgeois Guitars' main job is to craft the tops (or soundboards) of the guitars. This is a multi-step process in which the luthier first "voices" the underside of the top. As noted in Chapter 2, Dana Bourgeois has become known in the acoustic guitar world for refining this technique of tap-tuning—literally holding the braced soundboard near one's ear while tapping on it in various places to listen for variations in sound and therefore vibration in the wood. This ancient but exacting technique identifies areas on the bracing that need to be thinned further, or left as is, in order to maximize the top's resonance for a particular type of guitar.[22]

Dana describes this soundboard preparation process as follows: "Touchstone tops are voiced by my production staff, though I approve each top. Tops are first rosetted and profiled, then thicknessed to achieve a measured stiffness, then braced. Final brace shaping is accomplished by hand, using the tapping and flexing method to bring out a variety of resonant top responses at desired stiffness."[23]

Once prepared in this way, the Touchstone tops are then shipped to the Eastman factory in China for installation on the guitars' bodies, which that factory builds according to Bourgeois' specifications. The Chinese factory then ships the now-finished guitars back to Lewiston for a final step. According to Dana, "they ship them to us, and we check them for quality control, make any adjustments that need to be made, and make sure all is well. If there are any problems, they go back [to China]. So it's very important, especially early on, that every guitar is right." I ask Dana what name is going on the headstock? He quickly responds, "Bourgeois," then he adds: "the inside will carry a label. It hasn't been fully designed, but it will say something like 'Made in partnership with Eastman Music.'"

Finally, I ask Bourgeois how he would define or describe his partner. Searching for how to describe Eastman, he finally says, "I would say Eastman

Music is a product of Qian's Chinese heritage and his adopted American culture." According to Dana, "Qian is quite a guy, he's very visionary. And he's created an awesome company. Everyone there is amazing—they're fun to work with. I never leave a meeting with Qian without feeling energized."

As of 2022, the energy of collaboration between Bourgeois and Eastman continues despite the challenges of operating in a global climate of Covid restrictions as well as trade and other tensions between the United States and China. Early that year, Bourgeois received an initial shipment from Beijing of 44 co-produced guitars, with regular, planned production of these instruments to be in place by the summer of 2022.[24] The true market impact of this collaboration—in effect, a kind of "reaching down" to a lower-price consumer market for Bourgeois and a "reaching up" for Eastman to a higher-price market—remains to be seen, but initial signs appear promising.

SO WHAT?

Impact of Imports on the Acoustic Guitar World

This chapter was initially drafted in the eighth month of the Covid-19 pandemic, which has, of course, massively disrupted national economies and global supply chains. Moreover, as of this writing the United States appears well locked into ongoing trade disputes with China, not to mention larger conflicts over global economic, diplomatic, and military supremacy. Thus, one cannot make any confident predictions about the likely course of Chinese-made imported guitars, since that course will be shaped by these looming, still-unresolved influences. One can, however, draw some conclusions about the impact of imported guitars in the context of the acoustic guitar's transformation during the past sixty years. The chief question is, "What difference has the rise of imports made in the world of the acoustic guitar?"

Just as the answer to many questions depends on whom you ask, we can address this question from two basic perspectives, that of producers and that of consumers. First, from the perspective of producers, it should be clear by now that the impact of imports has been greatest on the lower-priced, mass-produced segment of the market. As noted earlier, the arrival of Japanese-made guitars—both acoustic and electric—throughout the 1960s and into the following decade severely hurt US manufacturers such as Kay, Harmony, and even Gibson. Not only were the imported guitars less expensive because of lower labor costs, they were, in most cases, fairly close copies of American-made instruments. Lawsuits against trademark infringement—most notably Gibson's successful suit against Ibanez in 1977—became one of the few avenues for American companies to resist the onslaught of foreign competition in the guitar market.[25] Kathryn Marie Dudley sums it up in her authoritative study of major changes in the acoustic guitar industry during this period: "By the early 1970s, competition from Japan had effectively squeezed American guitar makers out of the low end of an increasingly global market for steel-string guitars."[26]

In this case, "squeezed" is another term for bankrupt. Harmony, for example, founded in 1892 in Chicago, was once "the production king of American instruments," accounting for over half the guitars built annually in the United States.[27] At its peak in the mid-1960s, Harmony employed about six hundred workers turning out about 350,000 instruments (guitars, mandolins, banjos, ukuleles) per year. By 1974, owing primarily to Japanese competition, the company had gone broke, closed its doors, and dissolved.[28] A similar fate befell the other large Chicago producer, Kay. What followed has been a story of imports: first from Japan, a bit later South Korea and Taiwan, and especially since the 1990s, China. Indonesia is the latest Asian player; in the past decade, it has become the second largest producer, behind China, of guitars imported into the United States.

This sea change does not imply that American companies are absent from the import sector, far from it. In fact, US distribution companies such as U.S. Music Corporation (Washburn Guitars), The Music Link (Recording King, Johnson, Savannah), and St. Louis Music (Alvarez, Austin) all source their guitars from Chinese original equipment manufacturers, who build the instruments to order and put the brand label on the headstock. Saga Music falls into this category as well; all its guitars, mandolins, banjos, violins, and other products are made in Chinese factories. Saga's owner, Richard Keldsen, does emphasize, however, that his company does not merely send production orders to Chinese manufacturers, but it is closely involved in the design, sourcing of components, and other aspects of the production process.

That Asian imports have eliminated American makers from the low end of the acoustic guitar market is not to say that these foreign suppliers have been eternally relegated to making low cost, starter instruments. In fact, many observers have perceived a steady increase in the quality of Chinese-made guitars, to the point that some premium models (all solid, premium woods, no laminates) retail for over $1,500, lifting those instruments into the broad middle range of retail prices.[29] I would summarize this trend with two terms: learning curve and ceiling. First, Chinese guitar manufacturing has indeed been on a learning curve, especially in incorporating precise manufacturing tools such as CNC machines. Second, as Dana Bourgeois remarks, there is still a price ceiling beyond which the average buyer—at least in the United States—is unwilling to pay for a Chinese-made guitar and will instead opt for a Made in America instrument.

This combination of trends leads to two further conclusions about the impact of imports on American guitar makers. The first is something of a nonevent. Given that imported guitars from mass producers in China and elsewhere face consumer resistance above a certain low- to mid-range price point, the influx of imported guitars is not a concern for the high-end producers profiled in Chapter 2. In my interviews with builders such as Bill Collings, Jeff Huss and Mark Dalton, Richard Hoover, and Michael Millard, the threat of imports never came up. This premium segment of the producer world has been little affected, if at all, by imported guitars.

This is not true, however, for producers such as Martin, Gibson, and Taylor, which aspire to capture the middle range of the market, and this is the second conclusion: these quality mass producers—whose premium instruments retail for at least $3,500—also seek to appeal to this middle-range component of the consumer market by offering lower-priced instruments. To do so and remain profitable, these companies have gone to offshore sourcing. For example, Taylor Guitars, as mentioned in Chapter 3, operates a factory in Tecate, Mexico, producing its two lowest series of instruments (100 and 200), while Martin manufactures its Road Series guitars in Navojoa, Mexico. These instruments typically retail for between $800 and $1,600—a price point that rivals the top instruments being built in China. So there is some competition between these leading American makers and premium level, Chinese-made instruments.

What about the impact of guitar imports from the consumer's perspective? Here the answer is evident: guitar buyers are the big winners. In the lower-price market segment in which imported guitars vie for customers, these instruments offer far more value than their equivalent offerings of five or six decades ago, namely American-made, mass-produced guitars such as Harmony and Kay.

I offer subjective, albeit persuasive, data from my own experience. As mentioned in the Introduction, in 1972 I bought my first guitar: a used Harmony Sovereign, likely made in Chicago during the previous decade. It was a serviceable starter instrument, although it had high action, meaning that the strings were relatively high above the fretboard, and one had to press hard to play a note without buzzing. The Harmony *sounded* like a guitar, but it had no sonic qualities that particularly caught my attention. The price I paid—$75—is worth $508 in contemporary, inflation-adjusted dollars (ca. 2022).[30]

Recently, as described earlier, I purchased a *new* Eastman acoustic guitar, made in Beijing, from my local guitar store. The price was $405, considerably less in comparable cost to the Harmony. In my judgement, based on playing hundreds of guitars during the past five decades, this Eastman is a superior instrument. Aesthetically, the Eastman is far more attractive, with a cutaway body, solid spruce top, fine-grained (albeit laminate) back and sides, and spotless fit and finish. Moreover, my Eastman comes with a built-in electric pickup for amplification, versus no pickup in the Harmony. Finally, the Eastman, in my hands, plays as easily and sounds as loud, balanced, and resonant as a guitar that might retail for hundreds of dollars more. By contrast, a guitar of the quality of my 1960s Harmony would likely sell today for perhaps $150–200—much less in inflation-adjusted dollars than I initially paid five decades ago. From my limited but telling cost/quality comparison, I draw one clear conclusion: in terms of value—that is, the ratio between expenditure and product quality—today's lower-priced acoustic guitars, now mostly imported from China, offer much more than their comparable predecessors of fifty years ago. The guitar-buying public—especially those on a budget and/or just starting to play—is all the better for it.

Chapter 5

GIBSON

Driven by Innovation?

> Don't over-romanticize the making of these guitars—they are just boxes, for crying out loud.
>
> *—HENRY JUSZKIEWICZ, CEO, GIBSON BRANDS (1986–2018)*
> *(QUOTED IN JOHN SOUTHERN, "BIG SKY BUILDER," PREMIER GUITAR,*
> *SEPTEMBER 19, 2008)*

> Fender's bread and butter is still Stratocasters and Telecasters. Martin is still dreadnought flattops. When they've tried to do other things . . . they didn't sell. A company can become victimized by its own tradition.
>
> *—WALTER CARTER, OWNER, CARTER VINTAGE GUITARS*
> *(WMOT PODCAST, APRIL 23, 2018)*

We return for a last virtual walk-through of the three music retailers that frame this study: the Shreveport Music Company in 1960, Evanston's Guitar Works today, and internet sellers. We note again all the major changes that have transformed the acoustic guitar world during the past six decades, beginning with the sheer growth in supply. One immediately notices the disparity between the large number of instruments on display in Guitar Works, not to mention the seemingly endless offerings online, versus the Shreveport Music

Company's paltry collection. This difference testifies to the huge rise over time in consumer demand for acoustic guitars. Although musical trends and fashions come and go, and the instrument's popularity has been eclipsed at times by other instruments, the acoustic guitar has more than held its own through the years, especially given its advantages of portability, price, and the relative ease of attaining basic proficiency.

The other major difference has to do with substance: the stores have a strikingly different cast of characters on display. In today's Guitar Works and online, long gone, except as "vintage" items, are the entry-level American-made brands of 1960 such as Harmony and Kay. Replacing them at this lower-price level are various imported instruments bearing such labels as Alvarez, Yamaha, Takamine, and Eastman. Even household brands such as Fender are produced abroad. Without exception, this range of guitars have been manufactured in Asia—in China, Korea, Taiwan, and Indonesia. In addition, Guitar Works carries craft-level, limited-production brands unknown sixty years ago, such as Collings, Bourgeois, Santa Cruz, and Froggy Bottom. Finally, there are several models bearing the label of Taylor, a mass-production company that did not exist earlier. During the past four decades, Taylor Guitars has thrown down the challenge to guitar producers up and down the price chain, offering a wide range of price points from $500 to more than $5,000. The eyes and mind grow a bit dizzy with the profusion of new brand names. Has anything remained more or less the same?

Finally, our eyes light on two brands that were present in the Shreveport store of 1960 as well as Guitar Works today: Martin and Gibson. Ah, there seems to be some continuity in the acoustic guitar landscape! Our inquiring mind wants to know: How is this possible? What explains the longevity, persistence, and endurance of these classic brands that have their roots in the nineteenth century? How have they been able to withstand the competitive pressures and major upheavals in the guitar industry during the past six decades?

Perhaps some initial clues can be found in the quotes heading this chapter. Taken together, these words hint at the opposed imperatives that both companies have had to face and somehow balance throughout this period. On the one hand, Walter Carter, the author of well-regarded books on both companies,[1] underlines the victimizing force of tradition on Martin Guitars—a kind of embedded public expectation that limits the company's ability to do other things besides make its bread-and-butter D-style guitars. On the other hand, Henry Juszkiewicz, who headed Gibson for thirty-two years until forced to resign in 2018, seems to scoff at tradition, denouncing the over-romanticization of guitars while implicitly embracing change and innovation. These, then, are the apparently contradictory constraints—tradition and innovation—that both long-established companies have had to juggle as the competitive landscape has become transformed during recent decades. The question then becomes: How have these companies managed these conflicting pressures?

MARTIN V. GIBSON

A First Cut at Comparison

"If Gibson and its chief competitor in the flat-top market through the years can be compared to automobiles," argue Eldon Whitford, David Vinopal, and Dan Erlewine, "Martin guitars should be likened to a Mercedes-Benz: undeniable quality predictably reproduced in instrument after instrument and sold to a relatively affluent customer. The populist Gibsons are like Chevys and Fords, Studebakers and DeSotos, Packards and Cadillacs, pickups and sedans, coupes and convertibles—different sizes and shapes and prices, a model for everyone, rich and poor alike."[2] Automobile brands and other parallels aside, even a cursory reading of the two companies' histories points to two fundamental differences between them.

The first is the range of their respective product offerings. Although C.F. Martin & Co., founded in 1833 by German immigrant Christian Frederick Martin, has periodically ventured into making such instruments as archtop guitars, mandolins, basses, and even solid-body electric guitars, its output during the past six decades has been almost exclusively flattop guitars.[3] By contrast, if you ask a musician "What do you think about Gibson?," the response is likely to be another question: Do you mean Gibson *mandolins*? Gibson *banjos*? Gibson solid-body *electric guitars*? Gibson *archtop guitars*?, or Gibson *flattop guitars*? Since its 1894 founding by luthier Orville Gibson in Kalamazoo, Michigan, Gibson has become known for such top-of-the-line instruments as the F-5 mandolin, the Mastertone banjo, the Les Paul and SG electric guitars, the L-5 acoustic archtop, the ES-series of jazz archtops, and its J- (for Jumbo) series of flattop guitars (notably the J-45, J-50, J-160E, J-185, and J-200). Beginning in the early 1920s and extending into the early 1960s, Gibson created all of these instruments, and, with the sole exception of the banjos, they remain in production today.

A telling quantitative gauge of this basic difference between the two companies—Martin's focus on flattops versus Gibson's instrumental eclecticism—can be grasped quickly by perusing the most recent "bible" on historical fretted instrument production: *Gruhn's Guide to Vintage Guitars*.[4] Therein is listed all the data available on such instruments made by the major brands, including model types, years of manufacture, serial numbers, etc. The Gruhn Guide's listings for the various Gibson instruments just mentioned consume a total of 216 pages, whereas Martin merits a mere 68 pages, most of which describe its various flattop models (D-18, D-28, D-35, D-45, etc.), along with a handful of other, sporadically manufactured instruments.

A second major difference will be obvious by listing the names of the last six CEOs of the two companies. For Martin,[5] it is:

> C. F. Martin Sr. (1833–73)
> C. F. Martin Jr. (1873–88)
> Frank Henry Martin (1888–1945)
> C. F. ("Fred") Martin III and Frank Herbert Martin (1945–86)
> C. F. ("Chris") Martin IV (1986–present)[6]

For Gibson, the last six CEOs have been:

> Stan Rendell (1968–76)
> Carl Spinosa (1976–78)
> Jim Deurloo (1978–80)
> Marty Locke (1980–86)
> Henry Juszkiewicz (1986–2018)
> James ("JC") Curleigh (2018–present)

This list makes it obvious that the Martin family has kept control of the company since its founding nearly two centuries ago, whereas there has been nary a family member involved in Gibson since the company's founder,

Orville Gibson, got his operation up and running. Since the 1910s, controlling ownership of the Gibson corporation has been held by a succession of ownership groups as well as large, diversified corporations. Perhaps this factor alone—Martin's stability of family ownership versus Gibson's shifting patterns of ownership—gives some hint of the two companies' respective fortunes in the marketplace.

This and the following chapter seek to understand these old guard guitar makers on two levels: first, each company on its own terms (its own history and development), and second, in comparative terms. This chapter focuses on Gibson, while the following chapter examines Martin.

GIBSON

Driven by Innovation?

The foregoing is not to imply in any way that Martin is all about genuflecting to tradition whereas Gibson is all about pushing innovation. Rather, as stated earlier, the challenge for both companies is how to juggle and balance the public's expectations and desire for both traits, even from a single company. A company dedicated solely to preserving and replicating what it has always done can become stultified, lacking creativity and inventiveness, while a company focused solely on bringing new products to market can easily overextend into unknown, risky, and ultimately money-losing endeavors.

Although its overall track record in balancing tradition and innovation is considerably more uneven than Martin's, there is no question that Gibson today can draw on a tradition of making excellent instruments that have stood the test of time. For visual evidence, I need only glance across my study, and my eyes fall on a prized possession: a 1943 J-45 "Banner" flattop, built by a wartime workforce of women in the old Kalamazoo plant.[7] This guitar compares well in terms of sound, playability, and overall craftsmanship with an equally prized possession sitting next to it: a 1947 Martin D-18. My microlevel view of the guitar landscape reinforces a more general sentiment among guitar aficionados that the Gibson brand rests, rightly, on a history—a tradition—of making high-quality acoustic instruments that have achieved iconic status.

That tradition goes back, of course, to the original vision of the company's namesake, Orville Gibson (1856–1918). Having grown up on a farm in upstate New York, the young man, in his mid-twenties, migrated west to seek his destiny, settling eventually in the 1870s in the small southwestern Michigan town of Kalamazoo. A naturally gifted and inventive woodworker, Gibson worked menial jobs while he made instruments in a shop in his living quarters, and by 1898 he had received a patent for making those instruments in a radically new way that gave them both a different shape and superior sonic quality. To that point, the European-derived mandolin had a bowl-shaped back consisting of thin, bent strips of wood glued together side-by-side. (Not for nothing were these instruments colloquially called "tater bugs.")

Orville Gibson's innovation was to create a top and back that were slightly arched and thus needed no internal bracing. This was achieved by carving those components out of solid pieces of wood. In looks alone, Orville's mandolins bore little similarity to the dominant bowl-back model of his day. In his patent application, Gibson also claimed that even the best bowl backs of the day did not have optimum "sensitive resonance and vibratory action," whereas in his own design "every portion of the woody structure seems to be alive with emphatic sound at every touch of the instrument."[8] Hyperbole or not, there is no doubt that Orville Gibson's contributions to stringed-instrument making—which were later extended to the guitar as well—were original, representing, in the words of one authoritative source, "an abrupt departure from accepted styles and the beginning of a new type of instrument."[9]

Although his instruments found public acceptance for their sonic qualities as well as their unusual appearance, Gibson's business skills did not match his creative talent. Needing financial backing to expand production, he joined with five other men (including three lawyers), in 1902, in formally founding the Gibson Mandolin-Guitar Company. Unfortunately, these partners soon took over Gibson's patent rights and gained control over the new company's direction. Within a few years, Gibson became merely a paid employee with a modest salary. Along with declining status within the company that he cofounded, he also suffered from declining health, and the last decade of his relatively short life of sixty-two years—from 1907 to his death in 1918—were mainly spent convalescing back in his home territory in New York state.[10] Since there was no Gibson family successor to the fledgling instrument company, the company's ownership since the early 1900s has been a series of small partnerships and larger corporate overseers—some decidedly more successful than others.

Orville Gibson's departure did not permanently diminish the new company's ability to produce innovative designs, however. Over the course of the twentieth century, the company developed many such instruments including not only the mandolin, but also the mandola, guitar, flattop guitar, banjo, and even the electric guitar. Two periods in Gibson's history during the past century stand out as especially fertile in pioneering new instrument designs. The first was the so-called Loar era from 1919 to 1924, during which a young engineer, Lloyd Loar (1886–1943), served as the company's instrument designer. One such instrument that he developed was the L-5 guitar. Gibson's four previous models of the L-body arch top, which became popular in early jazz styles, had a round or oval sound hole, but Loar replaced that with two violin-style f-holes, which thereafter became the standard for virtually all guitars of all makes. One of the most iconic pictures in all of country music is that of the Carter Family trio, with Maybelle Carter, the sister-in-law of A. P. Carter, chording her trusty L-5 Gibson and appearing ready to start playing "Wildwood Flower" with her signature "Carter scratch" fingerpicking technique.[11]

Loar's key contribution to instrument building came, though, with the mandolin. By the time he arrived at Gibson, the company had been producing mandolins for over two decades, but Loar proceeded to redesign the instrument completely. In his newly christened F-5 Master Model, Loar not only installed, as he had done with the L-5 guitar, two violin-style f-holes in the top, thereby replacing the traditional single oval hole; he also lengthened the neck, which required repositioning the bridge, and changed the internal bracing. Taken together, these changes gave the Loar mandolin "a deeper tonal character . . . and a more powerful sound than any other mandolin on the market."[12] A few years later, an inventive young musician, Bill Monroe, became a virtuoso on his Loar-built mandolin and went on to create a new genre of acoustic-based music—bluegrass—built around rapid-fire solos by mandolin and other instruments. The type of instrument that the "Father of Bluegrass" played, beginning in 1943, was the F-5 model, which became *the* standard for bluegrass, and the so-called Master Model—down to the precise specifications that Loar established—is still produced by Gibson today. The actual instruments that were made during Loar's period at Gibson and bearing his signature on the interior label are considered the Holy Grail of all mandolins, and such instruments typically command about $150,000 in the vintage instrument market.

In the two decades following Loar's departure in 1924, Gibson remained an independent company run by a small ownership group. During this period the company focused on building a new line of flattop guitars to go with its established line. These included small body guitars (L-0 and L-1) along with a series of full-size "jumbo" (Advanced Jumbo, J-45) and even "super jumbo" (SJ-200) guitars. All of these models were well received by the public and worked their way into the hands of blues and country musicians such as Robert Johnson and Ray Whitley.[13] The big innovation among the offerings during the 1930s was the introduction of an electric pickup for amplification, and this began the ES (for "Electric Spanish") series of guitars that became—and still are—prominent instruments in the jazz field.

During the World War II years, demand for musical instruments dropped, and production at the Kalamazoo plant was largely limited to the "Banner" guitars made in part by women workers, referenced earlier. With financial challenges along with the original ownership group having passed from the scene, Gibson was bought in 1944 by Chicago Musical Instruments, a distributor of musical instruments owned by Maurice Berlin. During the early postwar years, Gibson faced obvious needs of modernizing its equipment and replacing its general manager. Especially critical was the latter issue since the general manager since 1924, Guy Hart, was in ill health and not performing to owner Berlin's expectations. So in 1948 Berlin hired a thirty-eight-year-old engineer, Ted McCarty (1910–2001), to replace Hart and run Gibson production.

McCarty, who remained general manager and president from his hiring in 1948 to his resignation in 1966, directed the second truly innovative period in Gibson's history. Recall that the first innovative period, 1919–24, was spearheaded by acoustical engineer, Lloyd Loar, whose chief contributions, in those pre-electric days, were the radical redesign of acoustic instruments, specifically mandolins and guitars. For those innovations Loar has been rightly termed "the single most important and influential Gibson employee of the pre–World War II period."[14] Brilliant though he was, Loar's career at Gibson was also brief. By contrast, McCarty took Gibson through a long period of maintaining quality production across a burgeoning, even bewildering range of instruments, both old and new, acoustic and electric.

As a clear gauge of Gibson's prolific instrument making under McCarty, one need only thumb through the company's 1957 Price List, mailed to all Gibson dealers. This seven-page, single-spaced document catalogs the company's standard instruments and their retail prices. There are, of course, various types and models of guitars: acoustic flattop, electric flattop, classical, carved top (archtop), Electric Spanish (hollow body, solid body, thin line), electric steel, and tenor. Also on the list are the types and models of mandolin, banjo, ukulele, and bass. In all, this list contains a total of seventy-one models of guitar, seven mandolin models, nine models of banjo, and two ukulele models. How, one wonders, could one manufacturing facility produce such a profusion of instruments while maintaining a solid, even revered, reputation in all of them? In addition to overseeing this production, McCarty also engineered the 1957 acquisition of Epiphone, a respected but money-losing maker of arch tops and other instruments, and moved its production to Kalamazoo. Such were McCarty's managerial skills that the best study of his tenure at Gibson is subtitled "Ted McCarty's Golden Era."[15]

The golden jewel in McCarty's crown was not, however, the acoustic guitar, but rather the electric guitar. Yes, McCarty-era acoustic guitars, both flattop and variety, are today considered high-quality instruments, but these longtime mainstays represented continuity from the prewar period rather than dramatic departures.[16] The real money in guitars in the 1950s was in louder . . . and who says louder says built-in electric amplification. An acoustic guitar, even played into a standup microphone, could not compete with amplifying electronics, otherwise known as pickups, that could be installed as a guitar was being built.

As mentioned, Gibson was already well into amplification in the 1930s, with its well-received line of Electric Spanish (ES) guitars. For example, the jazz great Charlie Christian played Gibson's ES-150 (so named for its price of $150 for the guitar and matching amplifier) in the late 1930s. Under McCarty the company further refined the ES line, culminating in the highly regarded ES-335—a thin, semihollow-body guitar with a double cutaway—that remains in production today as a standard instrument in jazz circles.[17] A fancier spinoff of that instrument, ES-355, also became prominent in blues and early rock and roll as the instrument of choice for the likes of B.B. King and Chuck Berry.

In the 1950s, however, the true gold in the hills of guitar amplification lay in *solid-body* electrics. This was the instrument of choice for the pioneers of the new genre of rock and roll. Popular performers such as Bill Haley, Little Richard, Ricky Nelson, and many others were backed by ensembles featuring a solid-body electric guitar.[18] Among the early discovers of that gold was the Californian Leo Fender (1909–1991), who came out with two solid-body electrics—the Telecaster (1950) and the Stratocaster (1954)—both of which became immediately popular.

Gibson under McCarty was right there as well, partnering in 1952 with the guitar maestro Les Paul (1915–2009) to bring out a solid-body model named for him. Gibson's aim was conservative in the sense of creating a guitar whose tone resembled the mellow sounds of Gibson's hollow-body electrics.[19] First produced in 1952, the Les Paul Standard model was designed to be "almost incapable of producing an ugly or unbalanced sound. It was a solid-body electric with none of the raffishness or bellicosity of the Fender; a guitar for tuxedos and velvet-curtained theaters rather than ten-gallon hats and dusty honky-tonks."[20]

Early sales of the Les Paul model were not as robust as expected, and in 1960 Gibson discontinued the original model, replacing it with a radically redesigned model having a double cutaway and painted red. This new model, however, displeased Paul so much that he insisted that his original design remain in production. In the short term, he lost that fight and even wound up promoting the new model, but by 1962 Gibson was producing both the original single cutaway Les Paul model and the redesigned double-cutaway guitar, now dubbed—simply, without Paul's name attached—the SG (for Solid Guitar). By the time McCarty resigned in 1966, both models were flourishing, as were other new solid-body models such as the Flying V, Explorer, and Firebird.[21] As he departed, McCarty could look back on a productive, creative career at Gibson. During his tenure as president, Gibson's instrument production increased from 20,000 units in 1948 to 160,000 units in 1965, and all his additions to Gibson's hollow-body and solid-body electric lines remain in production today.[22]

One could say that McCarty jumped Gibson's ship just in time, as the market for American guitars sagged in the late 1960s with changes in musical fashion and the influx of Japanese-made instruments. The company's total output plummeted from its 1965 high of 160,000 total units to less than 60,000 in 1969.[23] One fallout from this slump was that the company's corporate owner, Chicago Musical Instruments, was purchased by another conglomerate, Ecuadorian Company Limited (ECL), which soon thereafter renamed itself Norlin Musical Instruments.[24] Thus began, according to one historian, "a fall from grace that would last almost 20 years."[25] Under Norlin from 1969 to 1986, Gibson struggled in terms of both its bottom line and its production quality. Gibson's "long decline" during that period included not only a diminished reputation for its guitars but also a risky move in 1974 to expand electric guitar production by building a new factory in Nashville. That ultimately meant closing the Kalamazoo plant that had operated for nearly seventy years, from 1917 until 1984. By then, "Gibson's reputation was at an all-time low, and Norlin was sinking fast. The only question was whether Norlin would take Gibson down with it when it went under."[26]

A side story emerged in 1984–85 as Gibson seemed headed to the next Chapter (11?) in its history. It was—and still is—a story of devotion and persistence; in effect, a second act for the historic Kalamazoo plant at 225 Parsons Street. When Gibson announced its plan to close the plant and move its extant production to Nashville, it told its Kalamazoo employees they could keep their jobs by coming to Nashville as well. For most of them, such a move was out of the question. No matter, Gibson moved ahead, and the Kalamazoo plant was put up for sale. Up to that point, the scenario resembled the classic one that played out in the automobile, textile, and other industries: another (unionized) northern factory closes and moves production to a southern right-to-work state. But a group of now-former Gibson employees were so attached to place and work that they bought the Parsons Street factory and, in 1985, revived production under a newly formed company, Heritage Guitar Inc. Well over three decades later, Heritage Guitars persists, producing well-reputed, Gibson-style solid-body and electric guitars.[27]

As for Gibson under Norlin, as often happens when a company with a broadly recognized name falls on hard times, outside investors swooped in looking to buy cheap, fix up, and resuscitate the enterprise. This happened to Gibson in 1986 when a threesome of so-called Harvard Boys—young

MBA-trained investors—bought Gibson, thereby saving it from insolvency. Writing a few years after this purchase, one analyst—lacking, of course, a crystal ball but having a clear rearview mirror—observed: "If Henry Juszkiewicz, David Berryman, and Gary Zebrowski hadn't purchased Gibson in 1986, there would probably be no new Gibson guitars today."[28] The purchasing part was easy: for a paltry sum of $5 million, the trio took ownership. The fix-up part, however, was another matter. The analyst just cited remarked, in vivid terms, "Gibson was much like a nice-looking car, but with dismantled engine parts in the front seat, transmission in the trunk, and four flat tires—a real 'fixer-upper.'"[29]

Having rescued the company from bankruptcy, the new owners set out to fix up Gibson. Emerging as first among equals within the three-member ownership group was thirty-three-year-old Henry Juszkiewicz, and for the next thirty-two years he remained the company's CEO and public face. Juszkiewicz had big ambitions for his new acquisition. Although these efforts ultimately resulted (spoiler alert) in an actual Chapter 11 process in 2018, no one could accuse Juszkiewicz of lacking vision. That vision—a drive to innovate—can be summarized by "three Re-'s": re-vive, re-locate, and re-brand.

Re-vive... Acoustic Guitar Production in Bozeman, Montana

At the time Juszkiewicz and his partners took over, Gibson's production of its fabled flattop acoustic guitars was basically at a standstill. A few instruments were being made in the Nashville plant, but these were considered to be of poor quality, well below Gibson's historical standards. More generally, the acoustic line was adding little to the company's bottom line; during the two previous decades, electric guitars, led by the Les Paul model, had become Gibson's biggest sellers. Therefore, the first challenge the new management faced was the revival of the acoustic side of the business. The question was how and where to do that?

Opportunity presented itself in 1986 with the appearance of two young luthiers from Montana. In Bozeman, Steve Carlson had founded his own mandolin label and shop, Flatiron Mandolins, in 1979. By the mid-1980s, the small company was doing well, turning out about twelve mandolins and twelve guitars per week. In 1985, Carlson made a key hire, taking on Ren

Ferguson, a native Californian who had moved to Montana some years before and gained a reputation as a skilled craftsman. The next year the two men, aware of Gibson's dismal output of acoustic instruments as well as the company's recent change in ownership, attended the music industry's annual trade show, the National Association of Music Merchants (NAMM). Their intent: to meet the new Gibson owners and propose to produce mandolins for them under the Gibson label.[30] At the Gibson booth, Carlson and Ferguson introduced themselves to Juszkiewicz, then handed him an example of their wares: a Flatiron mandolin that closely resembled a Gibson F-5 model. Juskiewicz took the instrument, looked it over, then said: "I'll sue you and put you out of business." Following that meeting, Carlson received a cease-and-desist letter from Gibson. Any kind of partnership between Flatiron and Gibson looked to be a nonstarter.[31]

Fortunately for both parties, a year later, in 1987, an intermediary convinced Juszkiewicz to buy Flatiron, and a deal was struck. Shortly thereafter, Juszkiewicz asked Carlson and Ferguson to revive *all* of Gibson's acoustic guitar production . . . in Bozeman. This was not just a simple process of shipping tools and equipment from Nashville to Montana. Most of the existing tools and equipment were outmoded, so that for some guitar models, Ferguson and Carlson had to make their own molds. At one point, Carlson drove to Denver and bought $3,500 worth of machines that made tennis rackets but could be converted to guitar making. Finally, a new building was needed. Over the course of 1988 and the first half of 1989, the two Montanans supervised the whole process: both construction of a new factory and the installation of all machinery and equipment.

Finally, in the summer of 1989—two-and-a-half years after the confrontation between Juszkiewicz and the Flatiron duo—the new Bozeman plant was up and running. Within two or three years, says Ferguson, "we were making the best Gibson guitars since the1940s."[32] This perhaps-biased judgment from the principal luthier of this revival was echoed in the words of a visitor to the Bozeman operation in 1992. Observing the new team of workers "collaborating, brainstorming, and setting long-term goals," the visitor commented, "As a result the Gibson flattop, which by 1988 was lingering near death, had been resuscitated with unexpected success, the new guitars exhibiting the quality of the best vintage Gibsons ever made."[33] No less a guitar maestro than

Ren Ferguson, master luthier for Gibson, 1989–2012. Photo by author.

Jorma Kaukonen, lead guitarist for Jefferson Airplane and Hot Tuna, paid the ultimate compliment: "The folks in Bozeman have restored my faith in the American way of life."[34] Within a few years, Gibson's acoustic instrument production, now located fifteen hundred miles from company headquarters in Nashville, had been decisively revived.

Re-locate: . . . Gibson and Epiphone Production Facilities

A second main element of Juszkiewicz's strategy was to relocate production of specific lines of instruments in order to lower costs, both at home and abroad. On the home front, Gibson opened a new factory in Memphis in 2000 to produce its line of ES models—electric guitars with semihollow bodies. Abroad, Gibson had new plans for its subsidiary, Epiphone Guitars. In 1957, the previous CEO Ted McCarty had bought the failing Epiphone, which, along with Martin, had been a chief Gibson rival during the three previous decades. McCarty's plan was to make Epiphone instruments into a lower-priced clone of Gibson's guitar line, and that basic strategy has remained ever since. At first, Epiphones were built in the Kalamazoo plant, but in 1970 the new Norlin management outsourced Epiphone production to Japan. A decade later, Norlin moved its Epiphone manufacturing to Korea, in the process following the typical pattern of companies hopscotching countries in search of lower wage costs. The latest step in this process was a shift to China, which Juszkiewicz made in 2004.

Re-brand . . . Gibson as a Musical Lifestyle Business

By far the most consequential—and ultimately fatal—element of Juszkiewicz's tenure as CEO can be immediately grasped by the headline that appeared in a Nashville news service on June 11, 2013: "Gibson Guitar Corp. changes name to Gibson Brands." No longer was the company that Orville Gibson built a guitar-focused manufacturer of musical instruments. Rather, under Juszkiewcz, it had become a generic brand offering a gamut of music- and audio-related products. Gibson said in a press release that the change was made to "reflect Gibson's expanding range of products and evolving lifestyle orientation." That phrase was a euphemism for saying that Gibson had gone on a buying spree to create a lifestyle-brand image. "Of course," Juszkiewicz said in the press release, "the Gibson Guitar Corporation remains a vital, and crucially important, division of Gibson Brands. . . . But," he continued, "with the recent acquisitions . . . Gibson now encompasses the entire music and sound chain—from the first chord played by a songwriter on a Gibson guitar, until the music reaches the consumer through Onkyo's premium high-fidelity systems."[35] That "music and sound chain," put together through purchases during the preceding decade, included a total of eighteen other companies in addition to Gibson Guitars.[36]

Acquisitions cost money, of course, not all of which Gibson Brands had on hand, and so it borrowed heavily. Unfortunately, the company went too far in 2014 by floating a $375 million bond issue to acquire the consumer electronics division (Woox Innovations) of a Dutch conglomerate, Philips NV. With sales of all its audio products declining, Gibson was unable to pay off the bond issue when it came due in 2018.[37] The only option was to declare bankruptcy, which it did on May 1 of that year.

Obviously, Henry Juszkiewicz had some self-justifying to do, which he did as follows: "I had been driving to build the leading company in the *musical lifestyle business*, combining instruments and audio to engage musicians and music enthusiasts alike. I thought we could do this by acquiring the Philips electronics business. It was a bold and risky move, and I knew it at the time. We were taking on debt to acquire a much larger business. . . . If we had pulled it off, it would have been a huge win for Gibson, and for me personally."[38]

Several phrases stand out in this statement: "driving to build," "a bold and risky move," and "a huge win . . . for me personally." All of these point to Juszkiewicz's forceful character, which had both positive and negative aspects. On the positive side, he could certainly take credit for having resurrected Gibson in the wake of Norlin's mediocre management. As mentioned, he revived acoustic guitar production in Bozeman and relocated Epiphone's operations from Korea to China. On the other hand, under Juszkiewicz's "bold and risky" leadership Gibson became overextended, unable to pay its debts, and went bankrupt.

According to two people who worked closely with him, Juszkiewicz's legacy of ultimate failure can be traced not only to faulty business decisions but also to his imperious, all-roads-lead-to-me management style. For example, Walter Carter, who worked under Juszkiewicz for over a decade as editorial director of marketing, does recognize the CEO's accomplishments: "He had a lean management style. He was able to restore confidence in the Gibson name. He eliminated factory seconds, upgraded the cases, and raised prices on Gibsons." This lean management style, however, had its drawbacks. Carter comments:

> There was very little middle management, and no one had a secretary. If you needed to copy something, you went and copied it. Occasionally you would see that he would fire the marketing director, and then he would become the marketing director until he hired somebody else. He didn't have time to be the marketing director, so marketing suffered. Meanwhile, there are people waiting for decisions to be made. Or he would fire a plant manager and then he becomes the plant manager. He'd do that continually. He bought a restaurant in Nashville,

and he wanted to approve every hire—even busboys. That level of micromanagement was one of the things leading to his downfall.

Micromanagement also had a public aspect, namely that Juszkiewicz insisted on being Gibson's sole spokesperson. Walter Carter adds, "Henry didn't want anybody to speak for the company except him. He didn't want any other 'stars' at Gibson. Even his partner, Dave Berryman, was way in the shadows. Henry was the one and only star of that company. So when somebody like Ren Ferguson rises to the top in terms of public perception, it's good on the one hand, but it's a challenge to Henry on the other hand. Someone with a narcissistic personality has a hard time sharing the glory."[39]

This judgment is echoed by Fred Greene, now a vice president at C. F. Martin & Co. (see Chapter 6), who worked for Gibson and Juszkiewicz for fifteen years, from 1988 to 2003: "Gibson is Henry. Its purpose for being is Henry. That's his prerogative as owner, it's his capital at risk. In some ways, people there are simply tools to be used and the means of getting whatever he perceives that he needs to achieve." According to Greene, making excellent guitars was of secondary importance to Juszkiewicz; the main objective was to transform Gibson into a huge electronics company. Greene goes on to say: "Diversification into other fields started to happen in the nineties. The guitar was rockin' along, and Gibson was doing well, it had money. I think Henry always wanted to run an electronics company, and guitars were a way to do that. The goal was to become a billion-dollar company. When they bought Baldwin, that was when I said, 'I gotta go.'"[40]

Ren Ferguson, the master luthier who guided the revival of Gibson's acoustic guitar production in Montana, reinforces this take on Henry. Reflecting on a theme underlined in Chapter 2—namely the cooperative, sharing subculture that exists among guitar makers—Ferguson says that Juszkiewicz would have none of it: "Among the acoustic people, and much against Henry's level of permission because he would never have given it, there is a cooperative effort among Bob Taylor, Martin Guitars, myself, Collings, Santa Cruz, and Larrivée. We all met regularly at conventions and brainstormed—how do we do this, how can we do things better? Henry was against this—it was against policy. . . . But I tell you, if he had allowed that cooperative engine to work with him at the management level, he would be way ahead of where he is by now."

In the end, Ferguson does give Juszkiewicz his due as a driver of the guitar industry, but with a note of regret and bitterness: "However you feel about him, history will have to concede that without his aggressive nature, we would not have all risen at the same rate. I still admire him. It's a real love-hate relationship. I love what he's accomplished, but I hate how he got there, because he missed the opportunity so many times to accelerate past where we end up. He's hired the most brilliant people in the industry, then used them up like sandpaper, and discarded them before they really had a chance to show their capacity."[41] Walter Carter concurs with Ferguson's view in saying that Juszkiewicz's weakness lay not in lack of vision or business savvy, but in his inability to carry out his plans: "Henry has done a great job of bringing Gibson back from near death in the mid-80s. The company's grown continually since then. It's still a major brand. What I've always said is his vision for the growth of the company and his recognition of trends in instruments and consumer electronics have always been correct. It's his ability to implement that vision where he's fallen short."[42]

In the ensuing bankruptcy proceedings and corporate restructuring to sell off most of the professional and consumer audio companies that Juszkiewicz had acquired, Gibson ended up in the hands of a private equity group, KKR. That group proceeded to name a new management team headed by CEO JC Curleigh, who left the position of president of Levi Strauss & Co.[43] Once in place, the new leadership team made clear its intent to recenter Gibson on its core product: guitars. Declared Curleigh, "Our vision of becoming the most loved, the most played, and the most relevant guitar brand again, is becoming a reality."[44] Accordingly, much of the new CEO's focus has been on quality control. As he puts it: "Attention to quality was number one. I said, 'Let's make fewer guitars—but improve quality.' . . . We're making sure we have the right balance of craftsmanship and automation to deliver the quality people expect."[45]

In becoming the latest in a succession of management groups that have headed the company since Orville Gibson lost control of his creation soon after the Gibson Mandolin-Guitar Company was founded in 1902, the new team led by Curleigh could draw some lessons from the history of the "Henry era." After he had led Gibson's turnaround in the early 1990s by focusing on guitar production, Juszkiewicz speculated on whether Gibson would need to issue bonds or stocks to raise cash for further expansion. He commented: "On the one hand, it's appealing because it would be a quick way to do it. But then I don't know if I could operate the way I want having to answer to other people."[46] In trying to balance the dual constraints of innovation and tradition, Juszkiewicz eventually tilted heavily toward the former by turning Gibson into a lifestyle brand instead of a guitar company. But ultimately, he found that he had to answer to other people . . . with disastrous results.

Chapter 6

MARTIN

Victimized by Tradition?

> And to me, as Martin goes, so goes the industry. Gibson's always been kind of a rogue, almost big guy, but Martin carries everybody with them to some degree, I think.
>
> —*MARK DALTON, HUSS & DALTON GUITARS (AUTHOR INTERVIEW, OCTOBER 8, 2014)*

> In terms of the production of good, playable guitars in lower prices ranges, I think if you injected Chris Martin with truth serum, he'd tell you that Martin has been playing catch up with Taylor since the 1990s.
>
> —*RICHARD JOHNSTON, COFOUNDER, GRYPHON STRINGED INSTRUMENTS, PALO ALTO, CALIFORNIA (AUTHOR INTERVIEW, FEBRUARY 6, 2015)*

I pulled into Nazareth. . . .

The lyrics of The Band's classic song, "The Weight" are in my head as I pull into the parking lot of C.F. Martin & Co., of Nazareth, Pennsylvania.[1] I'm not "feelin' about half-past dead," as in the song, but I am tired nonetheless, having driven 750 miles over two days from my home in Evanston, Illinois. My purpose: to visit Martin's headquarters and factory in an attempt to understand what makes this company tick. The company had kindly granted my request for a visit and arranged two days of tours and conversations with key managers and even the CEO and principal owner himself, Christian ("Chris") Frederick Martin IV. Whatever fatigue I feel is outweighed, so to speak, by anticipation.

Martin, as anyone familiar with the guitar world knows, is the oldest and best-known brand of American acoustic guitars.[2] As mentioned in the previous chapter, the company was founded in 1833 by Christian Frederick Martin, a thirty-seven-year-old instrument maker from Neukirchen, Saxony in Germany, who soon set up shop in New York City. A few years later, in 1839, he relocated to Nazareth, and since then instruments bearing his name have been crafted here. This is a record of longevity, by one family in one place, that no other American company can match. Today, with the sixth generation of the family still owning and overseeing operations, Martin maintains its reputation for fine craftsmanship, even as it produces more than five hundred guitars per day using both hand tools and advanced technology. With its instruments having been played by such figures as Elvis Presley, Merle Haggard, Eric Clapton, Paul Simon, and Stephen Stills, the company can claim, without hyperbole: "Embraced by artists all over the world, the Martin guitar has helped define virtually all genres of music, from classical and country to blues, folk and acoustic rock."[3]

As I walk into the reception office, I recall my imaginary visits to the Shreveport and Evanston guitar stores, with sixty years separating them. In both visits, Martin guitars are on display. What, I wonder, explains such endurance, such survival power? In particular, how, during the past six decades, has the company been able to withstand the competitive pressures and major upheavals that constitute what I have termed the transformation of the guitar industry?

As I contemplate those questions, I also reflect on the two factors that both Martin and Gibson have had to juggle and balance: innovation and tradition. As we saw in the previous chapter, one can reasonably conclude that Gibson's Achilles' heel during the past four decades was an overemphasis on innovation: the willingness to take too many risks in the name of expansion and acquisition. Henry Juszkiewicz's drive to reinvent Gibson as a lifestyle brand rather than a mere instrument maker ultimately failed, producing bankruptcy, restructuring, and new ownership. As for Martin, I recall the words of an authority on guitars, Walter Carter, cited in the previous chapter: "Martin is still dreadnought flattops. When they've tried to do other things . . . they didn't sell. A company can become victimized by its own tradition."[4] Is that true? How can you say that a family-owned manufacturer that has survived and even thrived for nearly two centuries is a "victim"?

I could well imagine that Chris Martin might take issue with Carter's statement. In any case, I will soon find out. I am here, to find out how Martin's leadership team views the guitar world and their company's place within it. More specifically, I'm seeking to understand how Martin tries to balance the two types of pressure just mentioned: on the one hand, market pressure on companies to innovate and create new products; on the other hand, the public's expectation that Martin pay respect to its long tradition of excellent acoustic instrument making. This involves consideration of such aspects as its product offerings, workforce, use of technology, and acquisition of materials.

WHAT MARTIN MAKES

A Victim of Tradition?

My first meeting is with the chief himself, Chris Martin, the sixth generation of the Martin family to own and run the company. Born in 1955, Chris Martin became CEO in 1986, at the tender age of thirty-one, and now, as I sit down with him, he has over three decades of leadership experience under his belt. I notice that he still projects youthful dynamism, along with a friendly informality. Encouraging me to call him Chris, he and I quickly fall into a spirited conversation, which I lead with a classic question: What do you consider your main contributions to Martin and the guitar industry?[5]

With no hint of victimhood regarding Martin's tradition of making acoustic guitars, Chris, in fact, embraces that focus on the acoustic guitar. But he also says he understands the criticism that has come his way for having such a focus: "I think, having watched my father and seen the industry, what I've enjoyed doing—and I've been criticized for it—is focus. I came to the realization that the majority of the people who know about the Martin brand want something from us that we're very good at doing, and so that's what I try to keep everyone focused on. Let's remember, what we're known for is high quality, flattop, steel-string, acoustic guitars. Fortunately, that's kept us busy enough."

Martin's remark about "having watched my father," refers to the years 1970 to 1982, when his dad, Frank Herbert Martin, ran the company, under the watchful eye of *his* own father, C. F. ("Fred") Martin III. During that period, Frank Martin embarked on a series of acquisitions that ultimately failed. In most histories of the company, he is portrayed as an ambitious but hard-drinking, erratic businessman who nearly mismanaged the company into bankruptcy.[6] Chris took the cautionary lessons of his father's failed acquisitions to heart and makes no apologies about that:

> What I've been criticized for is I've never made an acquisition. I've had a couple of interesting partnerships—the Backpacker, the X series—but I will not give my colleagues much chance to speculate on how green the grass is across the street. If we stop paying attention to our lawn, Bob and Kurt [Taylor Guitars] are going to open up the champagne and say "Chris is distracted, and that's exactly what we want." And I do not want to get distracted from the business at hand, which is making the best flattop, steel-string guitars that we can, in large volumes. That's what separates us from a lot of other people. There are a lot of good guitars being made today. If you can't make a good guitar, get out of the way, don't even bother. But I think we've figured out how to do it, more, than anybody else, especially at our price points. Bob [Taylor] makes a good guitar, but I've heard they struggle to sell guitars over $5,000. We're relatively successful selling very expensive guitars.

Later in the day, I meet with another of Martin's top managers, Chief Product Officer Fred Greene, whose job encompasses everything related to product (strategy, conception, development, innovation, management). In his mid-fifties and with Martin since 2004, Greene backs up Martin's emphasis on keeping the focus on what they do best: making flattop acoustic guitars. Greene, it turns out, is well positioned to talk about Martin's big picture in comparative perspective. As mentioned in Chapter 5, Fred worked for Gibson for well over a decade before coming to Martin; there, he supervised the production of Les Paul model guitars at Gibson's Nashville plant. When I ask him to compare the two companies, he talks first about key differences in what each company produces:

> The Gibson brand is an incredible brand in terms of strength, but very different from Martin. There's only one brand that has history and significant models,

important product, in acoustic guitars, electric guitars, mandolins, banjos, amplifiers, arch tops. Nobody covers that spectrum of product except Gibson. These are all incredible things. Fender is solid-body guitars and amps. With Martin, it's ukuleles and guitars—acoustic guitars only. Martin is probably the most narrow of the bunch, which is why it's consistently been the highest-quality product over a long period. Martin has never been interested in the world domination aspect that Gibson has had, since Gibson is a large business and not a family business.

Giving his former employer Gibson its due, Fred Greene is also quick to dismiss any notion that Martin's "narrowness" or focus on acoustic guitars is in any way opposed to innovation. For Fred, the distinction between tradition and innovation is a false one; Martin, he says, embodies and embraces both aspects. In our discussion, he makes two central points. First, from its origins, C. F. Martin & Co. was an innovator. The idea is simple and obvious: to become a traditional brand, a company must first establish its bona fides as a producer to be emulated. That means originality—innovation—at the very outset. According to Greene,

> Martin's been around so long, I think people sort of take it for granted—they don't understand how important it is. When you look at X-bracing, or just look at a dreadnought, or a double-0 (00) or a triple-0 (000) model—that's the absolute foundation for every acoustic guitar ever made in the United States. They all start with a Martin. Even Bob Taylor—his first guitars were dreadnoughts. From there he was able to form his own path, but his own path started, as a home base, with Martin. Much like a Xerox machine or Kleenex—these are things we don't think of as brands anymore. Our guitar shapes are like that.

Fred Greene makes a second point about tradition and innovation, namely that even given the broad public perception of his company as traditional, Martin continually strives to improve the craftsmanship and sound of its instruments, and that requires a constant attention to innovation. But innovation does not take place in a vacuum. The impulse to innovate cannot be separated from the imperative of turning a profit, and so Martin, like every guitar company, must survive in a highly competitive market even as it brings forth both improved current products and new, potentially risky ones.

Although the company does not state it as such, Martin's survival strategy for the twenty-first century is a kind of three-legged stool. For brevity's sake, I will refer to these as Standard-Classic, Navojoa-made, and Custom-Authentic. The first of these is the company's bread and butter, all made in the main factory in Nazareth, the full range of Martin's standard, classic models: its dreadnoughts (D-series—D-18, D-28, D-35, D-41, D-42, D-45), along with its 0, 00, 000, and OM series, and a small number of other standard models—twenty models in all.[7] Martin's innovations in this realm are marginal, mainly having to do with adoption of CNC technology where possible and various combinations of woods, finish, body type, electronics, and the like. These are not for the beginner or faint of pocketbook; MSRPs in 2022 range from $2,800 to $6,400.

The Navojoa-made guitars are all produced in Martin's own factory in the Mexican state of Sonora, about five hundred miles south of Tucson near the

Martin worker bending sides. Photo by author.

Gulf of California. In the 1970s Martin acquired Darco Strings, which were already being produced in this facility, to supplement its own Nazareth-made strings. During the next two decades, with increasing competition from imports and domestic producers such as Taylor, Martin decided, in the early 1990s, to begin production of lower-end guitars in its Navojoa plant. Newly designed instruments—mainly guitars but also ukuleles—have issued from there ever since. The company's director of international manufacturing, Jen Weiss, clearly states the plant's raison d'être: "We need to be able to compete with all the less expensive brands throughout the world."[8]

The first new guitar to come out of Navojoa was the Backpacker, an inexpensive (initially under $200), thin-body, travel guitar that proved popular. In the past three decades, Martin has developed other new lines and models, notably the X-series (high-pressure laminate, or HPL) and the Road Series guitars. As for the former, the company touts the durability and affordability of its nine models. The X-series guitars, states Martin's website, "are made for musicians that want the freedom to play how, where, and when they want without breaking the bank. Delivering legendary Martin tone, the X Series will easily make the transition from the couch, to the stage, to the great outdoors." Guitars in this series typically retail, in 2022, from $500 to $700.[9] In contrast, the Road Series could be considered a price/quality option between the lower-priced X-series and the Standard-Classic guitars made in Nazareth. Taking advantage of Mexico's lower labor costs and using less rare tone woods such as sapele or mutenye, instead of mahogany or rosewood, Martin can offer a solid-body guitar with onboard electronics at a 2022 list price between $900 and $1,600.

Finally, if the Mexico-made instruments are Martin's efforts to innovate down market in the face of intense competition and a slowly growing market, the company has also attempted to innovate by going up market, in both quality and price, in a paradoxical reversion to—and reverence for—the past. In large measure, this is a market-driven effort to respond to and compete with the high-end guitars being made by the new lutherie movement discussed in Chapter 2. In the early 2000s, Martin created a custom shop within its Nazareth plant, whose main task is to design and produce what is termed the "Authentic Series." These are guitars made the old way, by hand with premium woods that exactly match the specifications, to the millimeter, of the instruments Martin produced during the so-called Golden Era of the 1930s. Getting the custom shop and the Authentic Series up and running was a chief task of Fred Greene when he joined Martin in 2004.

Greene is quick to give credit to Chris Martin for this attempt to challenge the new luthiers on their own field of small-batch, true-craft production. Martin, according to Greene, was driven by his belief that craft luthiers and small shops such as Bourgeois, Santa Cruz, and Collings were trading on the idea that they were building "better Martins than Martin." Greene says that Santa Cruz, for example, has its Pre-War series, all of which have classic OM and Dreadnought shapes à la Martin. These, he claims are "dead knockoffs" of Martin-designed instruments from the 1930s.[10]

To be sure, Fred says, there was flattery because the new luthiers clearly recognized that the old Martin way was the best way to build guitars. At some point, however, that flattery became invidious because it implied that Martin today had lost the touch that it once had. Greene contends, "So our internal feeling was to show everybody that just because we're a bigger company doesn't mean we can't build guitars by hand, and that nobody builds a better Martin than Martin. And so we wanted to go out and do things that they [the new luthiers] weren't willing to do. They were taking some shortcuts and not talking about it so much. For example, they were making bolted-on necks, but they covered it up so you couldn't see the bolt. We wanted to show that we could go back and do the hard stuff, stuff that people don't like to do because it's just hard. We could not only do it, but we could it in big numbers."

How did Martin do the "hard stuff"? As mentioned, one of Fred Greene's first jobs was to create Martin's custom shop to build instruments comparable to those classics built seventy years earlier. He put together a team of four experienced builders, including one, Dale Eckert, who had worked at Martin for forty-seven years. Their first assignment: to replicate a 1937 D-18 guitar. This meant not only creating the instrument to spec (body design and dimensions, wood types, bracing, etc.), but also doing that in the tried-and-true, painstakingly slow, exacting, handcrafted way. At this point, old-school hand builders can go geek, detailing such matters as the use of hide glue, forward-shifted, scalloped X bracing for the top, and a T-bar instead of a truss rod for the neck, with all necessary parts made and installed by hand.

Unfortunately, there was no seventy-year-old Adirondack spruce lying around to use for the soundboard—the top and underlying attached bracing—so Martin did the next best thing: it used its own process of heat drying, or torrefaction, to create both the visual and aural effects of aging for this crucial component of the guitar. Torrefaction reduces the wood's moisture to near zero and in the process both yellows the spruce's light color and increases the wood's vibrational qualities, causing the torrefied top, once installed on the guitar, to appear aged and to produce a fuller, more resonant sound. Martin contracted with a local company that uses this process to treat outdoor lumber (for decks, fences, etc.), and then had that company modify its process to suit Martin's specifications. Martin has now dubbed this process as its Vintage Tone System, and it is now standard for the Authentic Series.[11]

Since its inception in 2005, this series, according to Fred Greene, has never crafted more than nine hundred guitars in a given *year*, compared with the company's total output (of both Nazareth and Navojoa production) of about seven hundred guitars *per day*. But volume is not the point, Greene says. The point of the custom shop's Authentic Series is to demonstrate to the guitar-buying public that Martin can not only compete on quality with any of the builders in the new lutherie community, but also produce instruments comparable to those of the celebrated Golden Age. Today, Greene implies, it takes innovation to replicate tradition, and Martin can do justice to both at the same time. A "victim" of Tradition? Martin's chief product officer would beg to disagree.

HOW MARTIN WORKS

Community and Commitment

To grasp how Martin works, I come quickly to understand, I must take account of where its operation is located and how that community and C. F. Martin & Co. itself developed. Start with basics: according to the US Census Bureau, Nazareth's population has remained remarkably stable over time. In 1930 its population was 5,505, and in 2020 it was 6,053, which was the highest in those ninety years. During that entire period, the decennial census stayed approximately within those limits, with a low of 5,443 (1980) and a previous high of 6,023 (2000). Nazareth lies in the Lehigh Valley of eastern Pennsylvania, with the larger towns of Allentown (about 120,000 population), Bethlehem (75,000), and Easton (27,000) all within twenty miles to the east and south.

At the beginning of our conversation, Chris Martin schools me on the history and sociology of the region. One of my first questions has to do with his employees: How, if at all, has the workforce changed since you became CEO in 1986? He replies that in his early days the workforce was about 90 percent male, but that changed greatly during the next two decades, and it is now about 50–50 male-female. He then recounts a story about changes in the region's work force, and I begin to understand how the concept of community plays such an important role here.

Martin begins by saying that few hourly workers will relocate from elsewhere to come work at Martin, so the company must largely rely on the local labor force. In "the old days,", he says, implying the decades before and after World War II: "Every little town in this part of Pennsylvania had what was called a blouse mill. So Dad would get up, early, and Mom would get him off to work—to go heavy, at Bethlehem Steel. Then she'd get the kids off to school, then she'd walk to the blouse mill and sew sleeves on shirts—like a banshee, because it was piece rate. They would stop around 2:30, so she would go home, deal with the kids—here's your snack—and she gets dinner on the table. Then next day she does it all over again." Then Chris adds, "But all that work—both the steel jobs and the blouse jobs—went away."

But many women remained in the area who had factory experience in the blouse mills, and these women became a theretofore untapped source of labor. When Martin experienced an upsurge in demand in the early 1990s following the success of MTV's *Unplugged* series of acoustic concerts, they wanted to hire more workers. "That was a boom, and women showed up," Martin says. He would ask the candidates whether they knew "anything about wood." The answer was most often no. He would then ask: "Have you ever worked in a factory?" And the answer was usually "Yes, I started working in the blouse mill at fourteen." Then Chris would say: "You know how to work in a factory, that's a good start." He concludes his history lesson by noting that the women's prior experience in the blouse mills more than made up for any lack of woodworking background, and the transition to an equal labor force of female and male workers has worked out fine.

Once hired, workers have a ninety-day probationary period, during which they can be let go for any reason. "The first 90 days is rigorous. It's almost like boot camp," Chris says. "The reason we're careful in the beginning is that it's very possible you're going to stay until you retire, so we want to make sure the relationship is appropriate for both of us. We don't want to waste your time either." One of the rites of passage of a new hire, he tells me, is the job of sanding. Some applicants say they want to work at Martin because they want to learn how to build a guitar. Chris typically says to them: "Well, over the course of your career, that's very possible, but initially you're going to learn to build part of a guitar, over and over. Are you into that? If you can get through the sanding, you'll be all right. It's not romantic, but the end product is romantic, and you're part of it."

Chris goes on to say: "What we want you to do is figure out the job, learn how to do it at a very high level of quality, repetitively and efficiently. And we'll give you the tools, the training and support because we have a goal in mind—that this job should produce this many parts in this much time. If you get into that sweet spot, you're good to go. Everyone wants you to get there because—that weakest link in the chain—we're part of a department that needs to get this many guitars moved to the next department . . . and we need you to do your part."

I follow up Chris's remark with a question about how Martin deals with the ups and downs of market demand. He begins by denouncing a common practice in publicly traded companies whereby the CEO will lay off workers during a slack period and then be rewarded by the board with a bonus for improving efficiency. This is "the worst way to run a company," Chris says. Ultimately, he contends, this kind of behavior becomes a morale issue:

> I've seen layoffs come way too quickly when a company decides they have too much stuff. Well, all right, who do you lay off? Is it last in, first out? So whoever you lay off, I'm assuming that up to that point, they were relatively productive. So you're telling someone who yesterday was productive, "today, you're done." They might not come back. You invested in them, you've asked them to go home and wait for a phone call. And when you call them, they may say "I've got another job." So all that investment is gone, plus the feeling of "keep your head down, don't make any waves, hopefully the boss won't even know you're here, because you might be next." So I think it's a morale issue internally when you begin that. Everyone thinks they might be next.

To avoid layoffs, Martin offers employees a combination of bonuses and profit sharing. These incentives go up and down with the company's performance, and so provide a financial cushion to cut back in hours in slack times. Moreover, when people are hired, they are asked if they would be willing to work forty-four hours a week, Monday through Thursday—with the four hours over forty paid as overtime. These and other measures build in some flexibility into the deployment of its work force so that Martin does not have to resort to layoffs during periods of decreasing demand.

Both Chris Martin and Fred Greene stress two other distinctive aspects of work life at Martin: opportunities for advancement and the commitment of its workers. First, Greene underlines the permeability between the salaried managers and the hourly workers, stating that most of his managers in the

Martin worker installing kerfing on inside of rim with glue and clothespins. Photo by author.

various departments (bodies, fingerboards, necks, etc.) were once hourly employees. "They've come up through the company. I and the plant manager came from outside the company, but everyone else in the management team has flowed up." He continues: "Everybody gets trained in everything, and ultimately it's assimilation. Can you work with other people? There's nowhere to hide, the building is not that big." Once one has advanced to a department head, they can also move into other departments to gain broader managerial experience. For example, the people who work in sales or marketing were once department managers. As Greene puts it: "It all flows from the manufacturing team out."

Fred goes on to say that Martin's work environment is "Old School and not the way the world works anymore. . . . Here it's an apprenticeship. You come in and you pay your dues. You work on the line, and you love what you're doing, and you understand how these guitars go together, and it's important to you . . . or you don't. For some people, it just becomes a job. They get really good at doing one thing, and they're satisfied to do that and feed their family. And we need those roles—not everybody can be a department manager or a plant manager. But for those who do, there's opportunity, as long as the business is growing, and they show an aptitude. By being here awhile and doing your job, you're also showing your commitment to the organization and if you can fit in with the team.

Based on his long experience at both Gibson and Martin, Fred Greene goes on to compare the work environment in each, relating this ultimately to differences in the nature of the local community and the commitment of the workforce. At Gibson in Nashville, he reports, one had to push people to do good quality work: "We were constantly testing and inspecting quality into the product." Fred attributes this issue to the transient nature of the workers there, who tended not to stay very long. Many of them, he says, were working musicians who took the job to pay the bills but whose main goal was "to go out and play country music."

It's a different world in Nazareth, Greene says. Compared to Gibson in Nashville, Martin has "a very closed environment feel. While it's welcoming to visitors from outside, in terms of working here, it very much feels like a closed community. I won't say outsiders aren't welcome, it's just going take you awhile before they trust you. 'You're not from this area, are you?' After

10 years, it's sort of like 'ay, he's okay.' It has that feel to it—like a fraternity."
Many people come to work at Martin as teenagers with no intention of ever leaving. Fred also notes many family connections, with "brothers and sisters, and their moms and their dads and their wives and their husbands—all working here—and trying to get their kids jobs for the summer. So there becomes a kind of 'don't embarrass me' mentality."

This mentality, Greene says, also translates into a "It's not good enough" commitment to one's work. With just a hint of complaint, he states: "The hourly employees are so picky, so quality conscious, that we're basically arguing with them, saying 'Look, that's good enough. I need a magnifying glass to see the speck on the down side of the guitar, which nobody will ever in a million years find, unless you told them it was there. I'll say 'It's okay, trust me.' And then they'll argue with that—are you sure, etc. It's the complete opposite of Gibson, because they've been here so long. They don't want to be the guy responsible for the slip, because they've been there before."

HOW MARTIN USES TECHNOLOGY

The Human Element

How to use technology in the making of guitars? This has been a fundamental question in the history of guitar making, and it remains relevant today. Although evidence is lacking from the nineteenth century, I can easily imagine luthiers' reactions when one of their number first used a bandsaw to cut the guitar body's top and back. I can well envision the outrage: What are they doing using a *machine* for that? Guitars must be made by hand—so use a hand saw, dammit! Today, the question among high-end guitar makers is not *whether* to use labor-saving technologies, but rather *when and how*.

With just a few exceptions, the day of totally handcrafted guitars is largely over. Even boutique builders such as Richard Hoover and Dana Bourgeois extol the use of CNC machines for certain operations. The crucial questions remain, however: What, if anything, is being lost in terms of human woodworking skill in the deployment of automated and/or numerically controlled technologies? What is the impact on overall employment of the adoption of automated technologies? If such technologies are, by definition, labor saving, then doesn't that mean fewer workers are needed to produce consistently precise instruments?

Who could be a better person to address these questions than the company's chief technology officer, Gregory (Greg) Paul, who has been with Martin since 1997. As we settle in for an interview in his office, Greg makes no apologies for Martin's long-standing openness to considering whatever technologies might be appropriate for its mission of making excellent instruments. He says: "People always ask us: 'When did Martin start to embrace technology? Was it in the '90s?' And I always answer 'No, it was in the '70s . . . the 1870s!' Our organization has always maintained a great balance between handcraftsmanship and technology." Paul explains that in the nineteenth century the original Martin factory in Nazareth added a steam plant that drove a wheel that powered a belt that provided energy for sawing, drilling, and sanding. How's that for automation? he seems to imply.

I then ask a purposefully provocative question: Isn't automated technology bad for workers by eliminating their skills and ultimately making them redundant and therefore replaceable by a machine? Not surprisingly, Greg Paul defends Martin's use of such technology, but he argues that for Martin it's not just a question of cost cutting and precision replicability; it's also a question of what is best from the workers' perspective. First, there is the ergonomic factor. There are many repetitive tasks in making a guitar, many of them requiring a modicum of skill while stressing the human body. The "Martin way," he says, has always been to search for technological ways to do those tasks. He uses the example of polishing: "Our application of technology has always been to aid our craftspeople by giving them the ability to focus on the important things that are going on. So where there's a repetitive kind of work to do, particularly where that has repetitive motion involved and ergonomic challenges, we work to deal with that. Take polishing guitars—it's physically difficult and involves a lot of wrist, elbow, and shoulder. So we've brought in robotic polishing machines. It's all to help people." Ultimately, Paul says, Martin's intention is to "help people" work longer: "We have folks who start here as teens, and we have people who routinely wrap up their career in their eighties. People come here, and they tend to stay. We want to make them safe and comfortable while they work here."

Beyond the justification of advanced technology for the purposes of improving workers' ergonomics and longevity, Paul stresses that Martin's deployment of such technology never results in worker displacement; workers are never laid off when automated machines are brought in. On this point, he is categorical: "We don't use technology to displace people—we never displace people. When we bring in automated equipment, there's always been a commitment to ensuring that those folks can learn how to bring their craft and their art to that piece of equipment, if they wish. Or, if they're interested in doing something else, we find them some other work that they would like to do."

Although I cannot independently verify Greg Paul's claim that no worker is ever displaced by new technology, it does stand as company policy, which was confirmed in my interviews with other Martin officials. Fred Greene, for example, says, "We have a philosophy about buying high-tech machinery. I can buy any machine I want, and Chris is fine with it. I won't say there's an open checkbook, but it's about as close to an open checkbook as one could want . . . as long as I displace no jobs. I can't lay anybody off." For Greene, the deployment of new technology has to do with market issues of supply and demand: "I'm really not any more efficient, because my labor numbers haven't moved at all. I've just bought a new machine. So generally when new machinery comes in, I've got to increase capacity. And if the machine helps me do that, I can redeploy the labor to help me someplace else. If capacity isn't needed or we're not growing, then I don't have a lot of impetus to add technology."

Finally, I asked Chris Martin himself about the desirability and impact of using advanced technologies (robotics, automation, etc.) in what has traditionally been largely handcraft production. Chris is unapologetic about using technology when it can make a better instrument: "My ancestors would have killed if they had had the access to technology that I do. They would have embraced it, particularly early in the process. The more efficiently and accurately you can make those parts, the better they fit together. The hand is still an integral part of what we do." Ultimately, the issue is how to integrate new technologies into the process of handcrafting: "Our feeling is: let's take a look. If it's appropriate, and we can afford it, let's see if we can integrate it. Again, I don't lay people off. If we bring in a machine and if you can't learn how to work with that machine, we will find other work for you. You are not made redundant."

Martin follows up with a lesson he learned, almost literally, at his daddy's knee. His father, Frank Herbert Martin (President, 1970–82), was, according to Chris, a "technology enthusiast," but in one instance his dad failed miserably in the task of integrating technology. Frank Herbert bought expensive Italian-made tooling machines for the Martin factory in the early 1980s; however, he failed to consult with or integrate the workers who were doing the jobs the machines were designed to do. In three different instances, these machines were brought in and they failed at the job they were designed to do: fill in pores in the wood. Chris says there were "endless meetings of engineers in closed rooms," and the engineers spent hours tinkering with the machines, trying to get them to work. In the meantime, the workers continued to do the pore-filling tasks by hand, and they never learned how to use the machines. The machines ended up being left on the floor, bought but unused—"monuments to technological failure," says Chris. The clear lesson for Chris is that you have to bring the workers themselves into the process of adopting and adapting new technologies.

HOW MARTIN USES MATERIAL

Sustainably?

Everyone in the acoustic guitar industry is acutely aware of growing material scarcity, especially of the best tone woods: the lumber that make up the critical sound chamber of the guitar—its top, back, and sides. The tonal properties of these woods largely determine the sound that issues forth from the chamber once the strings are struck and their vibrations activate the top. At the top of the scarcity list are the premium woods of the recent past, most notably Adirondack, or red, spruce (for tops) and Brazilian rosewood (for backs and sides). These woods have become difficult, if not impossible, to secure.

In the case of Adirondack spruce, the original supply in the eastern part of the United States has been heavily depleted. In its place, most American luthiers have gone to another variety, Sitka spruce, that grows plentifully near the northwestern coast of North America from southeastern Alaska down to northern California. Sitka spruce is considered a good substitute for Adirondack spruce, but for connoisseurs it just doesn't have the same cachet, or sound, of Adirondack, and so guitar makers typically demand a premium for it, as much as a $2,000–$3,000 more per instrument.

As for Brazilian rosewood, it was used widely for high-end guitars from the mid-1850s into the 1960s, but in 1969 the government of Brazil banned export of whole logs because the trees were near depletion. Brazil's unilateral action has been supplemented by subsequent international agreements. Notably, during the early 1970s many other nations recognized the looming danger of resource depletion and environmental destruction throughout the world, and in 1973 a group of eighty countries signed the Convention on International Trade in Endangered Species of Wild Fauna and Flora.

As its name implies, this agreement, commonly called CITES ("sigh-tees") regulates—and in many cases, bans—exports of various types of fauna and flora, including Brazilian rosewood. Today, a total of 183 nations have committed to CITES regulations, and Brazilian Rosewood is on a list—so-called Appendix I—that includes "species that are the most endangered among CITES-listed animals and plants. They are threatened with extinction and CITES prohibits international trade in specimens of these species except when the purpose of the import is not commercial, for instance for scientific research."[12] The common substitute for Brazilian rosewood is rosewood from the eastern part of India. As with spruce, this widely available and perfectly acceptable substitute cannot claim the cachet or command the price of what is considered the best variety of rosewood. For two guitars that are similar in every other respect, a guitar with Brazilian rosewood back and sides will typically cost at least $4,000 more than its counterpart made of Indian rosewood.

These basic facts of life about the contemporary acoustic guitar world only begin to frame the broader issues of access to essential materials, and all guitar makers must wrestle with such questions as: Can we continue to acquire, in the near term, the best guitar woods at a reasonable price? What about the long run—can we raise and harvest the best woods in a sustainable way? In the meantime, what are some alternative woods can we use besides the classical ones that we've always used—spruce, mahogany, rosewood, maple, and ebony?

These questions are also on my mind in my Martin visit, and at the end of the day I sit down with the person most knowledgeable about them: Martin's vice president for supply-chain management, Nick Colesanti. I start with a basic query: What keeps you up at night thinking about Martin's ability to continue acquiring the best woods possible? Colesanti begins by describing the broad context. He underlines, for example, the swings, uncertainties, and vagaries of the global wood market, along with the sliver of that market that Martin and other guitar makers are interested in. Nick notes that only about 1.0 to 1.5% of all the wood that is being harvested around the world has the qualities suitable for making a guitar. Suitability in this case means that the wood they purchase must have certain traits in terms of species, grain characteristics, size, and aesthetic qualities. The obvious point is that guitar companies such as Martin are market takers rather than market makers—veritable saplings in a huge, towering forest.

This means, according to Nick, that the availability of suitable wood for a consumer such as Martin depends heavily on world demand for wood. Put simply, when world wood demand is strong, Martin has little difficulty securing the mahogany, spruce, maple, rosewood, and ebony it needs. When world demand sags, however, and these needed woods are either unavailable or too expensive, Martin scrambles for alternatives. Colesanti cites such a downturn a few years before when mahogany supplies became scarce, and Martin had to substitute Spanish cedar and other woods. Martin's vulnerability to shifts in the global wood supply means that the company must be forever adaptive, both in the immediate term and longer term.

Nick then details Martin's efforts to adapt, starting with its efforts to preserve the prized trees and forests that are under increasing threat of clear-cutting and depletion in developing countries. Martin's actions in this regard are twofold—with one effort being mandatory, the other voluntary—with an overall goal of promoting forest preservation and sustainable use of wood resources. First, who says forest preservation says "CITES," since that is the Convention's very purpose. For Martin, this goes well beyond the Brazilian rosewood case, given that almost all the woods it uses, except for spruce and maple, come from abroad. Complying with the Convention's regulations regarding the export of these woods, Colesanti says, takes much time and money: "I can tell you that the level of effort has increased exponentially, the amount of paperwork, the documentation, the time in country." Without a note of complaint, however, he quickly adds: "I think it's for the better, because I think the supply chains have cleaned up the atrocities that were going on—whether it be slave labor, people going around the law, abusing people, not paying people what they should be paid, ruining the environment. It's a great side benefit. From an environmental perspective, it's been a good thing."

Beyond complying with—and being held to account for—international strictures on illegal trade in specified woods, Martin goes a step beyond by voluntarily subscribing to certain forest-management principles and practices. Unlike Taylor Guitars, Nick says, "We don't go out and buy land, but we're active in other ways," notably the company's commitment to the work of the Forest Stewardship Council. The FSC, founded in 1993, is a multinational organization whose website claims it to be "the leading catalyst and defining force for improved forest management and market transformation, shifting the global forest trend toward sustainable use, conservation, restoration, and respect for all."[13]

FSC's modus operandi centers on a certification process whereby the primary actors with a stake in global forest management can gain a kind of Good Housekeeping Seal—viz., FSC certification—by adhering to sustainable forest-management practices as specified by the Council itself. The primary actors—those from one end of the wood supply chain to the other—include nations, special status groups within nations (e.g., native peoples within nations who have sovereignty rights within their territory), wood extractors and suppliers, and end users. As one such end user, Martin maintains its FSC certification by adhering to the organization's recommendations for how it acquires and verifies the wood it brings to the factory. Moreover, says Colesanti, "we actively promote to our supplier base their involvement with the FSC, so that they can get chain-of-custody certification if they're handling the wood, and they can get general forestry certification if they're growing and harvesting the wood."[14]

CONCLUSION

At the end of my interview-filled day at Martin as I prepare to pull out of, rather than into, Nazareth, I reflect on what I have learned. I must quickly remind myself that a one-day visit with a handful of highly placed company officials does not a full, objective analysis make. Was a message being spun by officials anxious to present a happy face and happy talk to an outsider? I cannot definitively answer this question since I must rely on my own impressions. My goal is not to arrive at some completely objective truth. That would be impossible in any case, and not the focus of this book. My aim in this instance is to explore Martin's story—its leaders' perspectives, values, and approaches related to their central task of guitar making. As in all my on-site visits and interviews, the first question I want to ask is: In the highly competitive world of guitar makers, how do you consider your company and its products *distinctive* compared with those of other guitar makers?

I come away with two main conclusions, both connected to the person at the top: Christian F. Martin IV, born in 1955 and the sixth-generation member of the family to head the company since its founding in 1833. The first conclusion is the universal, to-all-appearances genuine sentiment regarding Chris Martin that was expressed by the other people I interviewed. I never fished for such sentiment by asking my interviewees what they thought of him; rather, their perspectives came out unsolicited in the course of our conversations. A typical example came from Nick Colesanti at the end of my interview: "You asked me what makes our company distinctive. I can tell you unequivocally, it's Chris Martin. Everything that we do, our entire philosophy, the way we walk, talk, think, evaluate situations . . . ultimately, all comes from him. Right now he's the X factor here that drives this company. This is coming from many hours of hearing him, distilling what he has, working with suppliers, and connecting those philosophies, and asking How can I make this philosophy work in the supply chain. It's very different from the business school mentality I had when I got here." I pushed Colesanti to be specific. He said that Chris Martin wants to be fair to everybody:

> The great thing is that we'll sit here in meetings and say something about the operations in Nazareth, and he'll ask: "What about Navojoa, our operations in Mexico?" He'll say, "We're doing this here, why aren't we doing it there? Those people need the same consideration. They need to be treated the same way; they make the same products, so they should have the same respect as the people here." He'll say the same thing about other countries. "What are we doing there? Are we taking care of those people?" He doesn't have to do that, but he does it. He doesn't lay anybody off here.

A cynic could reply that Chris Martin is merely the latest in a line of benevolent paternalists, taking care of his employee flock. Perhaps that's true, Colesanti replies, but it works. There is an ethic, he says, coming from the top that says, in effect, we're all in this together.[15] During the 2008–9 recession, he points out, Martin told department managers, "Find a way to keep everyone here," and they found some creative ways to do it. According to Colesanti, this kind of approach makes Martin "really feel like an extended community that way. Then when the chips are down, people are jumping in to help." Nick concludes on the collective ethos that he credits Chris Martin with establishing: "But the idea is that there's enough to go around. If we keep doing what we do well, and we watch our brand, and we make the best products, and we are constantly innovating, and we treat everybody well, then things are always going to be good. That's the overriding philosophy and pervades everything we do, it really does."

Colesanti's remarks cause me to reflect on the contrast between the long tenures of Chris Martin (1986–2021) and his competitor at Gibson, Henry Juszkiewicz (1986–2018), discussed in the previous chapter. I give the last word on this topic to Walter Carter, who knows both companies well, having published major histories of each one.[16] Carter says that despite the companies' differences in ownership history, Gibson and Martin were longtime rivals in fairly similar condition when Juskiewicz and Martin, respectively, took over in the 1980s: "Ironically, the old-school guy who looked backwards for inspiration succeeded, while the forward-looking innovator ultimately failed."[17]

The second big takeaway from my visit to Martin concerns the future, not just for Chris Martin himself, but for the company that he has headed since 1986. As early as 2007, Chris, then just fifty-two and having served only two decades as CEO, was already thinking about the road ahead for his company. Ever the pragmatic manager concerned about resource accessibility, he said, "If I use up all the good wood, I'm out of business."[18] He was already thinking about how to sustain good wood supplies for the indefinite future.

Chris Martin went on to link resource sustainability to what one might term family sustainability. He said that he and his wife were already anticipating one possible future for his young daughter. In that 2007 interview just mentioned, Chris said, "I have a two-year-old daughter, Claire Frances Martin, and she can be the seventh-generation C. F. Martin. I want her to be able to get materials she'll need, just as my ancestors and I have over the past 174 years."

Thirteen years after this statement, in July 2020, Chris announced his intention to retire as CEO, and a year later, in June 2021, he did so at age sixty-six. His successor as chief executive, Thomas Ripsam, came from a long career in management consulting. Most recently working as a partner of PricewaterhouseCoopers, Ripsam was described in the local press as a "corporate growth strategist" and "avid guitarist."[19] Although retiring as CEO, Martin took on the title of executive chairman, and ownership of the company will remain in family hands. He defined his future role as follows: "I look forward to transitioning to the role of Executive Chairman of Martin Guitar where I will continue to be a cheerleader for the Martin brand. I am excited to work with Thomas as he gets to know all of us and shares the love we all have for the guitar."[20]

It remains to be seen what the future holds for young Claire Frances, who is still a teenager as of this writing. But a reasonable conjecture is that sometime in the not-too-distant future, C. F. Martin & Co., often pilloried for its adherence to tradition, may welcome its first female Chairperson and CEO.

Conclusion

THE AMERICAN ACOUSTIC GUITAR—
ON DISCOVERING A TRANSFORMATION

A snatch of a melody, steel guitar sings in harmony
And I'm moved, beyond words, by emotion.
At once comes a feeling that sends my soul reeling
What mystery set this in motion?

—*"SUDDENLY TEARS" — SONG LYRICS BY THE AUTHOR*

The process of imagining, researching, and writing this book has yielded two interrelated discoveries. The first one is personal: a gradual realization of the creative and emotional contribution the acoustic guitar has made in my own life. The triggering moments were ones I still visualize clearly: the musical evenings in the early 1970s at The Ark coffeehouse in Ann Arbor. Yes, there were accordions, fiddles, mandolins, banjos, and other acoustic folk instruments, but the star of the show was most often an acoustic guitar. For the first time, the sound of that instrument grabbed me, and I soon determined to try to make some of those sounds myself. Subsequent decades tell the story of my attachment to, and continued discovery of the guitar.

That discovery has entailed my share of woodshedding with the instrument: hours alone trying to master a new fingerpicking pattern, a flatpicked fiddle tune, or some song I like. I've also taken to writing songs of my own, always with guitar in hand. There is indeed the loneliness, but also the rewards, of the solo-practice player. But the true breakthroughs in my playing skills, creativity, and enjoyment have always been in social contexts. Playing with others—with my brother, friends, and especially Fast & Cheap, my folk band of the past twenty years—has brought the most fulfillment. The acoustic guitar—its simplicity, musical versatility, and last but not least, its portability—literally brings one out into the world. Did I discover the guitar, or did it discover me? Who cares?

As it turned out, we were suited perfectly for each other, and I intend to keep what I call this "instrumental affair" going, as the guitar and I keep discovering our affinity for each other. What is that affinity exactly? I've been reflecting on that question as I bring this project to a close. Yes, there is the satisfaction of learning a skill requiring manual dexterity, timing, and sense of pitch. To put it simply, the acoustic guitar has been the means by which I've gained an ability to make a pleasing musical sound—at least most of the time. And then there's the social aspect just mentioned: playing guitar has also been a means to deepen friendships and forge new ones. And yes, playing guitar, I have come to conclude, is a major channel for expressing whatever level of creative ability I have.

Ultimately, what all this comes down to for me is the emotional connection I have with the instrument, a connection I tried to capture, however incompletely, in the lyrics quoted above. I realize I am no Columbus here, charting undiscovered territory. Musicians and music lovers of all kinds have their own stories to tell about this ineffable aspect of music itself. But this is my story, and I'm sticking to it. Even as I always try to appreciate the specific qualities of other instruments, music made by an acoustic guitar touches me emotionally in ways that other instruments do not. That, for me, is the true affinity that the guitar and I share.

Complementing and reinforcing this first discovery is a second one: what I have described as the acoustic guitar's transformation. This too is a personal discovery in the sense of being the central conclusion I draw from trying to understand changes in how the instrument has been played and crafted since the 1960s. Those changes constitute a process of transformation in both of those dimensions: the making of the instrument and the use that musicians have made of it. This book has explored each of these dimensions.

The *playing* dimension, examined in Chapter 1, comes directly out of my experiences at The Ark coffeehouse in Ann Arbor, when I heard four guitarists who exemplify three distinct lineages of playing: the songster, flatpick, and fingerstyle traditions. David Bromberg was then, and remains to this day, a master of the songster tradition, in which the acoustic guitar, rather than being the main focus, has a supporting and enhancing role for the song itself. A perfect example is Bromberg's bravura seven-minute rendition of Jerry Jeff Walker's well-known tune, "Mr. Bojangles." After singing a couple of verses cum chorus, David breaks into a talking interlude about playing guitar with Walker and learning how Jerry Jeff came to write the song, which is then followed by two more verse/chorus rounds. After the second of these, with the chorus ending with the line "Mr. Bojangles, come on and dance," Bromberg plays a one-minute flatpicked guitar solo that can only be described as exquisite, one that conveys both the rhythmic dancer's hypnotic movements and a feeling of pathos toward the street dancer's hard times and rough life.

To illustrate the other two traditions of flatpicking and fingerstyle playing, I recall the performances of flatpicker Norman Blake and fingerstyle players Elizabeth Cotten and Paul Geremia, all of whom remained, like Bromberg, active musicians well into their seventies. An all-around instrumentalist who also plays mandolin, dobro, and fiddle, Blake has been mainly acoustic guitar-based and traditional in style, preferring songs that reference an earlier, bucolic era: fiddle tunes such as "Blackberry Blossom" and songs such as "When the Roses Bloom in Dixieland" and "Last Train from Poor Valley." Cotten and Geremia were also traditionalists in that their music, including their own original songs, was mainly rooted in pre-electric blues and folk idioms. All four of these musicians have their provenance and progeny—their predecessors and successors—in their respective styles, and my analysis in this chapter attempts to trace the dynamic, perpetually reinventing nature of acoustic guitar-made music since the 1960s.

This transformation of guitar-made music did not, of course, occur in a vacuum. Also being transformed simultaneously was the *making* of the acoustic guitar. As underlined in the introduction, this dual transformation was not merely coincidental; it was interconnected. Pinning down the causal factors in the transformation of the guitar-making industry itself is no exact science, but there were important changes in demand that stimulated increases in both the quantity and quality of the instruments produced.

Most notably, there was a shift in popular music styles, triggered by what came to be called the Folk Music Revival.[1] Paradoxically, old sounds sounded, well, not so old to many ears; in fact, they sounded new and vital—in a word, authentic. These songs included not just styles revived from an earlier time, including rural-based blues and traditional folk songs such as "Tom Dula" ("Tom Dooley"). The so-called revival also welcomed many young musicians performing old tunes in new ways or even writing original songs that somehow referenced an earlier time. The obvious example of the latter was Bob Dylan's early efforts to emulate Woody Guthrie and his "hard-travelin'" life of the 1930s.

Reinforcing this revived demand was the arrival of Baby Boomers to the music-listening market. This enlarged demographic cohort of young people born in the decade following World War II embraced not only an older generation of folk musicians such as Mississippi John Hurt, Reverend Gary Davis, Elizabeth Cotten, and Doc Boggs; they also flocked to concerts by performers of their own generation, most of them sporting acoustic guitars around their necks, including Dylan, Joan Baez, Tom Paxton, Taj Mahal, Joni Mitchell, Gordon Lightfoot, Dave Van Ronk, and many others too numerous to mention. The acoustic guitar became a kind of signifier of one's cultural identity; its low cost, small size, and ease of basic playing fit well with a rising generation's sense of itself as distinct from, even rebellious against, the status quo that many of them found stultifying.

The triggering effect of the Folk Music Revival has indeed been enduring. The acoustic guitar has remained a prime solo instrument, as successive generations of musicians have discovered innovative ways to draw sound from that wooden box and attract a buying public. Compared with the relatively prosaic role typically assigned to the acoustic guitar prior to the 1960s, the playing of the instrument has become transformed.

The popularity of the acoustic guitar has in turn promoted a growing, diverse industry of producers. In the typical interplay of demand and supply in a capitalist economy, supply soon responded to an increase in demand, and this dynamic has played out in the decades since 1960. This growth in both supply and demand has continued over time, albeit with ups and downs, to the point that one can take a long look back and discern some large trends on the supply side concerning the making of the acoustic guitar. As the reader will now be aware, these trends comprise what I believe to be a transformation in guitar making. As evidenced by our imaginary visits to the Shreveport Music Company store of 1960 and today's Guitar Works in Evanston as well as the massive "store" of offerings immediately available online, the landscape of the guitar industry has undergone some fundamental changes, including new entrants to the guitar-making industry as well as strategic responses by the oldest makers, Gibson and Martin.

Among the new entrants have been three vastly different sets of guitar makers. The first set, portrayed in Chapter 2, is what has been called the new lutherie movement: individual and small-scale producers who have come on the scene since the 1960s and established stellar reputations for the quality of their instruments. This chapter profiles just a few of the more prominent members. Many other equally deserving luthiers also comprise this movement.

Even within the cohort I had the fortune to visit and interview, one finds significant differences in scale of production, size of workforce, and range of products. Take, for example, two of them: Collings Guitars outside of Austin, Texas, and Bourgeois Guitars in Lewiston, Maine. Both companies are highly respected guitar builders, but they bear little resemblance to one another on the dimensions just mentioned. The company that Bill Collings (1948–2017) established in 1973 dwarfs Bourgeois's in scale and range of product. The Collings factory runs with about a hundred employees producing a total of about three thousand instruments a year—a mix of acoustic guitars (about 60 percent of total), mandolins and electric guitars. By contrast, Dana Bourgeois's company, set up in 1977, today produces just acoustic guitars—about four hundred per year—with about twenty production workers. Although the world of the new luthiers—most of whom are nearing retirement age—is highly varied, one thing is certain: the emergence and growth of this movement of small-scale shops and individual luthiers have had a decisive impact in raising the craftsmanship of the guitar-making industry as a whole. Although this cohort has been numerically dominated by men, Chapter 2 also notes the important contributions, both past and present, of female luthiers such as Linda Manzer, Judy Threet, Jayne Henderson, Rachel Rosenkrantz, and Maegen Wells.

A second important addition to the field of new entrants to the guitar field since 1960 is a single company, Taylor Guitars, established in El Cajon, California, near San Diego in 1974. As described in Chapter 3, Bob Taylor, then nineteen, and two other young San Diegans, Kurt Listug and Steve Schemmer, were making and repairing guitars at a small shop, American Dream, when they decided to set up their own independent operation, thereby giving birth to Taylor Guitars. After a decade of struggling, the combination of Taylor's technical savvy and Listug's business acumen enabled the fledgling company to gain a foothold among the competition.

Since the mid-1980s, Taylor Guitars has continued to grow in output volume, product range, and quality. As my interview with him made clear, Bob Taylor believes in growth as a goal in itself. He states directly, "I believe in the power of manufacturing," which has nurtured a kind of build-it-and-they-will-come mindset within the company. In effect, the company's leadership believes in a direct positive feedback loop between innovation and growth: innovation produces appealing products that bring growth and therefore profits, and those profits, in turn, become the financial resources to underwrite further innovation. Today, Taylor Guitars stands as the only guitar maker established in the past fifty years that has grown to rival in sheer output the historically dominant companies Martin and Gibson.

Finally, a third type of entrant to the acoustic guitar world since the 1960s has been what I term "globalizers," companies making instruments abroad. Imported guitars made by Japanese firms Yamaha and Takamine began arriving in American guitar shops in the 1970s, and these home-grown Japanese companies have remained fixtures ever since. Chapter 4 traced not only their emergence but also the subsequent rise since the 1990s of export-oriented guitar production elsewhere in Asia—in Korea, Taiwan, China, and Indonesia. Most of this spread in the locus of production has been accomplished not by companies native to those countries, but rather through a so-called OEM (Original Equipment Manufacturer) arrangement between an American contractor and a foreign manufacturer. A typical example would be that Fender contracts with a Chinese company to produce guitars according to Fender's specifications, including the all-important step of affixing the Fender label on the headstock. One of the more visible of these US companies is Saga Musical Instruments (or simply Saga Music). Established by Richard Keldsen in 1980, Saga imports all its instruments, including a wide range of Chinese-made instruments such as Blueridge guitars, Kentucky mandolins, and Rover banjos.

An interesting variant to this OEM model is a new partnership—a division of labor—between the Chinese-owned instrument maker, Eastman Guitars, and Bourgeois Guitars, by which Bourgeois provides the tops for a line of coproduced guitars with Eastman. As Chapter 4 describes, the first step involves Dana Bourgeois tuning the tops (selective thinning of the soundboard's braces), and then his shop installs the underside bridge plate and the sound hole rosette. Once finished, the tops are shipped to Eastman's factory in Beijing for installation to the rest of the box (back and sides), followed by attachment of the neck. Then the completed instruments are shipped back to Bourgeois for final setup and overall inspection. The two companies view this arrangement as a win-win. According to a leading music industry publication: "Dana Bourgeois' decades of guitar building expertise will be put to use enhancing the design and production quality of the approximately 40,000 guitars Eastman produces at its Chinese plants. Bourgeois, for its part, will gain access to Eastman's global distribution network and the ability to reach a broader customer base with more affordable instruments."[2]

Finally, Chapters 5 and 6 assess the responses of the two historic companies, Gibson and Martin, to these major changes in their competitive environment. How did they react to the new sources of supply coming from the new lutherie movement, Taylor Guitars, and imported instruments? With long legacies as high-quality, even revered, guitar makers, these two companies face the perpetual balancing act between two market imperatives, which I've labeled tradition and innovation. Notice that the word "and"—and not the word "or"—is placed between those two concepts, although we naturally think of these as opposed or mutually exclusive ideas. In the competitive world of the acoustic guitar, attention must be paid to both tradition and innovation. Martin and Gibson must balance the strategic emphasis given to producing those high-quality, traditional instruments for which they are known against that of developing innovative products or even a new corporate identity. To put the matter as simply as possible: too much of one strategic approach neglects the other. Hewing too closely to a company's traditional line of products while rejecting innovation may eventually produce stasis and stultification, whereas a company's pursuit of innovation to the neglect of its traditional line of instruments also runs the risk of losing money on uncertain investments and diluting the brand's identity. These two chapters are contrasting case studies of how Gibson and Martin have handled this balancing act.

In Gibson's case, the trio of young Harvard MBA's headed by Henry Juszkiewicz who bought Gibson in 1986 from its corporate owner, Norlin, most decidedly opted for innovation over tradition. This is not to say that the new owners completely neglected Gibson's core production in acoustic guitars. Chapter 5 recounts the revival of excellent guitar and mandolin production, headed by master luthier Ren Ferguson, in a new factory that Gibson built in Bozeman, Montana. Over time, however, the Juszkiewicz team sought to transform—to innovate—Gibson's identity from primarily that of a guitar, mandolin, and banjo builder to a polyglot collection of eighteen music-related instrument and audio companies.[3] In a clear symbolic move, Gibson Guitar Corporation underwent a name change to Gibson Brands. This strategy to innovate the very identity of this historic company ultimately failed because of unprofitable acquisitions and a debt load that led to bankruptcy in 2018. With financial reorganization also came new ownership, with Gibson's new leaders promising to recenter its operations on its core traditional products and reclaim the company's historic legacy as a "guitar company."[4]

In contrast to Gibson, Martin under the leadership of C. F. (Chris) Martin IV (born 1955) has tended to emphasize its own historical heritage. As noted in Chapter 6, Martin became CEO in 1986, with a determination to back away from the unsuccessful direction that his own father, as president, had taken the company during the 1970s and early 1980s. That direction had included a series of failed acquisitions as well as a public perception of decline in quality of Martin's Nazareth instruments. Chris Martin told me he was determined to learn from his dad's mistakes and to "focus" (his term) on making the best guitars possible. He wants employees to "remember, what we're known for is high quality, flattop, steel-string, acoustic guitars." He and other Martin executives I interviewed were quick to say that this focus on the company's traditional bread-and-butter instruments did *not* preclude innovation; in fact, this focus encompassed what I term a three-legged stool of producing: (a) the best standard, classic guitars that the company has produced since the 1920s, using precision CNC technology; (b) a new line of lower-priced guitars made in Mexico; and (c) a line of higher-priced authentic models, built by hand to the exact specifications of the so-called Golden Era instruments of the 1930s.

Taken together, the changes in the playing and making of the acoustic guitar during the past few decades have led me to a central conclusion: the world of the acoustic guitar has been dramatically transformed since the early 1960s. Far from being eclipsed, as many had predicted, by the electric guitar or new versions of electronic/digitally produced music, the acoustic guitar has held its own in the performing world. The key factor in the instrument's staying power has been the many innovations in its playing, as guitarists have continued to discover new techniques, melodies, tempos, chords, and arrangements that find their receptive audiences.

The acoustic guitar's lasting popularity is also related to innovations in the instrument itself, which has both qualitative and quantitative dimensions. Stated concretely from a guitar customer's viewpoint, the range of choices in terms of both price and quality is far wider than it was a few decades ago. The gamut begins with solidly built, imported instruments starting at $200, then proceeds through a mid- to high range (roughly $1,000–$5,000) offered by high-volume producers such as Gibson, Martin, and Taylor. At the very high end, fine quality instruments made by small-scale shops and individual luthiers begin at about $5,000 and range well into the five figures.

THE VIEW FROM HERE: OF COVID AND BEYOND

This book has focused mainly on the recent past and immediate present in trying to make sense of how and why the acoustic guitar world has changed in recent decades. Starting this project a few years ago, I was not especially focused on the future, assuming plausibly that whatever I was discovering would likely continue into the foreseeable if not indefinite future. After all, what unknown factor was out there to stop the flow of creative energy that both guitar players and makers are pouring into the instrument? Yes, there are worrisome long-term challenges to the acoustic guitar's future in terms of both demand and supply, but these are well known within the world of guitar makers, sellers, and industry observers (see below). Moreover, the relative stability of recent economic conditions promised a general continuity in the trajectory—the process of transformation—that I was tracing.

Then, the year 2020 arrived—a year that may well go down as this country's *annus horribilis* of the entire post–World War II period up to that point, for both public health and political reasons. Early that year Covid-19 invaded the scene, creating a global pandemic that disrupted normal life and brought massive death and suffering. As I type these final paragraphs, more than two years since the pandemic's outbreak, I realize it would be remiss to end this book by not asking: How have those in the acoustic guitar world been coping with Covid? The following are some partial soundings.

Everyone can remember when the pandemic altered their lives. I was shopping in a local fabric store on Wednesday, March 11, 2020, for a birthday gift certificate for my wife, when I noticed two or three people wearing masks. I had *heard* about a new, dangerous virus making the rounds, but this was the first time the virus came to me in some concrete form. Two days, later, that store—plus my gym, coffee shop, guitar store, and all other nonessential businesses in the state of Illinois—were shut down. That scenario was being repeated all over the United States. The only thing certain in my mind and in the minds of my fellow citizens was a feeling of uncertainty: What is this virus? How bad is it? How long will this last?

In the guitar-making world, as in virtually every shop and factory across the land, a shutdown of operations began in mid-March and extended over the next several months. Most guitar makers had only questions with no answers. For example, when interviewed in April 2020, Fred Greene, Martin's vice president for production, was asked if he or anyone among his fellow guitar makers had a strategy at that moment, or was it "Let's just pray this is over by June"? Greene's immediate response was that it's impossible to have a strategy when there's no certain end date. He went on to say, "For now, it's about how best to take care of our employees. Everybody's in a holding pattern." All else, he said, was unknown: Will our dealers be able to maintain business? What is demand for guitars likely to be? Can we get the parts and supplies we need—things such as strings, tuners, bridge pins, and cases? Asked how he was keeping sane, Greene said, "The main thing is: get up in the morning, don't sleep in too late, don't stay up too late, fight every instinct in my body not to drink too much at night . . . and make sure I get enough exercise."[5] That sentiment of uncertainty—about production, sales, cash flow, and survivability in general—was prevalent among guitar makers during the early months of the pandemic.

Uncertainty can give rise to desperation, but it also prompts adaptation, and that has transpired within the guitar world. By June 2020, many guitar-making operations were resuming some level of production, aided by adjustments big and small. Small adjustments included the usual workplace reconfigurations of masking, social distancing, air-filtering systems, and use of plexiglass shields between workstations. Larger adjustments were required for the larger firms. For example, Taylor Guitars, as we saw in Chapter 3, runs two interdependent manufacturing operations that are thirty-five miles apart but separated by the US–Mexico border. The company has faced major supply and coordination challenges because of differing government-imposed shutdown-and-reopening dates. Taylor's main adaptation was to institute a restructuring of work shifts and hours in the Mexican plant in Tecate.[6]

Testimony from guitar makers about they how adapted to the pandemic's uncertainties goes well beyond the strictly technical aspects of resuming safe operations. What they often stress is the importance of mutual support and cooperation among other makers and suppliers. For example, Richard Hoover of Santa Cruz Guitar Company, looking back in July 2020 on those first weeks of shutdown, said: "We didn't survive this because we make a lot of money and have sacks of money to get through. We ran out of money in a hurry. The bank account we relied on is the bank account that we have from making investment every day in ordinary kindness and good will to the people we deal with, as vendors, friends, other builders . . . We all had a common foe, we all had to pull together here. We all worked together. That's what we're counting on to get us through."[7]

Guitar makers talk about staying in touch with one another, seeking both advice and solace. This is consistent with a theme noted in Chapter 2, namely that guitar makers have to compete in a market environment, but at the heart of that environment is an ethos of mutual cooperation. Fred Greene of Martin, for example, spoke of texting regularly with Bob Taylor, Steve McCreary at Collings, and others:

We've been talking and commiserating back and forth. It's all about trying to find comfort within the acoustic guitar community—trying to let each other know we're not going through this alone, that we're all facing the same challenges. Everybody's friends. . . . We recognize that if anybody's having success, that ultimately means success for the rest of us. That means people are getting more interested in acoustic music and instruments, and we're trying to move the craft forward. We visit each other's factories on a fairly regular basis, so we learn from each other. If somebody's doing something cool, they'll usually help you out, so you can bring it back to your factory and implement it there. So as a group, we can kind of stay healthy and efficient at what we're doing. We're lucky in that sense—we're not locked into a death match with one another.[8]

Some months later, in early 2021, Fred Greene recounted a specific instance of cooperation when Steve contacted him requesting some specialized wrenches (for truss rods), and Fred then put Steve in touch with Martin's supplier. "You have to cooperate like that," Greene notes, "You have to help each other out, especially in these times." He went on to stress the need to support their suppliers. These are typically small companies making "pieces and parts for all of us," and they struggle when overall guitar production is down. He concludes, "So if you find something cool, you'll let others know where you got it. That gives [the suppliers] more business and helps them survive."[9]

The big story among acoustic guitar makers and sellers during years one and two of the Covid crisis is that the public's demand for the instrument, far from declining, remained relatively robust. As Fred Greene commented: "It's blossomed into some craziness."[10] While pleasantly surprised, makers and sellers alike observed that the reasons for sustained demand were easy to surmise, given that the pandemic had imposed some fundamental changes in how many people live and work. Quarantining or isolating meant that, where feasible, people were staying and working from home. One's disposable time and income then came into play, as commuting to work and activities such as going out to restaurants and entertainment were (literally) off the table. Those fortunate enough to live under these conditions found themselves with more free time and discretionary income and wondered what to do with it. Why not fill that time and spend that income on learning a new skill or working on a skill that one has let languish, such as . . . playing guitar?

Many guitar makers not only had two or three months of backorders when they reopened during spring and summer of 2020, but demand remained steady thereafter. Here is a sampling of comments from builders:

- Steve McCreary, Collings: "Knock on wood, it's been trying, but we've been able to move forward, not at the pace we were before, not where we'd like to be, but we're progressing."
- Richard Hoover, Santa Cruz Guitar Company: "I'm suffering some survivor's guilt. Not only is everything going our way, but we're going to come out of this better than we went into it."
- Dana Bourgeois, Bourgeois Guitars: "Of course, we had to close during March, but now [September 2020] things are going well in terms of orders. We're backordered now until the second quarter of 2021."
- Chris Wellons, Taylor Guitars: "Essentially, we didn't miss much of a beat at all. . . . We recovered well, and we're looking at 2021 as the big, beautiful flower. We've got guitars on back order, we've got guitars to build, so that we can increase production this year, in the safest manner that we can."[11]

A similar story came from sellers, who had to do some adapting of their own. For example, Walter Carter, owner of Carter Vintage Guitars in Nashville, reported that although he had to close his doors for two months, he kept his online sales open. By the end of 2020, he was letting customers back in the store on an appointment basis. He commented, "This thing has forced all sellers to step up in terms of web presence. We're doing about half the total business we were doing before, but it's steady and we're getting by." As a Gibson dealer, he also reports, "Right now, they're going great guns. Bozeman is back producing at normal rates, and they're trying to hire for extra shifts. I get a trickle of new Gibsons; they're backordered."[12]

The same holds for Terry Straker, the owner of my local shop, Guitar Works. After over a year of being closed to walk-ins, the store reopened to all customers in 2021. The main frustration, Terry says, was not lack of demand but getting new instruments in the first place: "Supply is horrible. There's almost nothing where I can call Fender for an order and get it in a rational time frame. For a retailer, a rational time frame in normal times is 7–10 days. Availability now is in months, 3–5 months out on almost everything. Nothing is available now."

The silver lining in Straker's business, as in Walter Carter's, was online sales, which required a major upgrading in the store's website. The first change was to adopt a point-of-sale ecommerce system, whereby customers can purchase directly online, then have the item shipped to them. Before Covid, Guitar Works was selling only about one instrument a month through its website, but within a few months after Covid's onset the store was selling 12–15 instruments a month. That uptick in online sales, says Straker, made the difference between survival and going under.[13]

Perhaps the most official word about Covid's initial impact comes from the trade association for the music retail industry—NAMM, or the National Association of Music Merchants—which declared in its 2021 Global Report: "2020 laid to rest any concerns that the guitar was dead, dying, or entering a long period of decline. Immediately after stimulus checks began flowing from the U.S. government in late April, retailers noted a sizable influx of first-time buyers. . . . The clear takeaway is that fretted instruments retain their broad-based appeal."[14]

• • •

One generalization to come out of the Covid period is clear: all of those in the acoustic guitar world—including performers, makers, and sellers— have found that the difference between surviving and going under has come through making various adaptations to changing conditions. No doubt this generalization will continue to apply to that world post-Covid—whenever that may be—especially concerning the longer-term challenges of demand and supply signaled at various points in this book.

The demand side of the acoustic guitar world is, of course, impossible to predict, especially given the equally unpredictable ups and downs of the general economy over time. As anyone with a basic understanding of economics knows, periods of recession, rapid inflation, or general uncertainty tend to force consumers to tighten belts and focus on buying the essentials, whereas growth periods permit consumption above and beyond the essentials. While I, for one, certainly consider the guitar an essential possession in my life, I already have one (well, several), as do countless others. When times are lean, one's natural inclination is to forego nonessential spending such as buying another—or even a first—guitar. Much of the demand equation, therefore, is obvious: the demand for guitars will fluctuate over time.

What is less evident is how other factors figure into the basic ebb and flow of consumer demand for the acoustic guitar, especially at the higher end of the market—roughly speaking, instruments that sell for $3,000 and above. There are at least two aspects at play that must worry guitar makers who produce for this market segment: demographics and the vintage/used market. First, the age cohort that has driven this upper end of the market for the past two decades has largely been male Baby Boomers born between 1946 and 1964. Not only did this generation grow up with the acoustic guitar as a popular featured instrument, but since the turn of the century, most members of this cohort have reached their peak earning years, thereby acquiring the financial wherewithal to purchase more expensive guitars. Will this trend last? Alas, even the youngest members of the Boomer generation are now reaching their elder years, and most of this cohort will gradually pass from the scene during the next two decades. Moreover, both generations coming along behind the Boomers—Generation X (those born between 1965 and 1980) and Millennials (those born between 1981 and 1996)—are smaller in number and generally less affluent.[15]

Further throwing doubt on the sustainability of demand for new guitars is a second factor: the de facto competition from the large and still growing vintage instrument market. Given the acoustic guitar's exceptional durability—its capacity, if properly maintained, to age well in terms of structural integrity and sound quality—many buyers searching for a high-quality instrument consider both vintage and new instruments. As just one example, I quickly found two Martin D-18's for sale online, one made in the early 1950s and the other a new D-18 from Martin's Authentic Series; both instruments sell in the $6,000–$7,000 range. One can only conclude that Martin and other companies making high-end guitars are, in effect, competing against instruments—even ones they previously made!—easily found on the used and vintage market.

What about supply? As previous chapters noted, the larger companies such as Taylor, Gibson, and Martin publicly voice their concern over the future availability of the best tone woods, notably rosewood and mahogany for the back and sides, spruce for the top, and ebony for the fretboard and bridge.

Even a small-scale builder such as Richard Hoover of Santa Cruz Guitars frets about access to traditional supply sources: "The consumer demand for pretty wood, real wood, has seen an exponential growth over the last couple of decades, especially the last decade. It's being vacuumed up. . . . The giant moneyed interests come in, and they buy geography. They don't buy trees, they buy geography, the whole thing. They scrape it and take it back and process it, everything from pretty wood to pulp and construction materials. So it's cause for alarm."[16] A good way to start a conversation with any luthier is to inquire: What do you worry about most in your work, now and in the future? The chances are high that the reply will involve wood supply in two respects: accessibility and possible alternatives to the prime traditional woods just mentioned.

As a group, guitar makers today are engaged, to varying degrees, in three sets of activities vis-à-vis the global wood supply, which can be summarized as: obedience, advocacy, and experimentation. The first of these, *obedience*, means following the "rules and regulations," established by the US government, other national governments, and international regulatory bodies related to the general problem of deforestation, specifically the conditions under which tree cutting and the transport of lumber and finished wood products take place. Following those "R&R's" for a guitar company is an increasingly daunting task. Mentioned time after time in my interviews with guitar makers, especially with large producers such as Taylor and Martin, was the exacting, time-consuming job of documenting imported shipments of wood and outgoing shipments of finished instruments. For example, Martin's supply-chain manager, Nick Colesanti, remarked on the costs of compliance: "It's a lot of time and a lot of money. We're obtaining the same woods that effectively we've been obtaining for years. I can't necessarily tell you whether the volume or quality of woods coming out of Mexico, Central and South America, and Africa has increased or decreased over the years, but I can tell you that the level of effort has increased exponentially, the amount of paperwork, the documentation, the time in country."[17]

Terms that came up often in these discussions were "Lacey Amendments" and "CITES," which refer to the main regulatory regimes governing the extraction, international shipping, and importing of unfinished wood and finished products containing wood. The Lacey Amendments—specifically amendments made in 2008 to the original Lacey Act passed by Congress in 1900—make it unlawful to import, export, buy or sell within the United States any plant product (including wood) that was obtained in violation of any U.S. or foreign law that protects plants. Moreover, the Amendments require that any imported product containing wood or other plant material must be accompanied by an import declaration which specifies various aspects of the wood (genus, species, country of harvest, etc.).[18] As for CITES—the Convention on International Trade in Endangered Species, a multinational body formed in 1975—this body's goal, according to its website, is "to ensure that international trade in specimens of wild animals and plants does not threaten the survival of the species."[19]

Of most relevance to guitar makers are the Appendices, notably Appendix I, which designates Brazilian Rosewood (*Dalbergia nigra*) as an endangered species threatened with extinction and therefore prohibits its trade in international commerce.[20] If your eyes as a reader begin to glaze over as you read the previous lines, you can perhaps sympathize with guitar makers who must (a) pay close attention to these types of governing rules and (b) obey them by providing the required documentation. I concur with Dudley's conclusion that "the regulatory regime that luthiers face is not a unified system administered by the U.S. government but an intimidating patchwork of domestic, international, foreign, and tribal laws. This policy is further complicated by the political struggles that underlie it."[21]

How, then, beyond adhering to regulations, do guitar makers seek to deal with the challenge of deforestation? All guitar makers are "green" in the sense that they want to preserve and protect the environmental resource—the primary woods noted above—that is the very basis of their livelihood. Connected directly to this material interest is an image interest. According to one environmental scientist, "the concern is that the guitar industry is driving logging (though perhaps not complete forest conversion) in some specific areas of high biodiversity and conservation value, principally old growth forests of the tropics that are home to some of these target species (e.g., rosewood, mahogany, ebony, etc.)." Chris Martin once remarked, only semi-jokingly: "I've got an eleven-year old daughter, and I don't want her someday going to a NAMM show wearing a t-shirt that said, 'My daddy cut down the last tree.'"[22]

The answer of how to be green isn't obvious, since guitar makers well recognize that they are bit players in the world of wood dominated by other interests, both agricultural and industrial. The environmental specialist quoted above also notes that "from a purely quantitative perspective, guitar-wood driven deforestation is fairly minor compared to agriculturally driven deforestation. Agriculture drives at least 75% of deforestation globally, so everything else really pales in comparison." Thus the feasibility that guitar makers could own and/or control their own forests and wood supply is slight, and the guitar industry cannot rely on its market strength alone to incentivize forest owners and managers to follow preservation and protection practices that will sustain the forests.[23]

Rather, luthiers must engage in various forms of *advocacy* in favor of sustainable forest practices. This often means working with environmental groups such as Greenpeace and Greenwood to convince policymakers as well as forest owners and managers to adopt such practices. An example of this type of advocacy was the Musicwood coalition, a group of four major guitar makers—Fender, Gibson, Martin, and Taylor—brought together by Greenpeace to limit clear cutting in southeast Alaska. As noted in Chapter 3, this group met directly with the leaders of the Native American corporation, Sealaska, to try to convince them to reduce timbering of old-growth spruce trees in the Tongass National Forest.

Although that campaign ultimately failed to change Sealaska's timber practices, these larger guitar companies advocate for forest sustainability practices in other ways, notably by example. This means, in effect, acting as good forest citizens through affiliation with and support for environmental organizations that promote sustainability. Martin Guitars, for example, touts its partnerships with the Forest Stewardship Council (FSC) and the Rainforest Alliance—two organizations that carry out a certain division of labor between them. The FSC defines sustainable forestry practices and issues certification for products—such as guitar woods—that meet those standards. By contrast, the Rainforest Alliance works directly with businesses, including Martin, to help them meet those certification standards.[24]

Finally, the third way that guitar makers are addressing the challenges of diminishing supplies of prime woods is through *experimentation* with new types of wood and (gasp!) even nonwood materials. Beginning with Ovation in the 1960s, at least a dozen other companies have employed such materials as fiberglass and carbon fiber/graphite to constitute the guitar's back and sides. The use of relatively inexpensive raw materials and precision molding devices diminishes the uncertainties of resource sustainability and human handcraft variability. Moreover, the advantages are obvious of an instrument that both makes a pleasing sound and doesn't suffer the damage, as wood often does, caused by temperature and/or humidity changes or rough handling. Such positive qualities of their instruments have enabled such makers as RainSong, Composite Acoustics, McPherson, and several others to carve out a market niche among guitar buyers. Of particular note is McPherson, based in Sparta, Wisconsin, which makes a range of both wood and nonwood instruments—all of them incorporating other innovations that, it claims, enhances tonality, such as an offset (noncentered) sound hole and a cantilevered neck whose upper portion does not touch the top.[25]

Even though guitars not made of wood have gained a foothold within the buying public, they are likely to remain a small part of the overall market. There is still the "gasp" factor: a sense of resistance among many guitar buyers to even considering the use of nontraditional materials to make acoustic guitars. For the present and foreseeable future, however, it is safe to conclude that there is no significant demand or supply rush to build guitars from these materials that would threaten to displace that cool wooden box.

Little question, then, that wood of some type will retain its place as the essential material for making guitars well into the future. The real issue is: what kind of wood? As such classic tone woods as old-growth mahogany and rosewood grow scarcer—and therefore more expensive and even prohibited from logging or shipping out of the country of origin—guitar makers both small and large are experimenting with alternative woods. Bob Taylor, for example, sees the future this way: "I will say that the guitars are simply going to change. I'm going to make another little news flash for all you guitar players out there: that beautiful two-piece guitar top that you have, with perfect grain, perfect this, perfect that—that's a bit of vanity that we're all going to have to shed pretty soon."[26]

Guitar makers often praise such relatively unknown hardwoods as jacaranda (South America and other regions), zebrawood (Africa), cocobolo (Central America), bubinga (Africa), and other woods as suitable alternatives for the guitar's back and sides. For example, Jeff Huss of Huss & Dalton Guitars comments: "There are a lot of great woods out there that nobody knows about. There are a lot of guys in Australia trying to market their wood—they have all kinds of climate zones and lots of different types of wood. I think new woods will be used more and more. For example, sapele—nobody had heard of sapele ten years ago. It's an African wood, it's not a mahogany, but it's similar in appearance and tone."

Huss goes on to say that even domestic woods such as walnut, mango, and cherry make good guitars. He concludes, "The tradition is going to have to fade. A hundred years from now, people will still be building guitars out of wood, but it's probably not going to be mahogany, rosewood, and those kinds of wood." The silver lining for small builders like Huss & Dalton is that their need for the traditional woods is relatively small, and for the immediate future at least, they have little difficulty obtaining the wood they need. Huss views Taylor as leading the way in using alternatives because "they need so much wood to feed their beast." He concludes: "We don't do a lot of experimentation because we can wait for Taylor to figure out what works."[27]

It goes without saying that the future fate—indeed, the further transformation—of the acoustic guitar will hinge on whether those in that world will be willing and able to "obey the rules" of forest and wood protection, to advocate for sustainable forest practices, and to experiment with new types of woods and materials. Rather than employ the cliché that "only time will tell," I happily give the last word on the acoustic guitar's likely future to the ever-optimistic Richard Hoover, founder of Santa Cruz Guitar Company: "A guitar is such a cool sounding thing. Even with the cheapest, crummiest guitar, you can write a song on it and change the world. So we're going to love guitars made out of whatever, just as long as we can make them."[28]

To which I say: hear, hear, Richard—I heartily concur. This cool wooden box, after the transformation it has undergone during the past six decades, has a bright, enduring future.

Notes

INTRODUCTION

1. Guitar Works's fortieth anniversary was featured in an article—"Evanston's Guitar Works Marks 40th Anniversary"—in the trade journal *Music Trades*, June 29, 2019, 40–44.

2. The term "acoustic" refers to the fact that the instrument's sound originates in the vibration of wood (or other material, such as a metal cone in the case of a resonator guitar), which is caused in turn by contact with a vibrating string. The vibrating wood creates a sound that is, in effect, captured within "that hollow box" of air beneath the strings, as opposed to vibrations transmitted electrically, as in the case of the electric guitar. This is not to say, of course, that acoustic instruments—guitars, violins, mandolins, etc.—cannot be amplified by use of electrical attachments, or pickups, but the primary energy source in such instruments is always the vibrating material, usually wood. For a concise description of the acoustic guitar's anatomy, see Ralph Denyer, *The Guitar Handbook* (New York: Alfred A. Knopf, 1998), 33–48.

3. For sources and images of these variants, see, for example, for classical guitars: Tom and Mary Anne Evans. *Guitars: Music, History, Construction and Players From the Renaissance to Rock* (New York: Paddington Press, 1977), 15–167; on the resonator: Bob Brozman, *The History & Artistry of National Resonator Instruments* (Anaheim Hills, CA: Centerstream, 1998); archtops: George Gruhn and Walter Carter, *Acoustic Guitars & Other Fretted Instruments: A Photographic History* (San Francisco, CA: Miller Freeman, 1993)), 167–224); lap steel: Andy Volk, *Lap Steel Guitar* (Anaheim Hills, CA: Centerstream, 2003) and John W. Troutman, *Kika Kila: How the Hawaiian Steel Guitar Changed the Sound of Modern Music* (Chapel Hill: University of North Carolina Press, 2016).

4. See, for example, Richard Johnson and Dick Boak, *Martin Guitars: A History* (Milwaukee, WI. Hal Leonard, 2008), 17–34; Jeffrey J. Noonan, *The Guitar in America: Victorian Era to Jazz Age* (Jackson: University Press of Mississippi, 2008); Robert Carl Hartman, *The Larsons' Creations: Guitars and Mandolins* (Anaheim Hills, CA: Centerstream, 1996), 10–11.

5. Many sources detail the evolution of the guitar, in both its acoustic and electric versions. For useful overviews, see, for example, Teja Gerken et al., *Acoustic Guitar: An Historical Look at the Composition, Construction, and Evolution of One of the World's Most*

Beloved Instruments (Milwaukee, WI: Hal Leonard, 2003); Tony Bacon, *History of the American Guitar: 1833 to the Present Day* (Milwaukee, WI: Backbeat Books, 2011); Tom Wheeler, *American Guitars: An Illustrated History* (New York: Harper Perennial, 1992).

6. See Ray Bonds, ed., *The Illustrated Directory of Guitars* (London: Greenwich Editions, 2004), 88.

7. I could easily write a whole book on the variety, geography, tonal properties, end use, and many other aspects of these and many other woods that go into guitar making and other wood instruments. But somebody already has! By far the best recent book on the subject of guitar woods—and the forests and countries they come from—is by two Austriilian geographers, Chris Gibson and Andrew Warren: *The Guitar: From the Grain to the Tree* (Chicago: University of Chicago Press, 2021). For a basic education in instrument-grade wood, I am most grateful for the lengthy conversation I had with Steve McMinn, founder and owner of Pacific Rim Tonewoods, when I visited his operation in Concrete, Washington, on July 19, 2016. Also see PRT's website: http://pacificrimtonewoods.com. For background, see David Olson, "Sound, Spruce, and Science: Measuring the Variables of Guitar Tone with Pacific Rim Tonewoods," *The Fretboard Journal*, 48 (2021), 74–83.

8. According to my online Merriam-Webster dictionary, a luthier is "one who makes stringed instruments (such as violins or guitars)." For variety's sake, I use the terms guitar maker and luthier interchangeably throughout.

9. Larry Sandberg, *The Acoustic Guitar Guide* (Chicago: A Cappella Books, 2000), 24.

10. Sandberg, 24–25. One other significant detail about archtops relates to the question of projection (loudness), which is how the top—and back—are constructed. The arched top and back are made one of two ways: each is either *carved* from a single piece of wood or *pressed* into an arched shape using a heated mold and thin, laminated sheets of wood. The carved version typically provides greater projection than the laminated variety.

11. I cannot resist this one anecdote about my meeting with Stan. I told him I wanted to learn to play guitar and asked if he had any *left-handed* guitars, since I am a natural lefty in all things. Stan then gave me one of the best pieces of musical (and life) advice this natural left-hander has ever received. He asked, "Wait a minute, do you know how to play?" I replied no—I want to learn. "Then," he said, "I'd strongly suggest that you learn to play *right*-handed. Then you'll be able to play most any guitar you run across. If you learn lefty, you can play *your* guitar and, if you're lucky, maybe Paul McCartney's." Belatedly, I say: Thanks, Stan, you were right. I did learn to play right-handed, and it's worked out fine.

12. Essential sources on the so-called Folk Music Revival include: Robert Cantwell, *When We Were Good: The Folk Revival* (Cambridge, MA: Harvard University Press, 1996); Benjamin Filene, *Romancing the Folk: Public Memory and American Roots* (Chapel Hill: UNC Press, 2000); Ronald D. Cohen, *Rainbow Quest: The Folk Music Revival & American Society, 1940–1970* (Amherst: University of Massachusetts Press, 2002); Michael F. Scully, *The Never-Ending Revival: Rounder Records and the Folk Alliance* (Urbana: University of Illinois Press, 2008); Ray Allen, *Gone to the Country: The New Lost City Ramblers & the Folk*

Music Revival (Urbana: University of Illinois Press, 2010); David King Dunnaway and Molly Beer, *Singing Out: An Oral History of America's Folk Music Revivals* (New York: Oxford University Press, 2011); Stephen Petrus and Ronald D. Cohen, *Folk City: New York and the American Folk Music Revival* (New York: Oxford University Press, 2015).

13. One notable exception would be the development of acoustic guitar-based blues music in the early twentieth century, although that genre's general popularity came only with its "rediscovery" during the Folk Music Revival period. Of course, the blues as a music genre has generated a vast collection of books, articles, recordings, videos, and other portrayals and appraisals. Even my own modest personal library contains well over forty books and countless CDs, and so I will not test the reader's stamina by making an exhaustive list. But a few suggested "starter" books would include: Leroi Jones, *Blues People* (New York: Morrow Quill, 1963); Paul Oliver et al., *Yonder Come the Blues* (Cambridge: Cambridge University Press, 2001); Alan Lomax, *The Land Where the Blues Began* (New York: New Press, 1993); Robert Palmer, *Deep Blues* (New York: Penguin, 1981); Samuel B. Charters, *The Country Blues* (New York: DaCapo Press, 1959); William Barlow, *Looking Up At Down: The Emergence of Blues Culture* (Philadelphia: Temple University Press, 1989).

14. The story of Tom Dula/Tom Dooley was just one of many folktales that have generated ballads. Other standards in the folktale-to-folk song process include "Frankie and Johnny," "John Hardy," "Casey Jones," and many others. See the "true tales" that indeed inspired these and many other well-known folk songs in Richard Pollenberg, *Hear My Sad Story: The True Tales That Inspired Stagolee, John Henry, and Other Traditional American Folk Songs* (Ithaca, NY: Cornell University Press, 2015). Also see Sean Wilentz and Greil Marcus, eds., *The Rose & the Briar: Death, Love and Liberty in the American Ballad* (New York: W.W. Norton, 2005).

15. Author interview, May 17, 2016. The following quote from Chris Martin is from this same interview.

16. Author interview, May 23, 2016.

17. The first use of the term "New Golden Age" came in the January/February (vol. 3, no. 4), 1993, themed issue of *Acoustic Guitar* magazine: "Vintage '93: The New Golden Age of Handcrafted Guitars." Included in this issue is an article by luthier William R. Cumpiano, "Hand to Hand: The North American Renaissance of Individually Crafted Guitars," 49–54.

18. According to one reliable source, *Statistica*, annual unit sales of acoustic guitars in the United States increased from 1.1 million in 2009 to 1.60 million in 2020. See: https://www.statista.com/statistics/439891/number-of-acoustic-guitars-sold-in-the-us/.

19. In the United States, average annual unit sales for the 2010–2019 period were 1.41 million for acoustic guitars, compared with 1.13 million for electric guitars. Averages tabulated from data in *Music Trades*, April 2020, 68.

20. Some notable examples include Dave Hunter et al., *Acoustic Guitar: The Illustrated Encyclopedia* (San Diego, CA: Thunder Bay, 2003); Gruhn and Carter, *Acoustic Guitars*, and Tony Bacon, *History of the American Guitar: 1833 to the Present Day* (Milwaukee, WI: Backbeat Books, 2011).

21. On Martin, see Jim Washburn and Richard Johnston, *Martin Guitars: An Illustrated Celebration of America's Premier Guitarmaker* (Pleasantville, NY: Reader's Digest, 1997); Walter Carter, *The Martin Book: A Complete History of Martin Guitars*, updated ed. (San Francisco: Backbeat Books, 2006); and Richard Johnston and Dick Boak, *Martin Guitars: A History*, rev. ed. (Milwaukee, WI: Hal Leonard, 2008). On Gibson, see Walter Carter, ed., *Gibson Guitars: 100 Years of an American Icon* (Los Angeles: General Publishing Group, 1994) and Eldon Whitford, David Vinopal, and Dan Erlewine, *Gibson's Fabulous Flat-top Guitars: An Illustrated History & Guide* (San Francisco: GPI Books, 1994). Finally, for Taylor, see Michael John Simmons, *Taylor Guitars: 30 Years of a New American Classic* (Bergkirchen, Germany: PPVMEDIEN, 2003) and Teja Gerken, *Taylor Guitar Book: 40 Years of Great American Flattops* (Milwaukee, WI: Backbeat Books, 2015).

22. Examples include Tim Brookes, *Guitar: An American Life* (New York: Grove Press, 2005); Allen St. John, *Clapton's Guitar: Watching Wayne Henderson Build the Perfect Instrument* (New York: Free Press, 2005); Kathryn Marie Dudley, *Guitar Makers: The Endurance of Artisanal Values in North America* (Chicago: University of Chicago Press, 2014); Daniel Wile, *Randy Wood: The Lore of the Luthier* (Knoxville: University of Tennessee Press, 2020); and John Warnock, *Beauty: The Making of a Custom Guitar* (Tucson, AZ: Wheatmark, 2020).

CHAPTER 1

1. Francis Davis, *The History of the Blues: The Roots, the Music, the People from Charley Patton to Robert Cray* (New York: Hyperion, 1995), 86.

2. Quote from website of The Ark: https://www.theark.org/about/history. Founded in 1965, The Ark still operates today, in a different location, as an independent (not church sponsored), nonprofit organization that is, according to the website, "dedicated to the enrichment of the human spirit through the presentation, preservation and encouragement of folk, roots and ethnic music and related arts." The original Hill House was demolished in 1986.

3. "Statesboro Blues," the better known of the two songs, was written and first recorded in 1928 by Blind Willie McTell (1901–59). The song was later covered by the Allman Brothers, Taj Mahal, Rory Block, and many others, and it is listed by *Rolling Stone* magazine as ninth on its list of "100 Greatest Guitar Songs of All Time." See https://www.stereogum.com/10114/rolling_stones_100_greatest_guitar_songs_of_all_ti/franchises/list/. Luke Jordan (1892–1952) recorded his "Church Bells Blues" in 1927.

Lest the reader be led to believe that I have super-human memory that perfectly recalls details of a live performance I heard fifty years ago, I have drawn my description of Bromberg's performance of "Statesboro Blues/Church Bells Blues" from a live 1973 recording he did for a subsequent album; the song is included in a 1998 compilation album: *David Bromberg—The Player: A Retrospective* (Columbia). When I saw Bromberg at The Ark, he performed the song as on the 1973 recording.

4. Liner notes to CD *David Bromberg—The Player: A Retrospective*, Columbia, 1998.

5. The most detailed account of Dylan's then-controversial performance is Elijah Wald,

Dylan Goes Electric: Newport, Seeger, Dylan, and the Night That Split the Sixties (New York: Dey Street, 2015).

6. Brad Tolinski and Alan Di Perna, *Play It Loud: An Epic History of the Style, Sound, & Revolution of the Electric Guitar* (New York: Doubleday, 2016), 17.

7. See the website for David Bromberg Fine Violins, LLC: https://www.davidbromberg fineviolins.com.

8. This and the following quote are from Bromberg's website: https://davidbromberg.net.

9. Quoted in Michael Molenda, et al., eds., *The Guitar Player Book: The Ultimate Resource for Guitarists* (New York: Backbeat Books, 2007), 70. The quote originally came from a cover story on Raitt published in *Guitar Player* magazine, May 1977.

10. Robert Santelli, *The Big Book of Blues: A Biographical Encyclopedia* (New York: Penguin, 1993), 275.

11. For example, on his 1996 album *Phantom Blues*, he is the sole featured vocalist on all fourteen tracks, but he plays an instrument on just one, with that instrument being harmonica.

12. http://www.tajblues.com/biography/

13. The relevant "world music" recordings are *Buena Vista Social Club* (1997, Cuba), *Mambo Sinuendo* (2003, India), *A Meeting by the River* 1993, India), and *Talking Timbuktu* (1995, Mali).

14. Speedy flat-picking on the guitar developed first among primarily *electric* guitar players such as Otis Wilson "Joe" Maphis (1921–86) and Walter Louis "Hank" Garland (1930–2004). The electric guitar's amplification made it relatively easy, at least compared to the typically unamplified acoustic guitar, for the player to apply a lighter, and therefore quicker, touch to the instrument, thereby facilitating fast single-note picking.

15. Kent Gustavson, *Blind but Now I See: The Biography of Music Legend Doc Watson.* (New York: Bloomington Twig Books, 2012), nonpaginated front matter.

16. I pause here to note the extraordinary impact of Grisman (b. 1945), a wildly creative mandolinist, on the world of the acoustic guitar. In looking at his recorded output, one is struck by the level of collaboration he has had with several guitarists featured here, including not only Doc Watson, but also Norman Blake and Tony Rice. Grisman can not only play bluegrass-style mandolin at a Bill Monroe-level, but he has also fashioned his own brand of "Dawg" music that incorporates the jazz-inflected styles of Django Reinhardt and Stéphane Grappelli.

17. Quoted in Gustavson, *Blind but Now I See*, 309.

18. The description in this paragraph is drawn from this video of the "guitar jam" at the 1979 Telluride Bluegrass Festival: https://www.youtube.com/watch?v=J8Y6dp3lɪBU.

19. See Tony Rice's introduction to the traditional song "I Am a Pilgrim," that he and his band perform, on YouTube: https://www.youtube.com/watch?v=YwAX2_vkHqA .

20. Scott Nygaard, "Farther Along: The Guitar Revelations of Clarence White," *Acoustic Guitar*, June 1998, 64–65.

21. Tim Stafford and Caroline Wright examine Rice's collaboration with Clarence White in their insightful biography *Still Inside: The Tony Rice Story* (Kingsport, TN: Word of Mouth Press, 2010). As we shall see in Chapter 3, Rice later developed another type of

collaboration, with luthier Richard Hoover, founder of Santa Cruz Guitar Company, to produce a near-precise replica of the "Clarence guitar," including the modifications, such as enlarged sound hole, that Clarence made to the original Martin D-28. To my knowledge, Rice has always performed with either the original Martin or the Santa Cruz replica.

22. See the wonderful improvisational interaction between Bromberg and Cosgrove in the studio version of Bromberg's original song, "Diamond Lil": https://www .youtube.com/watch?v=XI_7otYJ71w. One music writer termed this song, which is firmly within the "rueful blues" genre of sadness and regret over a misspent life, as Bromberg's "reflection on all his friends and fellow travelers who partied too hard and too long and paid too high a price" (https://americansongwriter.com /david-bromberg-scores-big-success-on-big-road/).

23. For background on Elizabeth Cotten and her relationship with the Seeger family, see Irwin Stambler and Lyndon Stambler, *Folk and Blues: The Encyclopedia* (New York: St. Martin's Press, 2001), 132–34. See also various references in Ray Allen, *Gone to the Country: The New Lost City Ramblers & the Folk Music Revival* (Urbana: University of Illinois Press, 2010); Bill C. Malone, *Music from the True Vine: Mike Seeger's Life & Musical Journey.* Chapel Hill: UNC Press, 2011).

24. Valerie Turner, "Out of the Shadows: Undersung Women of the Blues and Their Vast Contributions to the Music," *Acoustic Guitar,* 327 (March/April 2021), 34.

25. Useful contrasts between the Piedmont and Delta styles of guitar playing are found in Dick Weissman, *Blues: The Basics* (New York: Routledge, 2005), 44–81. There is, to be sure, a massive literature on blues music, and it would be futile to try to compile a complete list of sources. An excellent overview is Lawrence Cohn, ed., *Nothing But the Blues: The Music and the Musicians* (New York: Abbeville Press, 1993). Also essential is Robert Palmer, *Deep Blues* (New York: Penguin Books, 1981).

26. *Somethin Gotta Be Arranged*, directed by Geoff Adams posted January 10, 2016, https:// www.youtube.com/watch?v=WPkw42L97Aw. This documentary has wonderful footage of a forty-year old Geremia playing guitar and singing the blues standard "Don't You Lie to Me," with pianist Blind John Davis (1913–85) in Davis's Chicago home.

27. Adams, *Somethin Gotta Be Arranged.*

28. Quoted in David Hamburger, "Talkin' Blues: A Roundtable with Roy Book Binder, Steve James, and Paul Geremia on Living and Learning the Blues," *Acoustic Guitar,* November 1997, 64.

29. *Somethin' Gotta Be Arranged.*

30. Robert Cantwell, *Bluegrass Breakdown: The Making of the Old Southern Sound* (New York: Da Capo, 1992), 30–31.

31. There is a useful brief tutorial on Travis picking at https://www.youtube.com /watch?v=m6b371mNkCw .

32. Tommy Emmanuel is the source of this quote in this video (about 3:11): https://www .youtube.com/watch?v=90IBzV3Rcdo.

33. Steve Waksman, relying on the work of Robert Cantwell, conjectures that Atkins's "broader musical palette" may also have resulted from the different way the two men learned to play guitar. Travis learned personally from some local guitarists in Muhlen-

berg County—notably Mose Rager and Ike Everly (yes, the father of Don and Phil, the Everly Brothers)—whereas Atkins was largely self-taught, with his major musical input coming from the radio. Waksman suggests that the "direct-and-personal" manner of musical transmission, à la Travis, may circumscribe one's playing to the style of playing being demonstrated, whereas self-teaching, à la Atkins, requires figuring things out on one's own, thereby encouraging a greater degree of experimentation and creativity. See Steve Waksman, *Instruments of Desire: The Electric Guitar and the Shaping of Musical Experience* (Cambridge, MA: Harvard University Press, 1999), 88–94 and Robert Cantwell, *Bluegrass Breakdown: The Making of the Old Southern Sound* (New York: Da Capo Press, 1992 ed.), 154–55.

34. *Chet Atkins: A Life in Music*, Produced by Gregory Hall (TH Entertainment, 2000), https://www.youtube.com/watch?v=FEswohCU6Ts.

35. For simplicity's sake, I will use the present tense in referring to both the deceased Atkins and the still-present Emmanuel.

36. See the video (around 6:45) of Emmanuel and Les Paul, jamming and conversing together in 2009: https://www.youtube.com/watch?v=90IBzV3Rcd0.

37. Tommy Emmanuel, in instructional video. See, at about minute 5:00: https://www.facebook.com/GuitarWorld/videos/the-tommy-emmanuel-guitar-methodchet-atkins-merle-travis-the-importance-of-tunin/10156861995538974/.

38. This and the following quotations by Fahey himself and Pete Townsend come from the documentary film *In Search of Blind Joe Death: The Saga of John Fahey*, directed by James Cullingham (Tamarack Productions, 2012).

39. See Fahey's full discography at https://www.johnfahey.com/pages/textlist.html. This website features a wealth of information about Fahey's life and work.

40. I am grateful to an anonymous reviewer of this manuscript for emphasizing Fahey's enduring influence on the world of finger-style guitar and for bringing these and other musicians to my attention.

41. Russell Letson, "One Guitar, No Borders: The New Solo Adventures of Leo Kottke," *Acoustic Guitar*, December 1999, 60.

42. Adam Levy, "Bruce Cockburn: The Canadian Songwriter/guitarist on Playing in Open Tunings and Keeping an Open Mind," *Acoustic Guitar*, July 2012, 32.

43. Levy, "Bruce Cockburn," 33.

44. Interview by Matthew Caws, "The Paste Happiest Hour," April 28, 2020, https://www.youtube.com/watch?v=DEPwHGBToUo. See also Cockburn's memoir, *Rumours of Glory: A Memoir* (New York: Harper One, 2014), and James A. Heald, *World of Wonders: The Lyrics and Music of Bruce Cockburn* (self-published, 2012).

45. Highly recommended is Thompson's lively, insightful memoir of his early years as a musician: *Beeswing: Losing My Way and Finding My Voice, 1967–1975*, with Scott Timberg (Chapel Hill, NC: Algonquin Books, 2021).

46. Grayson Haver Currin, "The Face of Solo Guitar Is Changing," *New York Times*, May 2, 2021, 8.

47. Currin, "The Face of Solo Guitar," 8.

48. As quoted on her website; see: http://www.kakiking.com/contact.

49. See Williams in this YouTube clip: https://www.youtube.com/watch?v=Y-4gVQd CXVM. See also Noah Lekas, "More Than a Guitar Hero: Fingerstyle and Beyond with Yasmin Williams," *The Fretboard Journal*, 50 (2022), 16–24.

50. Adam Levy, "Still and All: Richard Thompson Looks Forward and Back," *The Journal*, 35 (2015), 28.

CHAPTER 2

1. The first use of this term was in 1993, when the feature article and the cover of the magazine *Acoustic Guitar* announced "Vintage '93: The New Golden Age of Hand-crafted Guitars." As Dudley notes, "Founded in 1990, the periodical itself was a product of the market phenomena it commemorated and encouraged" (*Guitar Makers*, xii).

2. As the reader will notice, I quote extensively from my conversations with these lu-thiers. For convenience' sake, all such direct quotes from these individuals will not be footnoted.

3. Rick Davis, "The Pioneer: Michael Gurian's Life of Lutherie on the Third Planet from the Sun," *The Fretboard Journal*, 5 (Summer 2007), 41.

4. Orville Johnson, "Michael Gurian," *Acoustic Guitar*, October 2013, 60.

5. Personal information about Michael Gurian's life comes primarily from my interview with him on July 21, 2016. Other useful sources are articles by Rick Davis and Orville Johnson, cited above; Michael John Simmons, *Boutique Acoustics: 180 Years of Handbuilt American Guitars* (Milwaukee, WI: Backbeat Books, 2015), 73–77; and Dick Boak and Adam Perlmutter, "Peace, Love, & Guitars: Michael Gurian, Linda Manzer, Richard Hoover, and Steve Klein Remember the 1970s Lutherie Revolution," *Acoustic Guitar*, July/August 2020, 38–44. For a video of and about Gurian, see *A Rare Bird: A Portrait of Luthier Michael Gurian*, produced by *The Fretboard Journal* (2013), https://www.youtube.com/watch?v=IEoWHmPhaeA.

6. The classic texts on the so-called company man are Vance Packard, *The Hidden Per-suaders* (New York: David McKay, 1957), and David Riesman et al., *The Lonely Crowd: A Study of the Changing American Character* (New Haven: Yale University Press, 1950). Also essential for grasping the Zeitgeist of 1960s rebellion against the postwar status quo is the *Port Huron Statement*, the 1963 founding document of the Students for a Democratic Society (SDS).

7. The search for how to live an "authentic" life among primarily a generation of young White males is a key theme in Kathryn Marie Dudley, *Guitar Makers*. This book is the most penetrating study to date of the North American artisanal lutherie community. This theme also comes out in several books about individual luthiers, written by people who directly engaged and/or interacted with these luthiers as they built a guitar. See, for example, Allen St. John, *Clapton's Guitar: Watching Wayne Henderson Build the Perfect Instrument* (New York: Free Press, 2005), and Tim Brookes, *Guitar: An American Life* (New York: Grove Press), about Rick Davis of Running Dog Guitars; John Warnock, *Beauty: The Making of a Custom Guitar* (Tucson, AZ: Wheatmark, 2020), about Vincent Guidroz of New Orleans Guitar Company.

8. Tim Olsen, quoted in John Sangster, "Learning the Trade: Jean Larrivée and the Making of a Steel-String Tradition," *Acoustic Guitar*, July 1995, 60.

9. Whitney Phaneuf et al., "In Her Own Words: 14 Guitarists, Educators, and Luthiers Share Their Passion for the Craft," *Acoustic Guitar*, March 2017, 32.

10. Johnson, "Michael Gurian," 60.

11. Quoted in Patrick Sullivan, "The Magnificent Seven," *Acoustic Guitar*, June 2017, 67.

12. This quality of the guitar-making community came home to me again in the midst of the Covid-19 pandemic in 2020, which I report in the Conclusion. Several guitar makers spoke of the importance of cooperation and helping each other get through the shutdowns and supply problems brought on by the pandemic.

13. Dudley, *Guitar Makers*, 26. For historical background, see GAL's website: https://luth.org.

14. Collings died of cancer on July 14, 2017. See remembrances of Bill Collings by fellow luthiers and musicians in "Bill Collings Remembered: Musicians, Builders, and Customers Reflect on an Industry Giant," *The Fretboard Journal*, 40 (Fall 2017), 102–18.

15. "Bill Collings: Guitar Maker and Founder of Collings Guitars" (obituary), *Music Trades*, August 2017, 116.

16. For a useful article on Jean Larrivée's background, in particular his contribution as a mentor to younger Canadian luthiers, see Zak Morgan, "The Larrivée Tradition." Also see the following: Marc Greilshamer, "Chief, Cook, Bottle Washer: From the Jungles of India to the Factory Floor, Jean Larrivée Favors the Hands-on Approach," *The Fretboard Journal*, 10 (Summer 2008), 36–55; and Teja Gerken, "Larrivée Guitars," *Acoustic Guitar*, 184 (April 2008), 50–58.

17. Much of the personal information on Richard Hoover, as well any direct quuotations, came from my visit to Santa Cruz Guitar Company and my interview with Hoover on February 5, 2015. Useful background articles on Hoover and Santa Cruz guitars can be found in Teja Gerken, "California Dreams," *Acoustic Guitar*, August 2007, 74–81; Mark Segal Kemp, "Birth of the Boutique," *Acoustic Guitar*, October 2014, 70–73.

18. The full story of the White/Rice "Holy Grail" D-28 guitar is told in Art Dudley, "58957: Tony Rice and his Holy Grail D-28," *The Fretboard Journal*, April 2016, https://www.fretboardjournal.com/features/58957-tony-rice-and-his-holy-grail-martin-d-28/ .

19. I interviewed Michael Millard at his Vermont shop on May 24, 2016. Useful articles on Froggy Bottom Guitars include Scott Ainslee, "Life in the Woods: Michael Millard and the Natural World of Froggy Bottom Guitars," *The Fretboard Journal*, 19 (Fall 2010), 28–41; Adam Perlmutter, "Froggy Bottom Guitars," *Acoustic Guitar*, March 2012, 46–52.

20. According to the Froggy Bottom website, the term "'froggy bottom" refers to the river bottom land which flooded predictably every spring and was relegated to former slaves and sharecroppers. It was where the earliest juke joints sprang up and where the Blues were born." See froggybottomguitars.com.

21. I first interviewed Dana Bourgeois on May 23, 2016. For useful background information, see Art Dudley, "Hands On: How Dana Bourgeois Became New England's Biggest Guitarmaker," *The Fretboard Journal*, 32 (Winter 2013–2014), 78–95.

22. Ned Oldham, "Shenandoah Valley Boys, From the Cradle of Appalachia, Update

Guitar-Making Traditions," *The Fretboard Journal*, 18 (Summer 2010), 77. Also see Adam Perlmutter, "Virginia Is for Luthiers: Huss & Dalton Celebrate Two Decades Making Fine Guitars and Banjos," *Acoustic Guitar*, September 2015, 62–63.

23. Interviews with Steve McCreary, January 28, 2018 and June 15, 2022. See also the following interviews with Steve McCreary commenting on the current "post-Bill" era at Collings: with *The Fretboard Journal*, October 2020, https://www.fretboardjournal.com /podcasts/podcast-302-steve-mccreary-gm-of-collings-guitars-mandolins/; and with Artisan Guitars, January 28, 2020, https://www.youtube.com/watch?v=TGZz5TlgLD8.

24. David D. Berkowitz, "From the Ground Up: A Fellow Luthier Pays Tribute to the Trailblazing Work of Linda Manzer," *The Fretboard Journal*, 36 (Summer 2016), 94.

25. For an extensive list of female luthiers, see Mamie Minch, "50 Women Builders and Repairers in the Guitar Industry," *She Shreds*, March 12, 2020, https://sheshreds.com /50-women-builders-and-repairers/

26. The essential reference work for Henderson's guitar-making is Allen St. John, *Clapton's Guitar: Watching Wayne Henderson Build the Perfect Instrument* (New York: Free Press, 2005). This is an informed, vividly written story of Henderson and his guitars.

27. "Jesse Winchester, Wayne & Jayne Henderson," *American Routes*, May 31, 2017, http:// americanroutes.wwno.org/archives/show/1012/Jesse-Winchester-Wayne-Jayne -Henderson.

28. Quoted in Alexa Peters, "Sustainable Energy: Guitar and Ukulele Maker Elle Jayne Henderson Carves Her Own Niche," *The Fretboard Journal*, 39 (Summer 2017), 56.

29. Quote is from her Blogsplot website, "The Luthier's Apprentice. See http://theluthiers apprentice.blogspot.com.

30. Brian K. Saunders, "Bench Press: Atelier Rosenkrantz," *The Fretboard Journal*, May 2016, https://www.fretboardjournal.com/columns/bench-press-atelier-rosenkrantz/. Also see Rachel Rosenkrantz, "Sustainable Futures: A Luthier's Experiments with Some Truly Wild Biomaterials," *The Fretboard Journal*, 48 (2021), 17–24.

31. Kate Koening, "Innovation and Exploration: Kaki King is Still Pushing Boundaries on Her Latest Album," *Acoustic Guitar*, July/August 2021, 14. A good example of the *passerelle* bridge in action is this clip of King playing her tune "Bowen Island": https://www .youtube.com/watch?v=FlR_k7FZnsw.

32. E. E. Bradman," How I Learned to Make Guitars," *Acoustic Guitar*, March/April 2020, 27–28.

33. Mamie Minch, "Innovation Through Tradition: Four Modern Luthiers Discuss Their Craft," *Acoustic Guitar*, August 13, 2019, https://acousticguitar.com/innovation-through -tradition-four-modern-luthiers-discuss-their-craft/

34. Maegen Wells Guitars & Mandolins, 2018, http://www.maegenwellsguitars.com/.

35. Elizabeth Dale, "Maegen Wells Guitars and Mandolins One Woman Shop Pushes Lutherie to New Heights," NAMM, https://www.namm.org/playback/success-stories /maegen-wells-guitars-and-mandolins-one-woman-shop.

36. Dale, "Maegen Wells."

1. Miguel Ángel Ariza, "Masters of the Telecaster," *Guitars Exchange*, https://guitars exchange.com/en/psych-out/293/the-10-greatest-telecaster-guitarists/.
2. *James Burton Foundation*, 2022, http://www.jamesburtonfoundation.org/.
3. In this chapter, I will employ the terms Taylor Guitars and, simply, Taylor, interchangeably, to refer to the company. Context should make clear whether I am referring to Bob Taylor himself or the company that bears his name.
4. Author interview with Ren Ferguson, January 22, 2015.
5. Simmons, *Taylor Guitars*, 148.
6. Dudley, *Guitar Makers*, 119.
7. Especially valuable in my historical research have been two "anniversary" books: Simmons, *Taylor Guitars*, and Gerken, *Taylor Guitar Book*. Although clearly sponsored by Taylor to mark these celebratory milestones, both books contain much historical documentation and in-depth interviews with key figures.
8. Bob Taylor, *Guitar Lessons: A Life's Journey Turning Passion into Business* (Hoboken, NJ: John Wiley & Sons, 2011).
9. Taylor, *Guitar Lessons*, 5.
10. Taylor, *Guitar Lessons*, 5.
11. Any direct, unattributed quotations from Bob Taylor in this chapter are drawn from my interview with him on January 23, 2015.
12. Tim Luranc, "Dream Weavers: The Inauspicious Debut of Taylor Guitars," *The Fretboard Journal*, Summer 2008, 10.
13. Bob Taylor, quoted in Simmons, *Taylor Guitars*, 25.
14. See https://www.deeringbanjos.com and https://www.stellingbanjo.com.
15. Simmons, *Taylor Guitars*, 53.
16. Schemmer remained a partner with Taylor and Listug for the next eight years, until they bought him out in October 1982.
17. Taylor, *Guitar Lessons*, 78.
18. Taylor, *Guitar Lessons*, 78–79.
19. See especially Dudley, *Guitar Makers*.
20. On the nature of craft communities, see Richard Sennett, *The Craftsman* (New Haven, CT: Yale University Press, 2008). Sennett points to the Linux operating system as an example of a modern-day craft community based on sharing open-source information. My guitar-playing friend Paul Lucas, who works in the software industry, would concur with Sennett. In a private communication, he writes that the kind of information sharing and cooperation one sees among guitar makers "reflects a much larger social trend of 'open' collaboration in many areas/facets of endeavors. The software industry is a prime example of open collaboration. Open source software development is huge now and driving the most innovation in software. Of course, like the software industry, guitar makers are looking for ways to monetize the "product."
21. Author interview with Ren Ferguson, January 22, 2015.
22. Taylor, *Guitar Lessons*, 85.

23. Oral History Program, NAMM, May 31, 2012, https://www.namm.org/library/oral-history/tim-luranc.

24. Gerken, *Taylor Guitar Book*, 32. All production and employee figures in this and the following paragraph are drawn from this source, pp. 32–48.

25. In Taylor's purely acoustic line, for example—in which most models come standard with electric pickup—there are, by the company's own count, 115 different models from which to choose, with suggested retail prices ranging from $499 to $8,899. Taylor Quality Guitars, 2012–22, http://www.taylorguitars.com.

26. The Tecate plant manufactures the following models: 100 series, 200 series, Baby Taylor, Big Baby Taylor, and GS Mini. Retail prices on these models ranges from $300 to $1,300. Daily production by Tecate's 250 employees is about five hundred guitars per day.

27. Taylor, *Guitar Lessons*, 106.

28. Author interview with luthier who requested anonymity, February 5, 2015.

29. Taylor Quality Guitars, https://www.taylorguitars.com/about.

30. Specifically, the neck tends to warp even as it displaces upward, thereby distorting the guitar's original intonation and the causing the action—the distance between the strings and the fret board—to rise and thereby make the instrument harder to fret. As for the body, this string tension also tends to cause sinkage in the top because of the downward pressure of the fretboard. Sinkage may, in turn, cause cracks and loosening of the top's internal braces.

    A neck reset, a skilled repair person's job, requires removing the neck, making minute adjustments in the angle of the neck vis-à-vis the body, then regluing the neck. As I can attest from personal experience, such a repair can take weeks in the shop and cost hundreds of dollars.

31. According to one knowledgeable source, "Bolt-on necks have been around since the 1830s—some Stauffers and a few early Martins had a complex clock-key mechanism to hold the neck on, but it wasn't until the 1970s, when Bob Taylor introduced a bolted-on neck capable of supporting the tension of steel strings, that more builders began using bolts in favor of the traditional dovetail joint." Gerken et al., *Acoustic Guitar*, 37.

32. Taylor fret boards include a reinforcing layer of wood under the end that extends over part of the body. That part of the fret board becomes, in effect, part of the top itself and thereby helps resist the string tension that often causes the top to sink.

33. See https://www.taylorguitars.com/guitars/electric/features/series/t5z.

34. I use the phrase "at least rhetorically" to note that there is sometimes a gap between rhetoric and reality. A friend and astute student of guitars and their history, Paul Lucas, points out to me that, notwithstanding Taylor's claim to not be bound by the past, the company has borrowed such traditional terms as concert, orchestra, jumbo, and dreadnought to describe their guitar body sizes and shapes. S

35. An X-brace was first used by C. F. Martin & Co. in 1843, but not widely adopted in steel-string guitars until the 1930s. Until that era, most guitars were braced in either a fan or a ladder pattern. See Robert Shaw and Peter Szego, eds., *Inventing the American Guitar: The Pre-Civil War Innovations of C. F. Martin and His Contemporaries* (Milwaukee, WI: Hal Leonard, 2013), xvii.

36. According to one source, "Martin ceased scalloping its top bracing in 1945, as the absurdly high tension from string gauges intended for arch-top guitars caused too much "bellying" of the top around the bridge." See Gerken et al., *Acoustic Guitar*,157.

37. Email correspondence from Terry Straker, owner of Guitar Works in Evanston, IL, May 5, 2020.

38. Dudley, *Guitar Makers*, 120.

39. Author interview, January 26, 2016.

40. Author interview, January 22, 2015.

41. Taylor Quality Guitars, https://www.taylorguitars.com.

42. Bob Taylor, column, *Wood & Steel*, Winter 2015, 5.

43. A full description of Taylor's Ebony Project can be found on its website: https://www.taylorguitars.com/ebonyproject.

44. See the excellent documentary *Musicwood*, directed by Maxine Trump (Helpman Productions, 2013).

45. Bob Taylor, quoted in Gerken,*Taylor Guitar Book*, 124.

46. Quotations from Andy Powers in this and the following paragraph come from my interview with him, January 26, 2016. For further background on Powers, see Jason Verlinde, "Wave Lengths: Catching a Break with Taylor's Andy Powers," *The Fretboard Journal*, 42 (Summer 2018), 21–35.

47. "Taylor Transitions to 100% Employee Ownership Through an ESOP," January 11, 2021, https://blog.taylorguitars.com/taylor-transitions-to-100-employee-ownership -through-an-esop.

48. George Varda, "Taylor Guitars Announces Complete Transition of Ownership to Its Employees," *San Diego Union Tribune,* January 11, 2021.

49. "Will Taylor Guitars' Unique Funding Resonate with Other Companies?" The ESOP Association, June 3, 2021, https://esopassociation.org/articles/will-taylor-guitars -unique-esop-funding-resonate-other-companies.

50. Phone conversation, June 17, 2022.

51. Quoted in Gerken, *Taylor Guitar Book*, 20.

52. The most authoritative source for such figures is *Music Trades* magazine. In its April 2020 issue (p. 102), the publication reports that in 2019 Taylor had total sales revenues of $122,450,000 (rank #15 among North American "music supplier companies"), slightly ahead of C. F. Martin & Co.'s $118,404,000 (rank #16). Two other household names — Fender and Gibson—far outsell Taylor and Martin overall by virtue of the huge range of other products they produce, including electric guitars, amplifiers, and other sound equipment.

53. Simmons, *Taylor Guitars*, 191.

54. Simmons, *Taylor Guitars*, 191.

CHAPTER 4

1. A word of explanation at the outset of this chapter. As the diligent reader knows by now, I have made a point of direct observational research, including factory/shop visits

and interviews with guitar makers. Alas, the coronavirus pandemic trampled my plans to continue this type of research in China, and I have been unable to visit guitar shops and factories there. Fortunately, I have been able to draw on the knowledge of several Americans with ties to Chinese guitar producers, and these have been most helpful in trying to understand the rise of imported guitars since the 1960s.

2. The Gibson lawsuit against the maker of Ibanez, which was settled out of court, was just one of several such suits filed against Japanese guitar makers during the 1970s. Adirondack Guitar, "What Do We Mean When We Say Lawsuit Guitar?" January 18, 2019, https://www.adkguitar.com/blogs/news/what-do-we-mean-when-we-say -lawsuit-guitar; and Leonard Wyeth, "Ibanez 'Lawsuit' & Elger Guitars," 2008, http:// www.acousticmusic.org/research/guitar-information/large-shop-guitar-builders /ibanez-lawsuit-elger-guitars/.

3. See Country Joe's immortal three-minute performance at https://www.youtube.com /watch?v=eRl6-bHlz-4. The headstock of his Yamaha guitar can be seen clearly at minute 1:30 of the clip.

4. Takamine Guitars, "History," 2022, https://www.takamine.com/history.

5. Takamine's website features an extensive list of nearly eighty well-known artists who play Takamine guitars. See: https://www.takamine.com/artists. One can also take a virtual visit, via YouTube, of the main Takamine factory in Gifu Prefecture (near the south-central city of Nagoya) at: https://www.youtube.com/watch?v=A4xLqbbnYDw. At minute 33:30 of this clip, the narrator says, "This is where a Takamine becomes a Takamine" as he and his guide arrive at the station where pre-amps and pickups are installed. The luthier then proceeds to do so in the Glenn Frey model he is making.

6. For example, in 2020, one high-volume instrument retailer, Musician's Friend, lists new Alvarez Yairi models for $2,300–2,700, whereas "regular" Alvarez models list for $380–640. See https://www.musiciansfriend.com.

7. There is abundant literature on China's economic transformation since the late 1970s. An excellent recent book that places current-day China within this recent historical context is Elizabeth Economy, *The Third Revolution: Xi Jinping and the New Chinese State* (New York: Oxford University Press, 2019).

8. Data reported here for guitars—Chinese exports and U.S. imports—come primarily from two sources: the National Association of Music Merchants' (NAMM) Global Reports and the monthly publication *Music Trades*. NAMM's data does not break out acoustic vs. electric guitars but considers both types together as "guitars." As a rough guide, acoustic and electric guitars have approximately the same number of unit sales each year.

9. Saga Music, 2022, https://www.sagamusic.com.

10. Saga's website offers (1) banjos: 4 brands, total of 10 models, retail prices between $300–$2,000; (2) guitars: 8 brands, 206 models, price range $100–$3,500; (3) mandolins: 4 brands, 43 models, price range $110–$3,000; (3) ukuleles: 2 brands, 66 models, price range $40–$1,080; (4) violins: 4 brands, 188 models, price range $100–$2,400. https:// www.sagamusic.com.

11. The bulk of the information about Saga Music and Richard Keldsen presented in this section derives from various interviews and conversations I have had with Keldsen during the course of my research between 2015 and 2022. All direct quotations from him come from my interviews.

12. Keldsen says that the Blueridge guitars of that period—made with solid spruce tops and rosewood-laminate back-and-sides—were the least expensive rosewood guitars on the market.

13. Gerken et al., *Acoustic Guitar*, 362.

14. An internet search for "OEM guitars China" quickly produced a website called "Made in China" that features hundreds of producer/supplier companies that manufacture guitars under contract to a buyer who specifies such aspects as the number and type of guitar to be produced. See https://www.made-in-china.com/products-search/find -china-products/obonolimit/Acoustic_Guitar-4.html. At the 2020 annual trade show, I saw many booths of such OEM companies with names such as Guangzhou Vines Musical Instruments Co., Ltd.; Hanzhong Hawanas Co.; and Zhangzhou Elise Co.

15. True confession: I ended up buying the Eastman grand auditorium model and was quickly inspired to write a new song using it.

16. The following paragraphs are based on the author's conversation with Qian Ni at the 2022 NAMM Show in Anaheim, CA, June 3, 2022.

17. https://www.eastmanguitars.com/vision.

18. https://www.eastmanguitars.com/mandolin.

19. Email communication to author from Dana Bourgeois, May 30, 2022.

20. See Bourgeois website: https://bourgeoisguitars.com/an-important-message-from -dana-bourgeois/

21. Interview with Dana Bourgeois, September 30, 2020. Subsequent quotes from him come from this same interview. Also see the excellent interview conducted by Jason Verlinde in *Fretboard Journal*, "Interview: Dana Bourgeois on the new Touchstone Series of Guitars," in August 2021. See https://www.fretboardjournal.com/features /interview-dana-bourgeois-on-the-new-touchstone-series-of-guitars/.

22. Dana can be seen demonstrating this technique at https://www.youtube.com/watch?v =Ei5-DkVTrEE.

23. Email communication to author from Dana Bourgeois, May 30, 2022.

24. Author's phone conversation with Dana Bourgeois, March 8, 2022.

25. Brad Tolenski and Alan Di Perna, *Play It Loud? An Epic History of the Style, Sound, and Revolution of the Electric Guitar* (New York: Doubleday, 2016), 267.

26. Dudley, *Guitar Makers*, 321n47.

27. Wheeler, *American Guitars*, 230–37.

28. After Harmony's dissolution, one of its longtime executives, Charles A. Rubovits, reflected on the complex causes of the company's demise: "One reason Harmony folded was the Japanese competition. I always said it was my fault they came into the industry, because if we had put up five factories in the U.S., we never would've needed the Japanese. We had the know-how, but we didn't have the guts. We were too conservative.

We were very successful, so we didn't want to do more, and as a result the Japanese began to get a bigger and bigger share of the market." Quoted in Wheeler, *American Guitars*, 237.

29. David Knowles, "American Companies Are Producing Higher-quality Affordable A coustics in China," *Acoustic Guitar*, February 24, 2014, https://acousticguitar.com /american-companies-are-producing-higher-quality-affordable-acoustics-in-china/.

30. Inflation Calculator, USD Inflation, http://www.usdinflation.com.

CHAPTER 5

1. See Carter's essential reference books: his edited collection, *Gibson Guitars*, and *The Martin Book*.

2. Whitford, Vinopal, and Erlewine, *Gibson's Fabulous Flat-top Guitars*, 1. This book provides a comprehensive overview of the various models of Gibson's flattop guitars since the company began making the small-body L-0 and L-1 instruments in 1926.

3. Martin also maintains a modest production of ukuleles.

4. George Gruhn and Walter Carter, *Gruhn's Guide to Vintage Guitars: An Identification Guide for American Fretted Instruments*, 3rd ed. (Milwaukee, WI: Backbeat, 2010).

5. For a brief overview of these six Martin figures, see Jonathan R. Walsh, "A Tradition of Creativity: Six Generations of Martin Leadership," in the company's in-house publication, *Martin: The Journal of Acoustic Guitars*," 2020), 10–21.

6. Chris Martin (C. F. Martin IV) stepped down as CEO in June 2021 but remains as owner and executive chairman. See next chapter.

7. During the war, as most of its male workforce was drafted for military service, Gibson continued guitar production by hiring many women workers. Instruments made by these "Kalamazoo Gals" are generally considered to be among the finest instruments the company has ever produced, mainly owing to the dexterity and hand skills of the women. The headstock of the guitars made during this period (1942–45) carried a decal of a banner bearing the phrase ONLY A GIBSON IS GOOD ENOUGH. Hence this brief generation of guitars is termed "Banner" guitars. See the excellent monograph: John Thomas, *Kalamazoo Gals: A Story of Extraordinary Women & Gibson's "Banner" Guitars of WWII* (Franklin, TN: American History Press, 2012). Also see this 2022 video celebrating the hundredth birthday of the last surviving member of the "Kalamazoo Gals" cohort, Irene Stearns: https://www.youtube.com/watch?v=bu44dWDEqT8.

8. Walter Carter, *The Mandolin in America: The Full Story from Orchestras to Bluegrass to the Modern Revival* (Milwaukee, WI: Backbeat, 2017), 11.

9. Roger H. Simonoff, "Orville's Instruments," in Carter, *Gibson Guitars*, 26.

10. Roger H. Simonoff, "Orville Gibson," Simonoff Banjo & Mandolin Parts, 2021, https:// www.siminoff.net/orville-gibson.

11. For a video of this surprisingly intricate technique, see the following YouTube demonstration: https://www.youtube.com/watch?v=cc4AxMoNxa8. As of this writing, this video has had nearly 300,000 views.

12. Carter, *Mandolin in America*, 37. See also Roger Simonoff's excellent overview of Loar's career: "Lloyd Allayre Loar", Simonoff Banjo, https://www.siminoff.net/lloyd-loar.

13. Richard Johnston, "Vintage Gibsons: How a Pioneering American Guitar Company Cut a Twisting Path to Success," *Acoustic Guitar* (January 2002), 40–50.

14. Joseph E. Spann, *Spann's Guide to Gibson, 1902–1941* (Anaheim Hills, CA: Centerstream, 2011), 21.

15. Gil Hembree, *Gibson Guitars: Ted McCarty's Golden Era, 1948–1966* (Milwaukee, WI: Hal Leonard, 2007). The Price List referred to in this paragraph is found on pp. 25–31. Not wishing to test the reader's patience, I have not included some of the other items on Gibson's list, including double- and triple-neck guitars, Electraharps, amplifiers, Fingerrest pickups, and zipper covers.

16. McCarty did oversee the introduction of three new flattop models late in his tenure—the J-185 (1963), Hummingbird (1964), and Dove (1966). These also remain in production to the present.

17. The cutaway is the portion of a guitar's body that appears scooped out where the neck joins the body. The purpose of the cutaway is to allow the player easier access to the upper portion (the higher-pitched notes) of the fretboard. A single cutaway is always on the fretboard's treble side which has the highest pitched strings. A double cutaway has cutaways on both sides of the fretboard, giving easier access to all strings well up the neck.

18. Essential works on the rise of the electric guitar include: Steve Waksman, *Instruments of Desire: The Electric Guitar and the Shaping of Music Experience* (Cambridge: Harvard University Press, 1999); Brad Tolinski and Alan Di Perna, *Play It Loud: An Epic History of the Styles, Sound, and Revolution of the Electric Guitar* (New York: Doubleday, 2016); and Ian S. Port, *The Birth of Loud: Leo Fender, Les Paul, and the Guitar-Pioneering Rivalry That Shaped Rock 'n' Roll* (New York: Scribner, 2019).

19. Hembree, *Gibson Guitars*, 79.

20. Port, *Birth of Loud*, 89.

21. In 1966 McCarty clashed with Gibson corporate owners, and he proceeded to purchase and head Bigsby, maker of vibratos for guitars, from 1966 to 1999.

22. Hembree, *Gibson Guitars*, 73.

23. Hembree, *Gibson Guitars*, 73.

24. The name Norlin was derived by combining parts of the names of the two primary owners of ECL at that point, <u>Nor</u>ton Stevens and Arnold Ber<u>lin</u>, son of CMI founder Maurice Berlin.

25. Walter Carter, "The Peak of Production," in Carter, *Gibson Guitars*, 238.

26. Tom Mulhern, "The Long Decline," in Carter, *Gibson Guitars*, 261.

27. "About Us," Heritage Guitar Inc., BandLab Americas, 2022, https://heritageguitars.com/pages/about-us.

28. Tom Mulhern, "Harvard Boys to the Rescue," in Carter, *Gibson Guitars*, 281.

29. Mulhern, "Harvard Boys," 281.

30. This account of the meeting comes from my interview with Ren Ferguson, January 22, 2015.

31. For Ren Ferguson, this 1986 run-in with Gibson and Juszkiewicz was a bit of déjà vu all over again. More than a decade earlier, in 1973, Ferguson had run afoul of the company by replicating Gibson banjo necks from the 1920s and 1930s—and received a similar cease-and-desist order. See Dudley, *Guitar Makers*, 49–50.

32. Dudley, *Guitar Makers*, 49–50.

33. Whitford, Vinopal, and Erlewine, *Gibson's Fabulous Flat-top Guitars*, 145. For an in-depth walk-through of the Gibson Bozeman factory featuring Ren Ferguson, see Teja Gerken, "Making History," *Acoustic Guitar*, December 2006, 77–84.

34. Whitford, Vinopal, and Erlewine, *Gibson's Fabulous Flat-top Guitars*, 189.

35. "Gibson Guitar Corp. Changes Name to Gibson Brands," *Nashville Post*, June 11, 2013, https://www.nashvillepost.com/home/gibson-guitar-corp-changes-name-to-gibson -brands/article_6707d8ba-c3b6-5e97-8e71-fcbb1e89fbad.html.

36. The Gibson Brands portfolio in 2013 included the following thirteen instrument companies: Baldwin, Chickering, Dobro, Epiphone, Garrison, Hamilton, Kramer, Maestro, Slingerland, Steinberger, Tobias, Valley Arts, Wurlitzer. It also included five audio systems/equipment companies: Cerwin-Vega, KRK, Onkyo, Stanton, TEAC.

37. Between 2014 and 2017, annual sales of Gibson's audio products declined steadily by over half—from $1.7 billion to less than $800 million. See "Gibson Chapter 11," *Music Trades*, June 2018, 26–30.

38. "Juszkiewicz on What Went Wrong at Gibson," *Music Trades*, September 2018, 60.

39. Author interview with Walter Carter, October 29, 2020.

40. Author interview with Fred Greene, May 17, 2016.

41. Author interview with Ren Ferguson, January 22, 2015.

42. Craig Havighurst, "Gibson Is Strung with Debt: Walter Carter on an Iconic Brand's Future," Roots Radio News, WMOT 89.5, April 23, 2018, https://www.wmot.org /post/gibson-strung-debt-walter-carter-iconic-brands-future#stream/0.

43. In the current era of golden parachutes, Juszkiewicz was retained for one year as a consultant for $2.1 million. See Gibson Chapter 11," *Music Trades*, June 2018, 26.

44. "Gibson Unveils Three New Guitar Collections," *Music Trades*, June 2019, 28.

45. Emile Menasché, "American Icons: How James 'JC' Curleigh Is Using Lessons from Levi's to Spur Gibson Revival," *Acoustic Guitar*, September/October 2021, 70. There is an interesting, perhaps ironic side note to the post–Juskiewicz management team assembled by KKR. Although Curleigh vowed to refocus Gibson's production efforts on guitars, neither Curleigh nor the other new top executives had any background in the music-products industry, much less guitar production itself. A quick perusal of the "About Gibson" section of the company's website indicates that the leadership team— brand president and the chief commercial, production, and financial officers—came from other fields, including sporting goods products, kitchen and bath design, and asset management. See: https://www.gibson.com/en-US/About-Us.

46. Bryan Miller, "Saving Gibson Guitars from the Musical Scrap Heap," *New York Times*, March 13, 1994, https://www.nytimes.com/1994/03/13/business/saving-gibson-guitars -from-the-musical-scrap-heap.html.

1. The opening lyrics of "The Weight," written by Robbie Robertson, are as follows: "I pulled into Nazareth, was feelin' about half past dead / I just need some place where I can lay my head / 'Hey, mister, can you tell me where a man might find a bed?' / He just grinned and shook my hand, 'no' was all he said." Robertson has said that the Nazareth reference is to the home of Martin Guitars, since he wrote the song on his own Martin D-28 guitar. See Marc Meyers, "Anatomy of a Song: 'The Weight,' by The Band's Robbie Robertson," *Wall Street Journal*, September 29, 2016.

2. Accordingly, the bookshelf of titles on Martin is starting to groan under the weight. Worthy claimants to a spot on the shelf include the following: Jim Washburn and Richard Johnston, *Martin Guitars: An Illustrated Celebration of America's Premier Guitar-maker* (Pleasantville, NY: Reader's Digest, 1997); Philip F. Gura, *C. F. Martin and His Guitars, 1796–1873* (Chapel Hill: University of North Carolina Press, 2003); Dick Boak, *Martin Guitar Masterpieces; A Showcase of Artists' Editions, Limited Editions, and Custom Guitars* (Boston: Bulfinch Press, 2003); Carter, *Martin Book*; Richard Johnston and Dick Boak, *Martin Guitars: A History*, rev. ed. (Milwaukee, WI: Hal Leonard, 2008); Richard Johnston and Dick Boak, *Martin Guitars: A Technical Reference* (Milwaukee, WI: Hal Leonard, 2009); Robert Shaw and Peter Szego, eds., *Inventing the American Guitar: The Pre-Civil War Innovations of C. F. Martin and his Contemporaries* (Milwaukee, WI: Hal Leonard, 2013).

3. This quote I found on the Martin website ca. 2020 at https://www.martinguitar.com/about/. Subsequently, the website underwent a design makeover, and that quote no longer appears. I assume the company would still stand behind the claim.

4. Havighurst, "Gibson Strung with Debt," https://www.wmot.org/post/gibson-strung-debt-walter-carter-iconic-brands-future#stream/0.

5. Unless otherwise noted, all direct quotes from Chris Martin and other Martin executives come from my interviews with them on May 17, 2016. For an updating of Martin's position within the company's management since this interview, see the final paragraphs of this chapter.

6. During Frank Herbert Martin's period running the company, Martin acquired a string making company (Darco Strings), a banjo company (Vega Banjo Works), a drum company (Fibes Drums), and a Swedish guitar company (Levin), and established an importing arrangement with Sigma Guitars of Japan. Except for Darco Strings, all eventually foundered. One of the standard histories of the company states, "Under Frank, Martin was chugging full speed ahead, but by the end of the decade [1970s], it would be clear that Martin had become a locomotive without a track." See Washburn and Johnston, *Martin Guitars*, 192.

7. See Martin's website: https://www.martinguitar.com/guitars/standard-series/.

8. "The Heart of Martin Guitar in Navojoa, Mexico," *Peghead Nation*, July 14, 2018, https://www.pegheadnation.com/peghead-partners/inside-look/martin-guitar-navojoa-mexico/.

9. See: https://www.martinguitar.com/series-x-series.html.

10. Dismissively, Fred Greene also says about Santa Cruz's Pre-War series: "'Prewar' . . . what war are they referring to? The Gulf War? Because Santa Cruz didn't exist before any other war."

11. For a detailed description of the Vintage Tone System process, see the Martin video: https://www.youtube.com/watch?v=CXdibaNFz-Q.

12. See the CITES website: https://cites.org/eng/app/index.php

13. "Mission & Vision," Forest Stewardship Council, FSC International, https://fsc.org/en/about-us.

14. Nick Colesanti mentions the 2013 documentary *MusicWood*, about the attempt by a group of four guitar companies—Martin, Taylor, Gibson, and Fender—to change the forestry practices of native Alaskan groups within the Tongass National Forest in southeastern Alaska. This film is an excellent case study of the complexity of forest-use politics and the challenges of relatively small actors such as guitar makers to effect sustainable forestry practices in such circumstances. Colesanti himself was involved with others such as Bob Taylor and Dave Berryman of Gibson in an ultimately unsuccessful campaign to persuade the leaders of Sealaska—a self-described "for-profit Alaska Native Corporation"—to stop clear-cutting the old-growth, Sitka spruce forest.

15. A benefit of digital technology: in the age of YouTube, one can quickly view Chris Martin, in a 2012 clip, explain his upbringing, formative influences, and the Martin family tradition. See https://www.youtube.com/watch?v=B7MWiMq9lIo

16. On Martin, see Carter, *Martin Book*, 2006. On Gibson, see his edited collection, *Gibson Guitars*. Carter also worked for Gibson for nearly ten years (1993–98 and 2001–2005) in the company's editorial department.

17. Walter Carter, email message to author, January 6, 2021.

18. Glenn Rifkin, "Saving Trees Is Music to Guitar Makers' Ears," *New York Times*, June 7, 2007, https://www.nytimes.com/2007/06/07/business/smallbusiness/07sbiz.html.

19. See See Pamela Sroka-Holzmann, "Corporate Growth Strategist Named New CEO at Martin Guitar," June 14, 2021, https://www.lehighvalleylive.com/news/2021/06/corporate-growth-strategist-named-new-ceo-at-martin-guitar.html.

20. Quoted from Martin website announcement, "C.F. Martin & Co. Appoints New CEO," Martin & Co., June 14, 2021, https://www.martinguitar.com/news/about-martin-press-210615.html.

CONCLUSION

1. See the sources cited in Introduction n9.

2. "Companies to Watch: Bourgeois–Eastman, *Music Trades*, 2018, https://www.music trades.com/profile5.html.

3. See Chapter 5, n36, for the complete list of Gibson Brands companies.

4. See, for example, NAMM 2021: CEO JC Curleigh Talks What's New at Gibson, YouTube, January 22, 2021, https://www.youtube.com/watch?v=BxWRpgCOC7w. Curleigh notes, "We at Gibson have been working hard to re-earn that iconic status. . . .

We want to make the most relevant, the most loved, and the most played guitars in the world again.".

5. "Podcast 282: Fred Greene, VP of Martin Guitars," *The Fretboard Journal*, April 2020), https://www.fretboardjournal.com/podcasts/podcast-282-fred-greene-vp-of-martin -guitars/.

6. Chris Wellons, Taylor's vice president for manufacturing, told me that before the pandemic the Tecate plant was running three shifts a day, five days a week. To optimize coordination with the El Cajon plant Taylor management went to a pattern of two shifts a day, seven days a week. Phone interview with author, January 5, 2021.

7. "Santa Cruz Coffee Break #9: Zooming with Otis," Santa Cruz Guitar Company, July 7, 2020, https://santacruzguitar.com/videos-coffee-break-with-richard-hoover/.

8. "Podcast 282: Fred Greene," https://www.fretboardjournal.com/podcasts/podcast-282 -fred-greene-vp-of-martin-guitars/.

9. "Podcast 310: Fred Greene of Martin Guitars," *The Fretboard Journal*, January 2021, https://www.fretboardjournal.com/podcasts/podcast-310-fred-green-of-martin-guitars/.

10. Podcast 310: Fred Greene, https://www.fretboardjournal.com/podcasts/podcast-310 -fred-green-of-martin-guitars/.

11. "Podcast 302: Steve McCreary, GM of Collings Guitars & Mandolins, *The Fretboard Journal*, October 2020, https://www.fretboardjournal.com/podcasts/podcast-302-steve -mccreary-gm-of-collings-guitars-mandolins/; Coffee Break #9," https://santacruz guitar.com/videos-coffee-break-with-richard-hoover/; Dana Bourgeois, phone interview with author, September 30, 2020; Chris Wellons, phone interview with author, January 5, 2021.

12. Walter Carter, phone interview with author, October 29, 2020.

13. Terry Straker, phone interview with author, December 22, 2020.

14. 2021 NAMM Global Report (Anaheim, CA: NAMM, 2022), 11.

15. The Pew Research Center does extensive research comparing the basic traits and life experiences of three post–World War II generations: Baby Boomers (b. 1946–64), Generation X (b. 1965–80), and Millennials (b. 1981–96). For basic comparative data, see "The Whys and Hows of Generations Research," September 3, 2015, https://www.pew research.org/politics/2015/09/03/the-whys-and-hows-of-generations-research/.

16. Tony Bacon, "The Future of Wood in Acoustic Guitars," Reverb, April 22, 2021, https:// reverb.com/news/the-future-of-wood-in-acoustic-guitars. Again, I draw the reader's attention to a deeply researched, sprightly written book that explores, both historically and currently, the issue of wood supply, with a focus on the forests and societies from which guitar woods are extracted. See Chris Gibson and Andrew Warren, *The Guitar: Tracing the Grain Back to the Tree* (Chicago: University of Chicago Press, 2021).

17. Nick Colesanti, interview with author, May 17, 2016.

18. "Endangered Species," NAMM, March 22, 2022, https://www.namm.org/issues-and -advocacy/regulatory-compliance/endangered-species.

19. "What Is CITES?" Convention on International Trade in Endangered Species of Wild Fauna and Flora, http://www.cites.org/eng.

20. Appendices, CITES, http://www.cites.org/eng/app/index.php.

21. Dudley, *Guitar Makers*, 271.

22. "A Word from Chris: Martin Guitar and the Rainforest Alliance," Rainforest Alliance, YouTube, February 27, 2017, https://www.youtube.com/watch?v=ed5ozLoy-No. The quotes by the environmental scientist in this and the following paragraph are from Kemen Austin, PhD (Director of Science, Forest and Climate Program, Wildlife Conservation Society), email communication to author, July 11, 2022.

23. A partial exception to this generalization is Taylor Guitars, whose Ebony Project, examined in Chapter 3, seeks to control the extraction and initial sawing of ebony from a forest in Cameroon. Taylor also engages in two projects in Hawaii via a partnership, called Paniolo Tonewoods, that Taylor established with Pacific Rim Tonewoods (PRT) of Concrete, Washington. According to PRT owner Steve McMinn, one project seeks to salvage and build guitars with stunted koa trees on Maui, while the other is a reforestation effort on a tract of former pastureland on the Big Island (author interview, July 19, 2016).

24. Forest Stewardship Council, FSC International, https://fsc.org/en. and Rainforest Alliance, 1987–2022, https://www.rainforest-alliance.org.

25. McPherson Guitars, https://mcphersonguitars.com.

26. *Musicwood*, directed by Maxine Trump (Helpman Productions, 2013).

27. Jeff Huss, interview with author, October 8, 2014.

28. Bacon, "Future of Wood," https://reverb.com/news/the-future-of-wood-in-acoustic-guitars.

Index

Martin Guitars, 161–63, 179–80, 182–83, 191–92, 200, 209–10; compared with Taylor Guitars, 118, 120–21, 124; current production level of, 99, 235n52; during Henry Juszkiewicz CEO period (1986–2018), 159–61, 169–77; impact of imports on, 137, 155–56, 236n2; origins and historical development to 1986, 164–69; wood supply concerns of, 217, 220. *See also* Gibson, Orville

Gill, Vince, 93

Goodall, James, 66, 106

Goodall Guitars, 2, 106

Goodman, Steve, 58

Grateful Dead, 42

Greene, Fred, 175, 186–87, 240n40, 242n10, 243n5, 243nn8–10; compares Gibson vs. Martin, 182–83, 191; on distinctiveness of working at Martin, 190–91, 194; on working under Covid-19, 212–14

Greenpeace, 128, 220

Greenwood (forest preservation), 128, 220

Grier, David, 40

Grisman, David, 36, 227n16

Grossman, Stefan, 48

Guild Guitars, 3, 14, 30

Guild of American Luthiers (GAL), 65, 69, 83

Guitar Center, 76–77, 80, 131

Guitar Works (Evanston, IL), 2–3, 10–11, 13–17, 136, 149–51, 159–60, 207, 215–16, 223n1, 235n37

Gurian, Michael, 63–68, 80, 83, 230nn3–5

Guthrie, Woody, 31, 206

Haggard, Merle, 180

Hammond, John, 48

Harmony Guitars, 2, 5, 9, 15, 137, 144, 155, 157, 160, 237n28

Harris, Corey, 48

Hart, Alvin Youngblood, 48

Hartford, John, 35

Hartman, Courtney, 40

Hatfield, Andy, 39,

Havens, Richie, 11, 64

Hedges, Michael, 53–55

Henderson, Jayne, 15, 93–94, 208

Henderson, Wayne, 15, 66, 93, 226n22, 230n7

Henderson Guitars, 62

Hendrix, Jimi, 38

Heritage Guitars, 169, 239n27

Hiatt, John, 30

Hooker, John Lee, 30

Hoover, Richard, 66, 70, 77–79, 92, 156, 192, 231n17; on Covid-19 impact, 213, 215; on guitar wood, 218, 222; on Santa Cruz guitars' distinctiveness, 86; on Tony Rice model, 228n21. *See also* Santa Cruz Guitar Company

House, Son, 44

Hull, Sierra, 40

Hurt, Mississippi John, 30, 45–46, 54, 206

Huss, Jeff, 66, 73–74, 87–92, 156, 222, 244n27. *See also* Huss & Dalton Guitars

Huss & Dalton Guitars, 2, 16, 62, 87–90, 179, 222, 232n22

Ibanez Guitars, 137, 139–40, 155, 236n2

Imported Instruments (from Japan, from China, etc.), 136–42

Jackson, John, 44

James, Skip, 31, 44

James, Steve, 48, 228n28

Jarosz, Sarah, 40

Jefferson, Blind Lemon, 44–45

Johnson, Blind Willie, 31

Johnson, Lonnie, 11

Johnson, Robert, 11, 45–46, 166

Johnson Guitars, 3, 5, 140, 150

Johnston, Richard, 179, 226n21, 239n13, 241n2

Jones, Glenn, 54

Jordan, Luke, 25, 226n3

Juszkiewicz, Henry, 159, 161–62, 170–77, 180, 200, 210, 240n31, 240n38, 240n43. *See also* Gibson Guitars